THE STATION AGENT
AND THE AMERICAN
RAILROAD EXPERIENCE

RAILROADS PAST AND PRESENT

H. Roger Grant and Thomas Hoback, editors

Recent titles in the Railroads Past and Present series

The Diesel That Did It
Wallace W. Abbey

Crossroads of a Continent
Peter A. Hansen, Don L. Hofsommer,
and Carlos Arnaldo Schwantes

Narrow Gauge in the Tropics
Augustus J. Veenendaal, Jr.

Amtrak, America's Railroad
Geoffrey H. Doughty,
Jeffrey T. Darbee,
and Eugene Harmon

The Panama Railroad
Peter Pyne

Last Train to Texas
Fred W. Frailey

Transportation and the American People
H. Roger Grant

American Steam Locomotives
William L. Withuhn

My Life with Trains
Jim McClellan

*The Railroad Photography of Lucius
Beebe and Charles Clegg*
Tony Reevy

Chicago Union Station
Fred Ash

John W. Barriger III
H. Roger Grant

Riding the Rails
Robert D. Krebs

Wallace W. Abbey
Scott Lothes and Kevin P. Keefe

Branch Line Empires
Michael Bezilla with Luther Gette

Indianapolis Union and Belt Railroads
Jeffrey Darbee

Railroads and the American People
H. Roger Grant

Derailed by Bankruptcy
Howard H. Lewis

Electric Interurbans and the American People
H. Roger Grant

The Iron Road in the Prairie State
Simon Cordery

The Lake Shore Electric Railway Story
Herbert H. Harwood Jr. and
Robert S. Korach

The Railroad That Never Was
Herbert H. Harwood Jr.

James J. Hill's Legacy to Railway Operations
Earl J. Currie

Railroaders without Borders
H. Roger Grant

The Iowa Route
Don L. Hofsommer

The Railroad Photography of Jack Delano
Tony Reevy

THE STATION AGENT
AND THE
AMERICAN RAILROAD
EXPERIENCE

H. ROGER GRANT

INDIANA UNIVERSITY PRESS

This book is a publication of

INDIANA UNIVERSITY PRESS
Office of Scholarly Publishing
Herman B Wells Library 350
1320 East 10th Street
Bloomington, Indiana 47405 USA

iupress.org

Manufactured in the
United States of America

First printing 2022

Cataloging information is available
from the Library of Congress.

ISBN 978-0-253-06434-9 (hdbk.)
ISBN 978-0-253-06435-6 (web PDF)

For

THOMAS HOBACK,

who did much to make this book possible.

CONTENTS

Preface ix

Acknowledgments xiii

1 Formative Years 1

2 Maturity: Essentials 27

3 Maturity: Complexities 82

4 Decline 141

5 Legacy 159

Notes 171

Bibliography 191

Index 199

Figure 0.1. The Union Switch & Signal Division of the Westinghouse Air Brake Company disseminated this "Old Time Depot" drawing. It graphically exaggerates an old-timey and overworked station agent. Viewers today may chuckle, but people once understood the hectic nature of this occupation. (*Jeff Kovacs collection*)

PREFACE

BY THE TWENTY-FIRST CENTURY, THE OCCUPATION OF RAIL-
road station agent and operator had nearly vanished, though it was once
vital to American transportation. Although Amtrak and commuter roads
today employ agents, and clerks and dispatchers serve multiple carriers,
the small-town or country station has disappeared. (Technically, the
word should be *depot*; *station* is a named place and not a building.) Yet
for more than 125 years, agents, who once numbered in the tens of thousands and at times worked with "trick" operators (telegraphers before the
common employment of telephones), became widely recognized and re-
spected community personalities. These agents and operators to a lesser
degree had more contact with a multitude of people, both internally and
externally, than anyone else in this massive industry.

The numerous interactions of the agent with the local populace support the views of Thorstein Veblen, economist, sociologist, and author of
The Theory of the Leisure Class (1899) and *The Theory of the Business Enterprise* (1904), about the importance of villages and small towns in national
life. "The country town is one of the greatest American institutions," he
opined early in the last century, "perhaps the greatest in the sense that
it has had a greater part than any other in shaping public sentiment and
giving character to American culture." Historian John Stover put it this
way: "The locomotive whistle and small town depot were part of the very
warp and woof of nineteenth century America."

The nomenclature of *station agent* and *operator* is confusing. Railroads had varied usage. On the Chicago, Burlington & Quincy, for

Figure 0.2. Resembling steam railroads, electric interurbans might convert existing structures into their depots. The Fort Wayne & Northern Indiana Traction Company did just that in Wabash, Indiana. And no different from other carriers, steam and electric, the FtW&NITCo. was a civic booster, in this case promoting this county-seat town. *(Krambles-Peterson Archive)*

example, *agent* indicated *anyone* who was in charge. If the station were open longer than a single shift, that meant either the "official" agent or the trick operator. Yet on the neighboring Chicago, Rock Island & Pacific, only the person who worked the first trick—the designated agent—carried that title. If there were second and third tricks, these individuals were called operators or telegraphers.

Americans generally viewed agents, mostly white men, as the personal face of a railroad company. "At small or average stations, which constitute 90 per cent of the entire number maintained by carriers," observed the 1925 edition of *The Station Agent's Blue Book*, "the local agent is the only company representative known to the people of the community." The public experienced multiple contacts: planning itineraries,

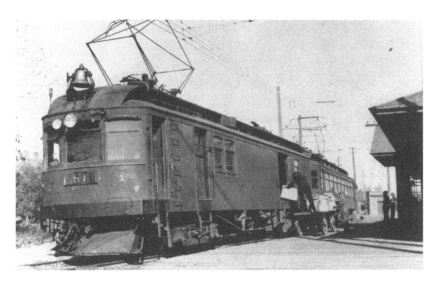

Figure 0.3. In Moscow, Idaho, the Spokane, Coeur d'Alene & Palouse Railway erected a depot reminiscent of ones used by steam carriers. LCL freight shipments are being worked on train No. 67 in readiness for a return trip to Spokane, Washington. By the time this photograph was taken on October 18, 1936, the interurban had become a Great Northern property. *(Herman Rinke photograph; Krambles-Peterson Archive)*

purchasing tickets, sending and receiving carload and less-than-carload (LCL) freight and express shipments, and handling commercial telegraph messages. At best, they likely had only a vague notion of how agents were hired and trained, how they facilitated train control, and how they conducted other railroad functions.

The story of agents is complex. It involves much more than the public perception. For decades, the job required the mastery of the cryptic Morse code. For some, this would be a daunting task. There were downsides, ranging from labor disputes over unionization, hours, and other workplace issues to managing unruly individuals who haunted depot waiting rooms. Still, the position held distinct attractions—possibilities for steady employment and advancement, decent wages, a safe working environment, workdays that were usually different, and community respect. Then there was that direct association with arguably the most fascinating business in the world—the railroad. The "romance of the rails" can't be minimized.

This study of agents is limited to steam railroads; after all, these carriers constituted the vast majority of trackage in the United States. Yet
there was a short-lived electric interurban era. This transportation alternative emerged during the mid-1890s, expanded explosively, and peaked
in 1916 with 15,580 route miles. But it died out rapidly following World
War I. Interurbans were commonly found in the Midwest, especially in
Ohio, Indiana, and Illinois, but they also appeared nationwide. In fact,
the largest was the five-hundred-mile Pacific Electric Railway, which
radiated out of Los Angeles. That company immodestly claimed to be
"the Greatest Electric Railway System in the World." Although these
"juice" roads frequently used commercial storefronts and hotels for their
stations and had an abundance of wayside shelters, they also had depots
staffed by agent-operators who resembled those employed by steam carriers and who might belong to the Order of Railroad Telegraphers. One
has only to look at such interurbans as the Illinois Terminal Railroad
(née Illinois Traction) in Illinois, Lake Shore Electric Railway in Ohio,
Piedmont & Northern Railway in the Carolinas, Portland-Lewiston Interurban Railroad in Maine, or the Spokane & Inland Empire Railway
in Washington State to find similarities.

Gaps exist in the academic literature of American railroad history.
They include multiple subjects. Leading ones involve corporate studies
of several major carriers and of recently created short-line conglomer-
ates, biographies of innovative mid-twentieth-century executives, and
the unheralded activities of such low-paid workers as crossing guards,
maintenance-of-way laborers, and track walkers.

The most glaring omission is that of station agents; they have been
largely ignored. Railroad scholars have written a limited number of journal articles that focus on this subject, and at best they have given only
passing references to them in their monographs. No one in any publication—article or book—has bothered to mention the wives of agents.
These women played an integral part in their husbands' professional
careers. Simply put, there is a lack of in-depth examination of this bygone
railroad occupation, something that this work seeks to rectify.

ACKNOWLEDGMENTS

RAILROADS HAVE LONG FASCINATED ME, INCLUDING DEPOTS and their agents and operators. In the early 1950s, Joseph (Joe) Beck Jr., a Minneapolis & St. Louis agent, and his wife lived briefly in the upstairs apartment of my family's house in Albia, Iowa. On various occasions, Mr. Beck, who knew that I loved trains, kindly took me to his office in the joint M&StL-Wabash railroad depot located on the eastside of town. I remember watching the daily work that took place and listening to conversations of section men, train crews, and the occasional customer or visitor. He also showed me how to use his "bug" telegraph practice set at home and the "real" one at the depot.

While I was in high school, I struck up a lasting friendship with Robert C. Brown, the Chicago, Burlington & Quincy agent in Pleasantville, Iowa. An avid collector of railroadiana, "Brownie" had converted much of the seldom-used waiting room in his neatly maintained combination depot into a makeshift museum. Here were displayed signs, hand lanterns, switch lamps, a copy press, and other assorted artifacts. Later, as a student at Simpson College in nearby Indianola, I joined him, and at times with a college buddy, on visits to scores of midwestern depots, ones that were not always officially closed. We gathered up various items ranging from brass wax sealers to porcelain signs. Brownie knew that agents who had a drinking problem or who were lazy might discard beer and liquor bottles, employee and public timetables, train orders, and other collectable trash behind freight-room walls. We frequently checked these spaces by removing the bottom wood sheathing, and we occasionally discovered hidden treasures. These outings involved more than fueling my railroad collecting obsession; I learned a great deal about how agents performed their duties.

In the course of my work on the station agent-operator, I have incurred assistance from numerous people, including academic professionals, industry personnel, and other knowledgeable individuals. I am indebted to Elaine Artlip, Mike Avitt, Jack Barriger, Robert Baudler, Chris Burger, Josh Catalano, Simon Cordery, Robert Edmonson, Henry Frick, Nick Fry, Bob Hanson, Tom Hoback, Don Hofsommer, Chris Hausler, Berne Ketchum, Jeff Kovacs, Jerry Lachaussee, Al Langley, Ray Lichty, Scott Lothes, Art Peterson, David Price, Martha Purchis, Lamar Robinette, Jim Rueber, Dan Sabin, Rich Saunders, Ben Safourek, Jerry Speer, Carlos Schwantes, Mark Vaughn, Guus Veenendaal, Inga Velten, and those academics, railroaders, and others whom I have known or have interviewed over a course of more than fifty years.

It is worth repeating the observation made to me by Bob Hanson, author, enthusiast, and former railroader: "The rail enthusiast network will usually provide what help they can when asked. And sometimes when they aren't." This has been true with this project.

Although I have already mentioned their names, several individuals have read all or parts of this manuscript at various stages in its development. A special thank-you goes to Don Hofsommer, Tom Hoback, Jerry Lachaussee, and Dan Sabin. And there was my go-to "answer man," Jim Rueber. This retired Chicago Great Western and Chicago & North Western dispatcher provided me with answers and insights to a host of questions. He *never* tired of responding to my persistent queries.

There has been institutional support for my research and writing. I am indebted to the interlibrary loan department (recently renamed the Information Sharing Office) of the R. M. Cooper Library at Clemson University. Its skilled staff borrowed a variety of publications, some of which were rare and difficult to locate. Also, Anne McMahan Grant, subject librarian for the Department of History, made possible my online use of Newspapers.com. And I appreciated the repeated assistance I received from Kay Crocker, the dedicated IT specialist in my College of Architecture, Arts and Humanities. Since 2006, I have benefited from an endowed chair at Clemson, serving as Kathryn and Calhoun Lemon Professor of History. This financial support permitted me to travel before the COVID-19 pandemic curtailed that activity. Lemon funds also helped me to acquire appropriate illustrations. Lastly, I wish to thank the Railway & Locomotive Historical Society. I became the recipient of its 2019 John H. White Jr. Research Fellowship, providing much appreciated monetary assistance.

There is one thing that I missed with this undertaking: my wife, Martha F. Grant. Over the years, she had been my best critic for more than thirty book projects, but unfortunately she is a victim of Lewy body dementia and resides in a skilled nursing facility. I know that if Martha could, she once more would have gladly helped.

H. Roger Grant
Clemson University
Clemson, South Carolina

THE STATION AGENT
AND THE AMERICAN
RAILROAD EXPERIENCE

ONE

FORMATIVE YEARS

THE RAILROAD DEBUTS

Not long before the Railway Age, or the Age of Locomotives, dawned in the United States, it made its debut in Great Britain. In the latter part of 1825, the British nation was abuzz with news of the breathtaking success achieved by George Stephenson, the "Father of Railways," and his son Robert on the Stockton & Darlington Railway. This historic event ushered in a land transportation revolution, effectively breaking down the barriers of distance that had separated humanity for millennia. Their Stephenson & Company built *Locomotion*, the groundbreaking steam motive power for this twenty-six-mile, four-foot, eight-inch (a half inch was added later) gauge coal carrier in the English Midlands. In 1829, another Stephenson triumph occurred. At the famed Rainhill Locomotive Trials, which took place near Liverpool on the thirty-five-mile Liverpool & Manchester Railway (L&M), which linked Britain's greatest port with its premier manufacturing center, the Stephensons demonstrated the stellar performance of their recently perfected *Rocket*. This steamer reached the unheard-of speed of thirty miles per hour and easily eclipsed its several competitors. The following year, they scored another noteworthy feat when the *Rocket* pulled the world's first intercity passenger train. This service, which began on September 15, 1830, operated over the L&M between its namesake cities. By the following year, the Stephenson firm had supplied that company with multiple well-performing locomotives. Soon British railroad construction exploded. By 1860, most of its core network had jelled, only three decades after the L&M had carried its first passengers.[1]

Americans were close behind the "mother of railroads" with railroad development. Although the United States, like England, had for some time operated wooden industrial pikes, powered by either animals or gravity, it would be on August 8, 1829, that the *Stourbridge Lion*, a Stephenson-built locomotive, appeared on the railroad division of the Delaware & Hudson Canal Company, a northeastern Pennsylvania coal hauler. Even though this seven-ton wood and iron steamer made a successful initial run along this sixteen-mile line, its rigid wheelbase and weight, which proved to be too heavy for the iron-capped wooden rails and weak timber bridges, precluded a second trip. The *Lion* never achieved any practical railroad use.[2]

A year before *Stourbridge Lion* arrived on American shores, historian James Dilts called the Baltimore & Ohio Railroad (B&O), chartered in 1827, "the nation's first railroad," or, more correctly, America's first common carrier. This pioneer company relied on horses, not steam, for its start-up motive power. It would be on New Year's Day 1830 that a horse-drawn car took dignitaries over a short stretch of the newly finished standard gauge (four feet, eight and a half inches) line between Pratt Street, Baltimore, and the Carrollton Viaduct. By May, the B&O opened for regularly scheduled freight and passenger service on the fourteen-mile section between Baltimore and Ellicotts Mills, Maryland. It would take almost twenty-five years before the rails reached the Ohio River at Wheeling, Virginia (West Virginia).[3]

The first steam-operated railroad would not be on the B&O but rather on the South Carolina Canal & Rail-Road Company (commonly called the Charleston & Hamburg Railroad or the South Carolina Railroad). Chartered the same year as the B&O, this Charleston-based carrier opted for steam, receiving the *Best Friend of Charleston*, the product of the West Point Foundry Association of New York City, in October 1830. On Christmas Day 1830, this novel piece of motive power became the first steam locomotive to pull a scheduled passenger train on American rails. Although this train ran only a short distance, the Charleston & Hamburg by 1833 stretched 136 miles across the Palmetto State to the Savannah River, making it the longest railroad in the world under a single management.[4]

Steam locomotives rapidly replaced animal power, and track mileage soared from a paltry 23 miles in 1830 to 2,818 by decade's end. The 1840s saw another 6,203 miles, and more trackage was either under construction or planned. Pundits proclaimed that this developing network of iron rails would annihilate time and space and shrink the continent. Indeed, the nation was awash in railroad dreams and schemes. Who would run these railroads? That question, though, was quickly answered.[5]

NEW OCCUPATION

With a developing transportation industry, new occupations emerged. Since antebellum railroads were mostly short-line operations, usually less than one hundred miles in length, the process of hiring workers lacked complexity. Owners and managers used common sense. Their approach could be readily seen when it came to train personnel. Passenger conductors often hailed from existing transportation concerns, being physically and mentally fit individuals who knew how to deal with the traveling public. "The position of a railroad conductor is one of great difficulty," opined the *American Railroad Journal* in 1848, "and requires a man of firmness and discretion." Some had been stagecoach drivers or canal packet or steamboat captains, especially ones who had worked on the nation's extensive river systems. These men had experience supervising employees and managing passengers and freight shipments. Locomotive engineers, or "engine runners," the other principal crew position, frequently shared backgrounds where they dealt with things mechanical. These men might have been involved with blacksmithing, foundry work, or agricultural equipment. They may also have worked with steam engines on watercraft. In addition to needing a mechanical aptitude, locomotive engineers required bodily strength, good eyesight, and a sober lifestyle.[6]

The trackside occupation of agent likewise appeared. In this nearly all-male Euro-American workforce, the person generally had been recruited from the local mercantile and commercial community. The employee needed to be literate and able to perform elementary mathematical tasks. Records had to be kept, reports made, and money collected and safely transmitted. Ideally, the agent possessed people skills and the ability to learn how to manage station equipment, including signals, switches, water-tank pumps, and woodsheds. It was not unusual for hotel or tavern workers to take on these duties. Such persons might have been in charge of a stagecoach stop where they sold tickets, oversaw baggage, handled US mail, and assisted passengers. In fact, some hotels became railroad stations. A rapidly shrinking canal network likewise supplied the first agents, possibly ones who had been toll collectors, lock keepers, or associated with commercial businesses at canal locks and ports. Dating from the dawn of railroading, the station agent never gained in the public's eye the prestige enjoyed by the locomotive engineer and maybe by the smartly attired passenger conductor, often known as "captain." But all three became familiar to the public. Take this joke from an early-twentieth-century vaudevillian routine:

> **Passenger**: That last station was my destination, sah.
> Why, sah, didn't you stop thar?
>
> **Conductor**: We don't stop there anymore.
> The engineer's mad at the station agent![7]

The initial method of station agent recruitment in the United States largely resembled what had taken place in Great Britain. As the process was being devised, employees of public houses, where stagecoaches commonly stopped, might transfer to newly opened railroad lines. Clerks and others with similar backgrounds also became agents, although in this class-conscious society, "railways did not employ gentlemen for any ordinary jobs." These men from the middling classes were presumably literate and capable record keepers with basic mathematical skills.[8]

On the European continent, similar hiring patterns occurred but with variations. The developing railroad network in the Netherlands is an example. The first station masters of the Holland Railway were recruited heavily from the ranks of the army. "The 'war' with upstart Belgium had ended in 1839 and a lot of officers and NCO's were looking for service," the Dutch railroad historian Augustus Veenendaal Jr. noted. "They had learned to give and obey orders and were thought suitable for railway service. Also innkeepers and supervisors of the old established diligence (mail coach) services, now superfluous, were deemed suitable." Veenendaal added, "When the State Railways [privately owned] opened the first lines starting in 1863 the situation was very much different. They had to look elsewhere and had trouble in finding the right personnel." Yet management found suitable agents. "A fairly large number of Germans were recruited and part of the printed regulations and general instructions of the company were issued in both German and Dutch. Station masters, coming in direct contact with the public, had to be Dutch-speaking, of course, as they were the staff representing the company toward the traveling public. In technical positions Germans were predominating in the early days of the State Company."[9]

Who hired American station agents? The process varied. During the antebellum period, it was likely a ranking official, often the superintendent of the railroad or a division superintendent (if the railroad had operating divisions). Even the board of directors or company president might enter the selection process. Using procedures employed by British railways, the Schenectady & Troy Railroad, for one, initially had its six-member board of directors vote on the hiring of agents and clerks. According to its *Organization and General Regulations*, adopted in 1852 by the New-York & Erie Railroad board of directors, the president played the pivotal role. "The President will appoint, subject to the confirmation of the Board the following Officers, viz:—General Freight Agent, General Ticket Agent, Express Freight Agent, the Wood Agent, and all the Station Agents and their Clerks."[10]

In a requirement that later disappeared, a railroad might demand that perspective agents sign security bonds of from $100 to $5,000 before they could be officially hired. The Chicago, Burlington & Quincy (Burlington), for example, ordered a $300 bond for a station that took in less than $10,000 annually to $5,000 for one that generated revenues in excess of $30,000 annually. "The agents themselves were to secure sureties from prominent businessmen in the communities they served," explained historian Paul Black. This arrangement reflected British practices.[11]

As the American railroad network expanded, growing rapidly between the end of hard times triggered by the Panic of 1837 and the advent of the Panic of 1857, the number of station agents spiked. While there is no exact count of these employees during this time, a likely representative numerical ratio when compared with other railroad positions can be found in this 1856 Illinois Central (IC) employee census: "44 officers, 134 station agents and clerks, 616 station labors, 153 track foremen, 1,359 track laborers, 23 construction foremen, 266 construction laborers, 28 shop foremen, 633 shop laborers, and 325 trainmen and enginemen." Monthly compensation to agents ranged from $33.33 to $75.00, depending on the business transacted at their stations; locomotive engineers earned $60.00–$65.00, conductors $60.00, and laborers, $25.00–$30.00. But with the onset of depression in 1857, which severely struck the Midwest, the IC reduced pay by 10 percent for all employees. These wage figures were probably typical of the industry, but variations occurred. Early on, the B&O oddly compensated agents with a percentage of revenues collected from their station's freight shipments.[12]

What duties did these agents perform? The most widely recognized involved meeting the traveling and shipping public. They sold tickets, but usually this was an easy task. "The first railroad tickets were simply thick white cards, bearing the name of the company of the two stations the ticket could be used between," an early agent remembered, "the agent at the selling point writing his name at the bottom for identification and to prevent counterfeiting." He added, "There were no complicated ticket cases, with tickets for hundreds upon hundreds of cities, towns, and villages; no coupons, no station-stamps." Some railroads opted instead for metal tokens made of brass, copper, or pewter. Agents also billed and received freight shipments, both carload and less-than-carload (LCL); collected payments; and notified customers when there were deliveries. And they possibly assisted with handling the US mail. These agents also posted arrival and departure times on train bulletin boards and helped maintain their depots and surrounding grounds, including watching over any water and wood facilities. Some became responsible for having excursion notices printed and distributed. If there was a station bell, likely found only in bustling stations, the agent was required to ring it to warn passengers of an approaching or departing train. That rather quaint responsibility ended with the advent of the telegraph, since noise from the bell interfered with deciphering the clicking messages. No matter the station's importance, agents needed to submit weekly or monthly reports, complete other paperwork tasks, and see that monies collected reached the appropriate party. These individuals, especially at smaller stations, were jacks-of-all-trades, and that occupational description lasted long into the twentieth century.[13]

DEPOTS

The first railroads frequently lacked depots for passengers, although they might maintain booking or ticket offices. These places were usually found in hotels and taverns. In 1833, the Paterson & Hudson River Rail Road, which initially used horses rather than steam, established its principal ticket office in the Congress House in Paterson, New Jersey. But by 1835, the company had relocated it to a commercial building across the street. It would be conductors who collected fares.[14] Not long after the B&O reached Ellicotts Mills from Baltimore in May 1830, officials decided that passengers could use the recently opened Patapsco Hotel near the end of track. Yet the infant carrier believed that it should erect a building in the town.[15] It earmarked its limited resources for a facility that could accommodate cargoes but not passengers; freight required protection from weather and thieves. Pioneer railroads might rely on other parties to erect warehouses for freight shipments. The Winchester & Potomac Railroad encouraged private individuals to build such structures on its property at six locations, designed solely for freight. "By this arrangement the company spared itself the expense of erecting depots, and also of appointing salaried agents," observed Franz Anton Ritter von Gerstner, a visiting European railroad expert, in 1843. He also noted that the Monroeville & Sandusky City Railroad in Ohio "has not constructed any *buildings* on the [fifteen-mile] line. The warehouse in Monroeville, which is served by several spurs, was built by private individuals." Early passenger trains might depart from a street or some other designated location. In 1834, the Mohawk & Hudson Rail Road announced, "Departure from State Street, Albany." Three years later, the Columbia & Philadelphia Railroad, a unit of the state's complex cross-state Main Line of Public Works, told patrons, "A through train for the accommodation of Western Passengers will leave the vicinity of Broad & Callowhill Streets [Philadelphia]." Arrivals were usually at or near the same places. Shortly after the Norwich & Worcester Railroad opened in Massachusetts, it skipped building or acquiring structures for "station houses" in smaller communities. The 1840 annual report for the recently opened Petersburg Rail Road of Virginia listed no expenditures for depots, and expenses for agents and station laborers amounted to only a small percentage of its operational costs. To enhance train movements, the Boston & Worcester Rail Road built a modest depot in Framingham, twenty-one miles from Boston, where its eastbound and westbound trains normally met. These railroads almost universally embraced this credo of management: "The maximum of traffic and the minimum of expense." When companies decided to erect depots, their "economical directors" made this point: "We are not bound to make decent looking buildings." By necessity, these early American railroads built cheaply; investment capital was dear. Not to be overlooked was the corporate feeling that by having a monopoly in their service territory, they did not need to pamper passengers.[16]

To meet the requirements of passengers (and agents), depots soon became more prevalent. This delay can be attributed to the corporate need to focus on securing land, surveying rights-of-way, laying track, obtaining rolling stock, and constructing shop facilities and other infrastructures such as water tanks and wood stations. If trackside structures appeared, they were intended to protect freight. After all, one writer commented that passenger-generated revenues were "not in itself a dividend-paying part of a line." Then as passenger volumes and revenues increased, proper accommodations became necessary. In 1856, the board of directors of the Galena & Chicago Union made this pronouncement: "At Belvidere, a Passenger House should be built, as the business is constantly increasing—especially the travel to and from the west that wishes to pass over the Beloit Branch, and the Beloit and Madison Railroad. The present building is required to accommodate freight at this point."[17]

When depots appeared, agents worked in a variety of structures, ranging from small to large and from wood to brick or occasionally stone. In many communities, especially smaller ones, station personnel later would hardly recognize the earliest workplaces. The adoption of the combination style, which became widespread after the Civil War, featured a practical tripartite floor plan: waiting room, office, and baggage-freight room. Original ones might be hotels and other commercial

Figure 1.1. The Delaware, Lackawanna & Western repurposed an existing two-story house for its depot at this unknown location in Pennsylvania. It is possible that the agent and his children are captured in this circa 1870s photograph. *(Author's collection)*

buildings, private homes, barns and other farm buildings, or shedlike shelters. Starting in the antebellum period and for years to come, it was not unusual for railroads in New England to use existing structures for depots. "[They were] just a building near the track, also housing a grocery store or perhaps a saloon or barber shop (though in a separate room)," observed transportation writer Alvin Harlow. "In numerous cases, the business and perhaps the building itself being the property of the railroad agent."[18]

The Cumberland Valley Railroad (CVR) exemplifies the utilization of existing buildings. This fifty-two-mile short line, which opened in 1837 between Chambersburg and Harrisburg, Pennsylvania, preferred non-railroad-owned space. "The company followed a policy of strict economy in providing passenger stations in [its] early period, building only one, at Chambersburg," noted company historian Paul Westhaeffer. "Since the railroad passed through the sizable towns on their main streets, the CVR arranged with trackside hotels to use their lobbies as ticket offices, waiting rooms, and LCL storage." In Shippensburg, it established a ticket office in the Dr. W. D. E. Hayes Drug Store, and westbound trains stopped in front of the Black Bear Hotel and eastbound ones in front of the Union Hotel. The agent likely had his office in the Hayes drugstore.[19]

There is a well-known example that reveals the pitfalls of a privately owned depot. When surveyors in the late 1830s located the Housatonic Rail Road through the Housatonic River valley in extreme western Connecticut, hotel owner Sylvanus Merwin and his wife at Merwinsville (later Gaylordsville) wanted railroad service, and so they wined and dined these men in their establishment. Their ploy worked. When the company built through the area, its tracks passed next to the Merwins' property, and trains on their run between Bridgeport, Connecticut, and Pittsfield, Massachusetts, made meal stops at the hotel. Moreover, the wife became the village's first agent. Apparently she lacked the requisite skills, and her inabilities to master train-control work resulted in an accident. The railroad fired her and sent a replacement. When the new man announced his presence, the angry husband asked, "Did you bring your depot with you?" The Housatonic had no choice but to build its own structure; the company placed it near the hotel.[20]

Railroad officials began to realize that existing structures, including trackside hotels, were not suited for the highest degree of station efficiency. Unlike the stagecoach, which could pull up directly outside the front entrance of a hotel, tavern, or some other place to accommodate its handful of passengers and their luggage, a passenger train was much longer and needed to be handled at multiple points. This required a sizable platform for maybe scores of travelers to leave and board cars. Baggage, express, and mail also had to be worked. Railroads wanted specially designed buildings and not repurposed ones. But financial restraints and other priorities often delayed the replacement process.

EARLY TRAIN CONTROL

Part of station work entailed assisting in facilitating train movements. For most antebellum railroads, this lacked complexity; they were not overtaxed with traffic. Even on main arteries, there were often only one or two daily or daily-except-Sunday scheduled passenger trains and a daily-except-Sunday freight train. On branch lines and small independent roads, it might be a lone daily-except-Sunday "up" and "down" mixed train, consisting of freight cars and a passenger coach or two. Yet one or more excursion trains became common on the Fourth of July, the nation's most celebrated holiday, and for other special occasions.

Before the telegraph played an integral part in train control, railroads operated on what was called the time interval system (TIS). The printed timetable served as the pivotal component. It appeared in a broadside format (perhaps for both the public and employees) with arrival and departure times listed for each station. The timetable frequently marked scheduled train meets in bold type and always designated those trains that were superior and inferior, meaning in which direction they were headed. Passenger and freight trains were classified, with the former being first class and the latter second or third class regardless of direction. The agent participated in making the TIS work.

These broadsides included military-inspired "Special Rules & Regulations," and they appeared below the timetable or on the reverse side. Although they were designed principally for train crews, agents needed to know this information as well. These instructions issued by the B&O in the 1850s illustrate the special rules in the pretelegraph era: "Trains following each other must be kept *one-half mile or more apart*—and no train must leave a station within five minutes of another, unless it be for a short distance to a hauling place, to enable another train to obtain needed accommodation at a station, or for some like purpose. Road repairers and station agents are required to report every breach and neglect of this rule which may come to their notice, and to give all practicable caution and assistance to their engineman for its observance."[21]

Even during the construction phase, railroads used these broadside timetables. When the Union Pacific built west from Omaha, the operating schedule, effective June 11, 1866, informed train crews that the "FULL-FACED FIGURES DENOTE MEETING PLACES." Rules 2,

TIME TABLE.

A. 23d, April, 1849.   **NEW YORK AND ERIE RAILROAD.**

No Train will be allowed under any circumstances to leave a station before the time specified in this Table, as regulated by the Clock at the Piermont office.

NAMES OF DEPOTS, STATIONS AND PASSING PLACES.	EASTERN TRAINS, Port Jervis to New York.							NAMES OF DEPOTS, STATIONS AND PASSING PLACES.	WESTERN TRAINS, New York to Port Jervis.							NAMES OF DEPOTS, STATIONS AND PASSING PLACES.
	Freight Trains.		MILK TRAIN	PASSENGER TRAINS.					PASSENGER TRAINS.		MILK TRAIN	Freight Trains.				
	NIGHT.	DAY.		WAY.	THROUGH	2C D A'N			Morn'g	Morning	After'n	After'n	Morning	DAY.	NIGHT.		
									Leaves	Leaves	Leaves	Leaves	Leaves	Leaves	Leaves	
New York			11 15	11 15	8 00	12 00		New York	7 00	8 00	4 00	4 00				New York
Pier	7 10	3 10	9 30	10 00	6 40	9 15		Pier	8 30	9 30	5 30	6 05	6 00	7 30		Pier
Piermont	7 04	3 04	9 26	9 56	6 36	9 11		Piermont	8 34	9 34	5 34	6 09	6 10	7 40		Piermont
Blauveltville	6 40	2 39	9 15	9 46	6 24	8 56		Blauveltville	8 49	9 46	5 46	6 24	6 40	8 13		Blauveltville
Clarktown	6 14	2 14	904	9 34	6 10	8 45		Clarktown	9 04	9 58	5 58	6 47	7 10	846		Clarktown
Spring Valley	5 58	1 57	8 53	9 26	603	8 33		Spring Valley	9 12	10 06	603	6 54	7 35	9 11		Spring Valley
Monsey	5 44	1 43	8 44	918	5 53	8 24		Monsey	918	10 11	6 11	7 12	7 50	9 26		Monsey
Suffern	5 12	1 10	8 22	9 03	5 36	8 01		Suffern	9 24	10 27	6 27	7 36	8 22	9 58		Suffern
Ramapo W'ks	5 00	12 57	8 13	8 50	5 29	7 50		Ramapo W'ks	9 31	10 33	6 35	750	8 37	10 14		Ramapo W'ks
Ramapo Sta'tn	4 54	12 51	8 08	8 54	5 27	7 47		Ramapo Sta'tn	9 37	10 40	6 42	8 07	8 42	10 20		Ramapo Sta'tn
Sloatsburg	4 43	12 38	8 04	8 50	5 19	7 38		Sloatsburg	9 42	10 43	6 48	8 18	850	10 31		Sloatsburg
Monroe W'rks	4 03	11 58	7 45	8 33	4 59	708		Monroe W'rks	1004	11 03	708	8 37	1004	11 16		Monroe W'rks
Turners	3 38	11 22	7 27	8 18	4 41	6 48		Turners	10 29	11 22	7 29	8 55	10 44	11 56		Turners
Monroe	3 05	11 04	7 02	8 07	4 33	6 31		Monroe	10 40	11 33	7 40	9 06	1104	12 14		Monroe
Oxford	2 50	1049	7 02	7 59	4 24	6 20		Oxford	1049	11 43	7 51	9 16	11 22	12 34		Oxford
Chester	2 24	10 17	6 50	7 49	4 14	6 06		Chester	11 03	1255	8 04	9 37	1155	1 04		Chester
Goshen	150	9 43	6 31	7 32	3 58	5 46		Goshen	11 25	12 12	8 25	9 44	12 40	1 50		Goshen
New Hampton	1 10	9 01	6 15	7 19	3 45	5 29		New Hampton	11 45	12 26	8 42	9 52	1 14	2 24		New Hampton
Middletown	12 40	8 30	6 03	7 07	3 35	5 16		Middletown	11 55	12 41	8 58	10 12	1 43	2 24		Middletown
Howells	12 09	7 59	5 45	6 54	3 17	4 57		Howells	12 13	12 57	9 13	10 27	2 20	3 26		Howells
Otisville	11 41	7 31	5 30	6 40	3 00	4 41		Otisville	12 30	1 12	9 30	10 42	300	3 56		Otisville
Shin Hollow	10 45	6 35		6 18	2 39	4 18		Shin Hollow	12 49	1 31	9 49		3 20	4 31		Shin Hollow
Port Jervis	10 20	6 10		6 00	2 20	4 00		Port Jervis	1 00	1 50	10 00		4 00	5 06		Port Jervis
	Leaves After'n	Leaves Morning	Leaves Morn'g	Leaves Morn'g	Leaves After'n	Leaves After'n										

The large figures shew the points of meeting of trains. The letter P is added where the expected train is a passenger train.
All passenger trains going East are entitled to the road; Passenger trains going West, will keep out of the way of the Eastern passenger trains.
When engines are transferred from one principal station to another, they shall follow one of the times of this table and be subject like extra trains to the
directions given in the 17th and 18th clauses of the Instructions.
In regard to gravel trains see the 17th clause of the Instructions.
The night freight trains until further notice will leave Piermont on Tuesdays, Thursdays and Saturdays, and will leave Port Jervis for Piermont on Mondays, Wednesdays and Fridays. They will not be put on the road when necessary.

Figure 1.2. The New-York & Erie Railroad in its operating timetable, which took effect on April 29, 1849, clearly identified where eastbound and westbound freight, milk, and passenger trains should meet. (*Author's collection*)

3, and 4 made clear how movements on this single-track line between Omaha and Columbus, Nebraska Territory, would be governed: "2. Trains going West will have the right to Track for one hour behind time. If not then at meeting point, Trains going East will proceed, keeping one hour behind card time until meeting Westbound Train. 3. At meeting points Conductors will allow five minutes for variation of time if Trains due have not arrived. 4. Trains going East will Side Track at meeting points."[22]

Another example of "Special Rules & Regulations" can be found after most but not all railroads employed telegraphic communications for train control. Employees' timetables, "For the Government and Information of Employees Only," now had emerged. Operating schedule No. 12 for the Mansfield & Framingham Division of the Boston, Clinton & Fitchburg Railroad (later Old Colony Railroad), effective October

Figure 1.3. The narrow-gauge Burlington & Northwestern Railway, which in 1880 opened between Burlington, Iowa, and its northern terminus in Washington, Iowa, initially used the time interval system for train control. A mixed train awaits at the Washington station while the agent appears near the waiting-room door. *(Krambles-Peterson Archive)*

30, 1871, listed Rules No. 4 and No. 5: "No. 4. All Passenger Trains from South Framingham will leave there on time, and have the right of road over all Passenger Trains coming from Mansfield, except Train No. 2, which will wait at Walpole until 15 minutes late, then proceed to Mansfield, keeping 15 minutes behind time. See Rule No. 5. Train No. 7, will have right of road to Walpole, over Train No. 2, until 2:35 p.m."[23]

A constant concern for management and workers involved safety; accidents had to be avoided. A small delay of one train tended to disrupt or slow traffic. Nevertheless, rigid operating practices based on the timetable and the rule book (the latter appeared as more antebellum railroads issued their increasing number of operating rules in a booklet format) seemingly created an acceptable degree of safety.[24]

Before telegraphic communications, the specific practices used by the New Albany & Salem Railroad (future Monon) reveal the timetable and rule book in operation. "Suppose a certain meeting place for two trains to have been established [by the timetable]. In case one was late and the other on time, the latter would wait five minutes and then move ahead," wrote company historian Frank Hargrave. "It would have the right of way over the other as long as it was not itself more than thirty-five minutes late. The late train would go forward by sending flagmen ahead to determine whether or not it was safe to proceed. If the first mentioned one ran behind more than thirty-five minutes both were said to be 'wild' and could continue onward only by keeping flagmen constantly in front to see if the track was clear until the two trains finally met." If there was no siding or "turnout," the meeting point presented a problem. Hargrave explained, "One of the trains would have to back up to the nearest switch much to the disgust and anger of both passengers and crew. Sometimes sharp quarrels arose as to which train was entitled to the right of way." During this pretelegraphic period, some railroads in their timetables or rule books required crews to "run curves." A train needed to stop at every visually obstructed curve and send a man ahead to flag down a possible opposing movement. After a prescribed delay, the train could proceed.[25]

One inherent weakness in the reliance on printed timetables became apparent following a head-on collision that occurred on the Paterson & Hudson River Rail Road on May 9, 1853. Although no deaths resulted, an investigation revealed that the Jersey City agent had failed to deliver the current timetable to the conductor of one of the trains involved, "and in consequence of which neglect the collision occurred."[26]

Early on, railroads saw the desirability to have station agents signaling locomotive engineers and ascertaining train locations. They might place a lighted candle in their depot window to indicate that it was safe for a train to proceed. There were also manual wayside signals, ones that had boxes or discs with flags by day and oil lanterns by night. Even a rotating signal board appeared. At the dawn of the Railway Age, the tiny New Castle & Frenchtown Rail-Road in Delaware introduced another device that became popular on antebellum railroads: ball signals. The company placed a thirty-foot signal pole every three miles between stations and had employees with telescopes relaying movements by raising or lowering these canvas balls. But for longer roads, the pole signal was impractical; it was used only at stations and where rail lines crossed. When a train passed the station or after a specified time lapse, the agent would raise the ball to indicate that the next train could proceed. (That practice explains *highball*, an enduring railroaders' term.) A ball lowered to the bottom required the arriving train to stop and wait. Yet before telegraphic communications, the agent usually had little or no idea about the exact location of a train. "When a train left a station, it was almost like a ship going to sea," observed transportation historian John (Jack) H. White Jr. "No one knew its whereabouts until it reached the next terminal." If a train were late to arrive, the agent hoped to see smoke on the horizon or hear a distant whistle or, when dark, to spot a flickering headlight. He might walk down the track or ride horseback to learn the reason for the delay. It could be a disabled locomotive, derailment, broken rail, washed-out bridge or culvert, or something else. An inspired and safety-conscious Boston & Worcester Rail Road opted for an apparently effective albeit expensive way to diminish accidents and extended delays. During its formative years, the company maintained a relay of horses at five-mile intervals along the route to allow their riders to report to the midpoint Framingham agent or other personnel the location of a stopped or delayed train. In the mid-1840s, there appeared this suggestion "deserving of more attention": audible signaling. Locomotives would have two whistles of different and easily distinguishable tones. "Let the appropriate whistle be sounded by every engine, day and night, along the whole route, at every mile post, or at every half mile post, if necessary; and where lines unite or cross each other, still more frequently." Crews and agents would gain a better understanding of train locations and could respond accordingly. Yet "the signals are not intended to supercede any of those now in use." Alas, this auxiliary signaling was never implemented. Another creative idea came during the antebellum years. An agent for the Nashville & Chattanooga Railroad suggested that all trains run southbound one day and northbound the next. Management, however, rejected this well-intentioned idea. (Some railroads eventually "fleeted" freight movements, dispatching three or four in one direction and then reversing the traffic flow.) Jack White astutely summed up the pretelegraphic train traffic situation: "There were a great many unknowns in railroading during its pioneering days."[27]

Ball signals nevertheless remained for decades part of wayside signaling, aided, of course, by the advent of telegraphic communications. Variations and refinements occurred. Noted the Erie Railroad in its Buffalo Division operating timetable effective May 16, 1864: "At the crossing of the Tioga R.R., Signal Poles have been erected, upon which a Red Ball by day, (with a Red Light in it by night,) indicates that the way is clear for Trains of the Tioga Road, and Trains of this Road must keep out of their way. When no signal is hoisted, the reverse is indicated."[28]

Railroads generally seemed satisfied with these primitive options. After all, traffic density was normally light, night running frequently exceptional, and train speeds slow. Yet in 1848, *Scientific American* castigated such devises with this caustic sentence: "The signals that are used on all the railroads are contemptible rags." Major transformations in train operations, which the telegraph made possible, would cause a sea change. By the 1870s, railroad dispatchers and station telegraphers had become the modern version of air traffic controllers.[29]

From the dawn of the Railway Age days, agents needed to manage matters less stressful than train control. Circular letters and notices became ubiquitous. These communiques came from either the central office or the division superintendent, and they often had the authority of a rule book entry. Over the ensuing decades, a blizzard of notices, ranging from directives on ticket sales to maintaining depots and station grounds, filled cabinets and shelves of depot offices everywhere. The Illinois Central Railroad offers an early example. Remarked US Senator Stephen A. Douglas, the "Little Giant" of Illinois politics, "[The IC] is one of the most gigantic enterprises of the age." The railroad, which in 1850 received the first federal railroad land grant, soon became heavily involved in land sales, outwardly more a real-estate operation than a transportation company. By the mid-1850s, agents received instructional circulars on land sales, and they were regularly updated. Another illustration of this type of directive comes from the North Missouri Railroad (future Wabash) in an 1865 "Circular to All Employees": "AGENTS will be careful to see that no dissatisfaction arises from the manner in which their duties to the Company and the public are discharged." The circular continued, "Hereafter it will be deemed proper, whenever it can clearly be shown that the Company sustained loss in freights, or in any other way, by the neglect of an Agent, that the loss be charged to such Agent. They must see that Cars left at their Stations be locked, and that they are blocked, and brakes set so that they can not be blown on to the Track, and see that Switches are right."[30]

AGENTS, OPERATORS, AND THE TELEGRAPH

As the industrial revolution evolved, invention after invention appeared in Great Britain, Continental Europe, and North America. Some worked, some worked not so well, and some failed to work at all. Resembling the development of the electric streetcar and other advances in transportation, the telegraph took years to perfect and even longer to become an essential tool for train control. After most of the major technical flaws had been resolved in this transformative communication form, scores of railroads—obvious users—showed reluctance to embrace it on a grand scale.

Although inventors both foreign—most notably in Great Britain with the work of William Fothergill Cooke and Charles Wheatstone—and domestic became interested in creating a practical electric telegraphic device, it would be Samuel F. B. Morse, Yale College educated, accomplished artist, and persistent tinkerer, who gained fame nationally for "inventing" the telegraph. Inventions, of course, are rarely the product of a single person. As early as December 1842, the American railroad community became aware of the possibilities of telegraphic communication. A letter from the Committee of Arts and Sciences of the American Institute to the *American Railroad Journal and Mechanics' Magazine* lauded Morse's accomplishments: "[The electro-magnetic telegraph] is admirably adopted to the purposes for which it is intended, being capable of forming words, numbers, and sentences, nearly as fast as they can be written in ordinary characters and of transmitting them to great distances with a velocity equal to that of light." Somewhat later, Morse received the welcomed news that a supportive US Congress had appropriated $30,000 for a demonstration trial. He learned, too, that the B&O, which had considerable municipal governance, agreed to allow his experimental telegraph line to be placed alongside its Washington, DC, branch. Yet the railroad issued this caveat: "[Tests to be conducted] without injury to the road or embarrassment to the operations of the company," and it demanded the right to remove the line if it proved a nuisance. On Friday, May 24, 1844, the historic event took place. Morse used the double-wire pilot line, which stretched along forty miles of the

B&O's right-of-way between Washington and Baltimore, to transmit from the US Capitol to the railroad's Mount Clare station this famous message: "What hath God wrought!" Additional messages followed, including, "What is your time?" This dramatic demonstration of near-instantaneous communications created a fundamental jarring of the public's perception of time and space.[31]

The Morse telegraph steadily evolved. After years of experimentation, this invention featured electric batteries and electromagnets to record messages in a coded form onto a moving strip of paper. Yet Alfred Vail, Morse's principal associate, deserves recognition, convincing Morse to place the copper wire lines on poles rather than burying them in lead pipes and also to refine the dot-and-dash code. Vail was especially pleased with the former. On June 3, 1844, he wrote to soon-to-be US Secretary of Treasury George Bibb: "If injury is sustained [to the wire], it is at once seen, and can be repaired ordinarily almost without cost." Morse, though, had believed that underground wires would be less subject to vandalism. Experiments abroad had also led to several failed ways to install long-distance lines, including employment in Russia of underground copper wires wrapped in resinate tape and later encased in glass tubes attached by this same adhesive. Somewhat after the famed Washington experiment, Morse launched the Magnetic Telegraph Company, and personal riches followed. Interestingly, he failed to realize that it was possible for "receivers" to read audibly a sent message from a sounder, making his recording device unnecessary. As for the talented Vail, he was frozen out of Morse's business activities and died in poverty.[32]

By the Gilded Age, Samuel F. B. Morse had become an icon among telegraphers, railroaders, and Americans in general. In 1878, for example, the W. J. Johnston Company of New York City, publisher of *The Operator: A Journal of Scientific and Practical Telegraphy*, offered a "Beautiful Engraving of Prof. S. F. B. Morse, Father of the Telegraph." For fifteen cents, the purchaser received a nine-by-ten-inch image "impressed on heavy, cream-tinted card-board, with a neat tint background." Grade schoolers from coast to coast learned the story of that first telegraphic transmission from their teachers and textbooks. Newspaper and magazine readers were told repeatedly that it was the "Morse telegraph." In 1904, industry expert Marshall Kirkman summed up the common feelings about

Morse's triumph: "But to Prof. S. F. B. Morse belongs the credit of adapt-
ing the many discoveries, and making the electro-magnetic telegraph
practical." The inventor cultivated his celebrity status at the expense of
collaborators and competitors alike.[33]

A landmark event for the railroad and the telegraph came in 1851. It
was best told in 1899 by Erie Railroad historian Edward Harold Mott. He
described how the New-York & Erie Railway (later Erie) could claim the
honor of being in the vanguard of utilizing the telegraph for railroad operations: "The Erie, through Charles Minot, and through his successor,
D. C. McCallum, attracted the eyes of the whole country to the value of
the telegraph as a vital agent in the management of railroads, the running
of trains, and the safety of passengers." Few, if any, informed observers
of Mott's day disagreed.[34]

Before this presumably first practical act of employing the telegraph
for train control, the New-York & Erie had shown interest in the Morse
invention. It would be the railroad's general superintendent Charles Minot, a Harvard College–trained lawyer turned railroader, who became
an early enthusiast for telegraphic communications. Two years before
"true" dispatching occurred, Minot, working with telegraph trailblazer
Ezra Cornell, convinced the company to construct a pole line along
nearly four hundred miles of right-of-way between the New York communities of Piermont and Fredonia, passing through most counties of
the state's Southern Tier. By 1851, the network, however, extended only
between Piermont and Port Jervis, a distance of less than sixty-five miles,
although the track to Dunkirk, New York, on Lake Erie, had recently
opened and had gained national fame as "the work of the age."

The famous dispatching event, which took place largely by accident,
allegedly occurred on September 22, 1851. But Edward Mott thought that
the exact date could not be determined, believing it "in early autumn of
1851, as near as the date can be now fixed." On that red-letter day, Superintendent Minot was aboard passenger train No. 1, the westbound express.
Being governed by the operating timetable and book of rules, his train
had to wait an hour at Turner's (later renamed Harriman), forty-seven
miles from New York City, for eastbound express No. 2 to pass. (Eastbound trains on the Erie had rights superior to opposing ones of the same
class.) It struck Minot that he could have the Turner's agent telegraph

the Goshen station, fourteen miles distant, to learn if the approaching train had arrived. The reply was negative. Next, he instructed the agent at Turner's to send this message to Goshen: "Hold all eastbound trains until I arrive." Minot then commanded his train to proceed: "To Conductor and Engineer, Day Express. Run to Goshen, regardless of opposing train."

When engineer Isaac Lewis read the order, he flatly refused. "Do you take me for a damned fool? I won't run by that thing!" Fearful of the outcome of Minot's directive, he jumped off the American Standard (4-4-0) wood burner and took a back seat in the rear car. Lewis and his colleagues believed that such an action was unsafe and violated established operating procedures. "Engineers [had] discussed the subject," explained Mott, "and resolved that they would not act upon an order sent by wire, and would not run their trains against a ruling time-card train." Convinced that the track to Goshen was clear, Minot took the throttle. At Goshen, he telegraphed Middletown, four miles away, and learned that the eastbound train had not reached that station. Again he ordered that the opposing express be held until his train arrived. The process was repeated for the next station, Port Jervis, twenty miles from Middletown, "where it entered the yard from the East as the other train came into it from the West." Minot's actions demonstrated that the telegraph could be an effective tool for train control. "An hour and more in time had been saved to the west-bound train," wrote Mott, "and the question of running trains on the Erie by telegraphy was at once and forever settled." Soon telegraphic-assisted train control with modifications was established on the entire railroad. The New-York & Erie could boast that it operated the most advanced railroad telegraphic network in the nation.[35]

The official New-York & Erie assessment of employing the telegraph for train control came in the 1853 annual report to shareholders. "The Company has in operation four hundred and ninety-seven miles of Telegraph, used exclusively for its own business, and fifty-two offices, and has sixty-five operators employed." The board of directors was pleased. "No expenditure which has been made on this work has proved more profitable than that made for this purpose. It has added to the safety of the passengers, and has given a feeling of security, to the managers and operatives of the road, against a large class of accidents, to which, without it, they are peculiarly exposed." It added, "During particular seasons of the year, on certain days of the week, and on special occasions, some of the [freight] trains are so heavily laden that they cannot make regular time between stations. In these cases, without the use of the Telegraph, however, the chief part of the delay in the other trains is obviated, as they can, with perfect certainty and safety, be moved forward to advanced stations for passing, and thus save the expense and inconvenience of tedious delays." The board's final thoughts: "There are many other incidental advantages, arising from the use of the Telegraph, which are so obvious, that it is unnecessary to mention them." Asserted D. C. McCallum, who replaced Charles Minot, "A single track railroad may be rendered more safe and efficient by a proper use of the telegraph than a double track railroad without its aid." He concluded, "It would occupy too much space to allude to all the practical purposes to which the telegraph is applied in working the road; and it may suffice to say that without it, the business could not be conducted with anything like the same degree of economy, safety, regularity, or dispatch." Later, McCallum castigated North Pennsylvania Railroad management for not employing the telegraph after that road experienced a head-on collision at Camp Hill, Pennsylvania, which claimed sixty-six lives.[36]

The Erie's euphoria for the telegraph was largely exceptional. Although during the antebellum period, some railroads, including the rapidly expanding Pennsylvania, B&O, and the gestating Galena & Chicago Union, employed the telegraph for train control for part or all of their lines, most did not. Reasons varied. There existed widespread distrust and doubt among officials. Principal concerns included safety risks and legal liabilities. Railroad officials worried that if telegraph lines were at trackside, poles and wires might fall on the rails, blocking or derailing trains. A wind, snow, or ice storm could play havoc to operations, resulting in service disruptions and expensive consequences. Acts of vandalism might also occur, usually theft of copper wire (or the occasional galvanized iron wire) and even poles and also destruction of the glass insulators by trigger-happy hunters and mischievous youngsters. It was more common for these pioneer telegraph lines to provide unreliable service; the technology frequently malfunctioned. Some officials worried that a telegraph operation violated their corporate charters; telegraph lines on their rights-of-way could be considered a commercial activity beyond that of a legally constituted common carrier. Another consideration involved conflict over patents and related contractual rights between a growing number of competing telegraph companies. If a railroad did not own its telegraph lines, a commercial firm might not serve the best interests of the railroad. Although it would become a frequent practice for the private company to provide free service and maintain the network, it might give priority to its own messages and not that of the railroad. Then there was an emerging ossification. Was there need for the telegraph? Many carriers did not see the natural affinity between rail and wire. In an era of relatively low freight and passenger volume and train speeds, the established time internal system seemed adequate. In New England, where by 1860 a multiplicity of roads had emerged, nearly all companies with substantial traffic opted for double tracking rather than implementing telegraphic dispatching. Yet the industry's influential trade publication *American Railroad Journal* questioned that philosophy. "Double tracks govern the capacity more than the safety of a road." One New England carrier, Eastern Railroad of Massachusetts, refused to embrace anything "as new-fangled and unreliable as dispatching trains by telegraph," but in 1871, it altered its position. In August of that year, a rear-end collision at Revere killed twenty-nine and injured fifty-seven, triggering public indignation. The outcry led to a management shakeup, and the new leadership agreed to dispatch by telegraph. Fortunately, wires already paralleled Eastern's tracks; the company had found telegraphy useful for commercial correspondence. Another consideration for the tardiness to adopt the telegraph for monitoring train locations was financial. If it were adopted, a carrier would need to expand its workforce, hiring personnel to manage that cryptic Morse code. Telegraphers and dispatchers would expect higher wages than those paid to existing trackside employees.[37]

Cost proved to be the contributing factor explaining why most British railroads initially showed reluctance to adopt the telegraph on a wide scale. Companies "grew alarmed" at the expense of adopting the technology, including installation, patents fees, and day-to-day maintenance. "Economy was pursued by some railways too far," concluded railway historian Jack Simmons, "it was a watchword enjoined on every one of them." By the late 1850s and early 1860s, that wariness had changed noticeably.[38]

The overall slowness of American railroads in adopting the telegraph for train control was hardly unique. There are other examples of a reluctance by the industry to embrace better, even superior replacement technologies. One was the refusal of steam locomotive builders to abandon what had become obsolete cast-iron tires. The development in the early 1850s of steel tires by the Krupp works in the German Ruhr Valley should have ended the use of iron driving wheels. Yet it took domestic manufacturers and railroads another twenty years or so to follow suit.[39]

The delayed response by the general railroad community, which questioned the value of the telegraph, is somewhat surprising. At the dawn of telegraphy, the perceptive *American Railroad Journal* anticipated the "Telegraph Age." Opined the publication, "We have no doubt that within a few years the wire will be placed along the lines of every important railroad and reach from one seaport to another, and from each seaport to every important inland city and town in the Union." Eventually this prediction came true. In fact, by the eve of the Civil War, approximately fifty-six thousand miles of telegraph wire spanned the nation.[40]

WATERSHED

There are decades in American history that can be classified as watersheds or turning points, whether the 1780s, 1890s, or 1930s. Shortly after the stock market crash of 1929, husband and wife historians Charles and Mary Beard argued that the 1860s was also one, calling it the "Second American Revolution." They believed that the captains of industry had begun their powerful assent and concluded that finance-industrial capitalism would forever rule the nation. "The Second American Revolution assured the triumph of the business enterprise." The Beards pointed to landmark probusiness Civil War–era legislation that made this possible. Three pieces passed in 1862 stand out: a protective tariff; the Homestead Act; and the Pacific Railway Act, which financed construction of the first transcontinental railroad. Others followed, notably the National

Banking Act of 1863, which launched a system of nationally chartered banks with authority to issue notes backed by government securities. The railroad and the telegraph became part of this watershed story.[41]

The blood-soaked Civil War demonstrated the value of the telegraph for traffic control. Disagreements still existed between railroaders who were wedded to the established time interval method based on operating timetables and rule books and those who endorsed the telegraph, advocating the coordinated employment of timetables, train orders, *and* telegraphic dispatching. This hybrid approach became known in the railroad world as the American System.

During this conflict between North and South, the federal government scrambled to produce efficient ways to manage a complex military rail network. Initially, Washington launched the US Military Rail Roads (USMRR) with a US Military Telegraph Corps (USMTC) unit. At first, the USMRR extended only between Washington, DC, and Annapolis, Maryland, but with military victories, it ultimately included large areas of the faltering Confederacy. In fall 1861, the USMRR and USMTC, however, were separated for political and bureaucratic reasons. For two years, the talented and determined Herman Haupt, a West Point graduate and former chief engineer and general superintendent of the Pennsylvania Railroad, headed the USMRR. He steadfastly opposed dispatching trains by telegraph. Haupt considered the technology to be unreliable and hence unnecessary, embracing the traditional time interval rule book method for traffic control. "All trains would run on set schedules with the telegraph being used only for administrative business, not for overseeing train movements," observed historian Benjamin Schwantes about Haupt's operating philosophy. On the other hand, D. C. McCallum, Erie veteran, military railroad superintendent, and later USMRR director, considered the telegraph an essential tool in making wartime train operations safe and efficient. He was not alone. At conflict's end, Anson Stager, who headed the parallel USMTC, expounded the anti-Haupt perspective. "The military telegraph has been an invaluable assistant in the construction and operation of the various military railroads. Trains have been run and many of the roads operated almost exclusively by telegraph." In the post–Civil War era, the McCallum-Stager view would triumph. Soon the nation's railroads overwhelmingly accepted the American System. Some citizens, though, continued to express mixed feelings about the Morse invention, seeing it with a mixture of awe and anxiety.[42]

What relationships developed between railroads and telegraph companies? The answer: cooperation and joint contributions. Contracts usually required telegraph firms to supply poles, wire, and telegraph instruments for those stations that would be commercially profitable. They would also provide the main electrical batteries. For their part, railroads offered free transportation for poles, wire, and other materials and complimentary passes for telegraph company employees when traveling on business. If problems developed with the trackside lines, railroads agreed to straighten poles and mend wires. Their transportation business was not to be interrupted by commercial messages, although all receipts received from public messages went to the telegraph partner. Furthermore, telegraph firms had exclusive franchise rights to operate on railroad properties, effectively shutting out their competitors. (After 1866, Western Union dominated the industry.)

There were exceptions to the most common agreements. One illustration involves the contract signed in May 1859 between Western Union and the New Albany & Salem Railroad (later Monon), which covered nearly two hundred miles of line. The railroad furnished and placed the poles between New Albany and Lafayette, Indiana, but Western Union provided wire, insulators, batteries, and maintenance. The railroad was given the exclusive control of the operation, but it was obligated to pay the telegraph firm $9,000 annually. These monthly payments were expected to come from receipts generated from commercial messages. In time, Western Union installed a second line, and the altered contract became the standard telegraph-railroad arrangement.[43]

Yet this may not have been a perfect marriage. "The two industries were drawn together though external factors such as war, increasing safety regulations at the state and national levels, and financial necessity on the part of the young telegraph industry," concluded Benjamin Schwantes, "rather than because railroad and telegraph officials perceived their industries as inherently linked or beneficial to each other."

Although adjustments occurred, both parties generally agreed that there were pronounced mutual benefits. Their symbiotic relationship endured for a century or so; they became inextricably bound.[44]

Americans surely stood in wonderment when in a relatively short time they saw the advent of steam-powered transport and the electric telegraph. They witnessed striking technological replacements in transportation and communication—stagecoaches and canal packets to railroads and visual signaling to nearly instantaneous telegraphic messaging. Technological advances continued, revealed by the inventive genius of Thomas Edison. In 1874, the "Wizard of Menlo Park" perfected the quadruplex telegraph for sending two messages simultaneously in each direction over a single wire, dramatically increasing capacity and reducing the costs of installing and maintaining additional wires.[45]

The telegraph created a major industry with thousands of employees and, for railroads, new occupations, significantly those of railroad station agent-operator, telegrapher, and dispatcher. In an exaggerated fashion, one commentator made this sweeping conclusion about the relationship between the telegraph and the railroad: "Without the telegraph the railroad might have been limited to use in industry and mining. Without the railroad, the telegraph would have lacked a right-of-way, a supply of operators, and a steady customer." Happily, this relationship provided the public long-lasting benefits.[46]

TWO

MATURITY: ESSENTIALS

HIRINGS

As the Railway Age matured, hiring practices for station agent-operators became firmly established. Yet some old hiring customs continued. When railroads, for example, penetrated remote regions of the West, especially frontier mining towns and camps, they once more might turn to hotelkeepers, who previously had served stagecoach operators. But failure to master telegraphy could prevent these agency hires from becoming permanent employees. In 1871, Robert Harris, president of the Chicago, Burlington & Quincy (Burlington), declared this nearly universal sentiment among management: "Almost the first requisite for a station agent now is that he should telegraph." Another Burlington executive, Charles Perkins, offered these thoughts on hiring: "So far as possible new men should be taken into service only in the lower grades; train service men should begin, for example, as brakemen, engine service men as firemen, station service applicants as clerks or assistants, and so forth. The higher grades should be filled by promotion. And in making promotions, those who are in authority should be able, from personal acquaintance, to judge of the men from whom they can select."[1]

The hiring of station agents commonly was the duty of the division superintendent. After all, divisions were the core units of the operating departments. If the railroad had a decentralized organizational structure, this seemed particularly wise. Variations existed. General managers might become involved. In naming agents for large, urban stations, top-ranking officials almost always did the selecting. When it came to employing telegraphers, the chief dispatcher frequently served as the decision maker. Occasionally, a traveling auditor facilitated a hire.[2]

As railroads matured, they might introduce a class of "special" station agents. Their titles varied, being called "appointive agents," "star agents,"[3] or by some other name. They assumed a number of tasks that traditional agent-operators did not perform. These employees were usually found in the larger towns with a strong customer base and where they worked closely with division sales personnel. They called on customers or potential ones and had authority to extend preferential services to major shippers. This could involve extra switching when needed. These special agents also had ties to the passenger department, often organizing special train or group movements. Additionally, they were frequently the first to interview new employees or employees who might be considered for promotion. Their appointments might or might not come from seniority lists, and usually division superintendents did the hiring.[4]

As in the past, a majority of applicants for agency service hailed from urban backgrounds. "No other labor-using institution is so well equipped to get the raw materials in labor as the railroad," observed a writer in *Railroad Man's Magazine* about agency employment. "It reaches out into the villages and picks it off." These young males considered this an attractive occupation. After all, railroads were those magic carpets of transportation, and they seemingly embraced the latest and most exciting technologies. "For generations country boys have wandered into country railroad depots, attracted by the dots and dashes spilling out of the telegraphic sounder and, mysteriously, creating words on the operator's pad," opined *Trains* editor David Morgan. These jobs meant a way to support themselves and their families, essential if the principal breadwinners were no longer present or were physically incapacitated. And they were considered safe, lacking the dangers associated with train service and track work. Nineteenth-century brakemen faced extreme dangers; hundreds died in service after only a few months or several years. Agency employment also offered opportunities for advancement, especially during the line construction boom of the 1880s and a second wave of expansion that occurred shortly after the turn of the twentieth century and continued until the outbreak of World War I. A future agent-operator might launch his career in a lonely, low-paying position but could advance to a larger station with a better salary. There would also be other financial benefits; the most common involved express company commissions. Since the railroad industry was the first in which the seniority system was formally developed to any extent, long-term job security became a realistic possibility. "One gets the impression usually from conversations with railroad people that seniority is an inseparable a part of a railroad as wheels and whistles," opined a research fellow at the University of Chicago School of Business. Since station work involved an extensive variety of assigned activities, ranging from serving customers to managing freight shipments, this know-how prepared a novice agent for greater rewards in either the railroad or the business world. "The variety in the duties of this position is a great advantage to the ambitious young man, because it serves to give him a good lift toward a valuable business education," observed *The American Railway* in 1890. "He can learn about the methods and knacks and tricks of many different kinds of businesses, and can profit by the knowledge thus gained." A veteran agent summed up how many youngsters viewed agency employment. "For many poor boys it was a break of a lifetime when they were able to learn a trade without cost and without having to live away from home while doing so, then step into a job in one of the most interesting industries in the world."[5]

Rural youth had similar feelings about agency employment. A repeated scenario was that these young males detested farmwork and country life. Agriculture involved those arduous and repetitive cycles of plowing, planting, cultivating, and harvesting. Living on a farm frequently meant physical isolation, lack of access to secondary education, and limited opportunities for social encounters. Furthermore, a youngster might not be physically fit or might lack talent for farming. A country boy was at a disadvantage, however; he needed ideally to make contact with a station agent or operator. Yet this might be possible, likely staying with a relative, friend, or someone else who lived in town. Perhaps the would-be telegrapher could borrow a key and sounder, battery, and wire locally or purchase them from a manufacturer, distributor, or mail-order firm. Occasionally, a young enthusiast built his own practice set; one creative lad learned by fabricating a device made from whalebone and wood.[6]

A not-to-be-overlooked aspect of the hiring process involved nepotism. While less widespread than the role played by shop and track foremen, an agent might become involved. He knew the "brass hats," who had the power to hire, and could lobby for a son (perhaps daughter), brother, or other family member. The agent may have taught the lad Morse code, station bookkeeping, and other required duties, making his nominee a strong candidate for employment. Still, an appointment might not be as an operator or agent-operator, however. It could be a lowly one, most likely that of station helper. (Yet not all railroads had such a position.) In all probability, the teenager who became a helper "might be the best paid young man in town and being a railroader it was going to be exciting."[7]

The greenhorn agent or operator revealed a common ethnic and religious background. Until the 1880s, when an influx of Eastern and Southern European immigrants entered the country, it would be native-born, old-stock residents who had family roots in Great Britain or Northern Europe. And they were overwhelmingly Protestant. Railroad hires therefore mirrored the makeup of the larger American population. That pattern changed. Take the Erie Railroad, which by the latter part of the nineteenth century had developed into an interregional carrier, having extended its main line from New York City to Chicago. By the twentieth century, its eastern end, New York, New Jersey, and Pennsylvania, reflected recent immigration patterns, having an identifiable Eastern and Southern European and Roman Catholic flavor. That also included agents and telegraphers. However, Erie's western end, Ohio and Indiana, remained a bastion for employees with traditional family ancestry and Protestant religious affiliations. During the Gilded Age and after, people of color were on agency payrolls, but these infrequent hires mostly worked as operators and not as agents.[8]

Although the railroad industry was a citadel of male employment, a few females appeared in agency work during the antebellum years, but more assumed similar positions during the Civil War and the following decades as the national workforce soared.[9] Elizabeth Cogley is unusual. This bright, well-educated Pennsylvanian had mastered Morse code from a telegrapher who had boarded with her family. After a short stint as a telegram messenger in her home town of Lewiston, Cogley worked as an operator for the Atlantic & Ohio Telegraph Company. During the winter of 1855–1856, that firm's Lewistown office consolidated with the one of the Pennsylvania Railroad, and "she became the first known female telegrapher to work for a railroad." During the Civil War there were military female telegraphers. In 1863, Louisa Volker, "a most estimable young lady" who worked at the St. Louis & Iron Mountain station in Mineral Point, Missouri, took on that assignment. She was able to transmit information about nearby Confederate troop movements to the Union army commander at Pilot Knob, Missouri. Cassie Hill is an example of a postwar agent-operator. Following the death of her husband in 1884, she assumed his duties at the Southern Pacific station in Roseville, California. Hill could "burn the wire up" and manage the office effectively. The majority of females, however, worked in commercial telegraph offices. Nevertheless, by the close of the nineteenth century, a few had advanced to train dispatcher. Likely the best-known woman dispatcher was Rebecca Bracken, a Michigander who during the Civil War had mastered the key and sounder. Encouraged by the wife of the Michigan Central agent in her hometown of Niles, Bracken applied to the company's superintendent of telegraph and soon became an operator. In time, she joined the ranks of dispatchers in Niles, the junction of four operating divisions. And Bracken excelled. "Miss Bracken bore the reputation of having more knowledge of time cards and how trains ought to move in relation to another in passing Niles than any employe [sic] or official on the road," wrote a journalist at the time of her death in 1905. As a further testimonial: "No wreck was ever traceable to carelessness or error on the part of Miss Bracken." Medora Olive Newell became another, albeit lesser known, dispatcher. After learning telegraphy at the age of fourteen, this Iowan served as a dispatcher toward the end of the nineteenth century for the Chicago Great Western (Great Western) in Des Moines and Dubuque. "A young woman presiding over the telegraph in offices and railway stations," observed women's suffragist and temperance advocate Frances Willard in 1897, "was so ordinary that one has ceased to have even a feeling of surprise at seeing them there." Still, females never became a sizable population of the depot workforce. Representative figures can be found in these two examples: the Philadelphia & Reading in 1901 employed 19 women out of 458 station agents,

Figure 2.1. About 1903, Catherine Carroll "Kate" Shelley (1865–1912), arguably America's best-known female custodian, poses in front of the modest structure used by the Chicago & North Western at its Moingona, Iowa, station. A few years earlier, fire had destroyed the original two-story depot. Since the main line had recently been relocated, Shelley did not need to learn Morse code and the ins and outs of train control. *(Author's collection)*

and the Pennsylvania five years later had 83 female agents out of a total agency workforce of 3,922. Railroads generally hired females because of their skills, their good work habits, and recurring labor shortages. These women furthermore usually accepted lower wages than did their male counterparts. Yet the positions of agent and telegrapher were gender neutral; both sexes were equally equipped to master the job and craft. Still, women commonly shied away from traditional station employment. Since it involved various amounts of manual labor, usually moving about less-than-carload (LCL) freight and express shipments and US mail sacks, working at a telegrapher's bench was deemed preferable.[10]

If females lacked telegraphic skills, they still might find employment in agency service. These were the less demanding custodial positions. Not that they needed only to sweep floors, maintain waiting room and office stoves, and perform other janitorial chores; they conducted the

Figure 2.2. The woman who stands at the entrance to the Wheeling & Lake Erie depot at Robertsville, Ohio, might be the custodian agent. Since there is no train-order board, the depot evidently lacks a telegraph connection. If this is correct, she must know only how to sell tickets and manage freight and express shipments. This station is located on the not-so-busy forty-two-mile branch between Canton and Sherrodsville, Ohio. *(Author's collection)*

traditional duties of selling tickets, handling freight and express, and contacting customers. These women nearly always worked in somnolent village stations, commonly located on the less trafficked lines.

A good example of a railroad hiring a custodial agent involves the heroine of a bridge washout on the Overland Route of the Chicago & North Western (North Western) west of Boone, Iowa, in July 1881. The young Kate Shelley endured wind and rain to warn an eastbound passenger train of a severed main line. The company recognized Shelley's bravery in several ways, including appointing her "station mistress" at Mongona, located near her farm home. The pressures of this job were minimal (as was the monthly pay of less than fifty dollars). Shelley's responsibility consisted mostly of handling ticketing and LCL freight and express shipments. There was no need to learn telegraphy because by the time of her appointment in 1903, the former main line had been relocated.[11]

It was not rare for the wife of an agent or operator to take a station custodianship. In the 1930s and 1940s, a Midwestern couple, Pete and Gerata (Jerry) Irelan, worked at different stations along the Burlington in Nebraska and in their home state of Iowa. "The enticement for my father would be the 'station and train order work' at the larger depots, which would pay considerably more than the job at Murphy [Nebraska]," explained his son. "Then in the spring [of 1938], my mother would become a CB&Q employee as the custodian at Murphy [eighty-three miles from Lincoln on the Billings, Montana, line], and my father would be sent wherever needed in that region, a standard procedure for agents with the least seniority." Later, Jerry served as a custodian closer to the family's roots in southeastern Iowa, becoming the custodian at Birmingham and later Salem, both on Burlington branch lines, and Pete worked assignments at depots and towers on the main line of the Ottumwa Division.[12]

When telephone rather than telegraphic communications became widely used, railroads hired more female agent-operators, especially during a labor shortage. When this developed during World War II, carriers sought to employ women for the "duration." In an autobiographical piece written in 1944 by Sue Morehead, this Tucson, Arizona, resident responded in the summer of 1942 to the Southern Pacific's plea for female operators. "I called the Superintendent's office for information about getting one of these new jobs," Morehead wrote. "They told me to go out to any little station along the line [Tucson Division], listen in, study the Book of Rules, and let them know when I felt qualified to take the examination. Being a telegrapher wasn't necessary for one of these spots." With the help of another woman operator, she began to master her work duties. "Mrs. Chaffin let me OS[13] the trains and report them coming, east or west, to the dispatcher," Morehead noted, "and that was my preliminary training for a job of my own." After passing her book of rules and a physical examination, her assignment became the second trick operator at Naviska, Arizona, about twenty-six miles west of Tucson. At first, Morehead struggled, but in time her performance improved. "Some of trainmen and engineers got peeved, and some laughed at me but most of them went out of their way to help when they saw that I was honestly trying."

Another woman who came to work during World War II was Elisa Ward Lindenberg. Initially this Santa Fe operator encountered a perplexing problem—the lingo of railroaders. "As part of my training, I was instructed to don the earphones and pay attention to what was said over the Santa Fe phone lines. They might as well have told me to listen and understand a Siamese dialogue well sprinkled with strong Indonesian expletives." She added, "Why, I asked myself with mounting despair, had no one ever thought of inventing a railroad dictionary and conversation manual for the benefit of idiots who, like me, want to know everything without asking?" Like most wartime "Rosie the Riveter" female "ops," Sue Morehead made this expected statement: "When the war is over I'll be ready and willing to step out and give the job back to a railroad man returning to his own work, but I shall miss it." Some women, though, continued as long as they could hold their jobs.[14]

TRAINING

For much of the Railway Age, agent-operators faced a number of standard tasks. Most, though, had to know how to send and receive American Morse code.[15] Ideally, he (or she) could develop into what contemporaries called an "ace lightning slinger," capable of sending and receiving messages at a rapid rate. These station personnel also had to understand how to manage a variety of bookkeeping and paper tasks, ranging from reporting ticket sales to giving orders to trainmen. Fortunately, most of these bureaucratic tasks could be learned through an agent's tutelage. Not to be ignored was that these employees needed to be physically and mentally fit.

No one questioned that mastering Morse code was a skill. "Sincere craftsmen" was an appropriate description. A novice needed to memorize the dots and dashes that represented the letters of the alphabet, numerical figures, and punctuation and also how words and phrases were abbreviated and shortened. "Then practice, practice, practice," a learning technique that was time well spent. Said Marshall Kirkman in his 1904 edition of *The Science of Railways*, "In taking up the study of telegraphy the student must remember that to become an expert operator requires time and an unlimited amount of patience and practice."

Some individuals picked up sending and receiving code with ease; others struggled; some never learned. "Telegraphers who were more capable wound up on jobs that required Morse," remarked a former operator and dispatcher, "while others, often somewhere on branch lines, could have been sending with their elbow instead of their hand." The most talented telegraphers became heroes of sorts, being "wizards of the electric wire." Perry Benjamin, a self-taught telegrapher for the Grand Trunk Western, was one. "He had a sure hand and often sent messages so fast that the chief dispatcher, who was no slouch himself, had to ask him to slow down." A common way to acquire this ability was to have an accomplished telegrapher—usually the agent—provide instruction. After striking up a friendship, the youngster usually performed odd jobs at the station in exchange for instruction in telegraphy. It was common for a would-be agent to set up his own key and sounder (with battery) at home and attach them to a small wooden board. This equipment might be connected to a makeshift line that reached the residence of the local agent, a friend, or perhaps the depot.[16]

A future Pennsylvania Railroad agent-operator and tower man, D. C. Sanders, described the process (and the excitement) of mastering telegraphy. This Hemlock, Ohio, lad haunted his hometown Zanesville & Western (New York Central affiliate) depot and became friendly with its agent. "Then, one glorious never-to-be-forgotten morning [in 1912] Pierce [Osenbaugh] handed me a sheet of paper on which was written, in his own hand, the Morse code. He said 'Why don't you memorize this?' Why don't I! I think I jumped up and down in delight. Then I ran home as fast as I could go and told Ma I was going to be a telegraph operator." Sanders faithfully followed agent Osenbaugh's advice. But he recalled this warning from his mother at berry picking time: "Now don't let that code business run through your head and forget to watch out for snakes."[17]

Although Sanders memorized the Morse code, he longed for a practice telegraph set. He found several listed in a Sears, Roebuck catalog, "but the cheapest was dismaying. Minus the battery, but with postage added, this was a bit over five dollars, and I didn't have five cents." Still, Sanders was determined to buy this equipment. He found a job as a stable boy for a local coal mine owner, and during the winter months, he trapped muskrats for their saleable pelts. It took Sanders nearly a year before he acquired the money needed to make that longed-for purchase from Sears, Roebuck. But he lacked a battery. Sanders happily learned that the telephone company had used, yet serviceable batteries that were available for only a nickel apiece. He was on his way to becoming a "brass pounder."[18]

What might come as a surprise, parents or family members may not have been pleased about the home telegraphy of would-be agent-operators. "I picked up a used telegraph key and car battery from an electrician, who charged the battery for a week," recalled a future agent. "I took it home, put it behind my dresser and hooked it to my key." Unintended consequences followed. "The battery was covered with acid, which was absorbed by my overalls, causing one of the legs to fall off. My parents didn't tell me then, but I found out later I almost drove them nuts."[19]

The largely self-help approach to mastering the necessary skills to become an agent-operator was not the sole path to this railroad career. By the post–Civil War years, there emerged a variety of private telegraphic schools. Arguably the best one, founded in 1868, was in New York City and started under the auspices of the Western Union Telegraph Company. It was housed in the Cooper Union for the Advancement of Science and Art, a unique institution established in 1859 by philanthropist Peter Cooper. He sought "to aid the efforts of youth to acquire useful knowledge, and to find and fill that place in the community where their capacity and talents can be usefully employed with the greatest advantage to themselves and the community in which they live." Cooper's ultraprogressive school provided free instruction and "the complete obliteration of all distinctions of class, creed, race, or sex among its beneficiaries." Most of its trained telegraphers found employment with commercial telegraph companies, usually the giant Western Union or its principal competitor, Postal Telegraph. Yet some took railroad jobs.[20]

If an individual sought this training, it more likely came from a for-profit telegraph school. Early in the twentieth century, the Morse School of Telegraphy, headquartered in Cincinnati, claimed to be the largest. "We furnish 75 per cent of the Operators and Station agents in America," the company boasted in a 1905 advertisement. "Our six schools are the largest exclusive Telegraph Schools in the world. Established 20 years and endorsed by all leading Railway Officials." There was this promise: "We execute a $250 Bond to every student to furnish him or her a position paying from $40 to $60 a month in states east of the Rocky mountains or from $75 to $100 a month in states west of the Rockies, **immediately upon graduation**." This may or may not have been truth in advertising, but the Morse School apparently attracted students. About the same time, Valentines' School of Telegraphy in Janesville, Wisconsin, and claiming to be "the Road to Success," made this exaggerated pronouncement to attract would be telegraphers: "The reputation of the school is such that there is no difficulty in placing our men in almost any part of the country they may prefer." In 1907, the Railway Commercial Training School, located in Elmira, New York, boasted, "We have the best Telegraph School in the United States. It is equipped with every modern appliance, including the use of a railway wire for practice purposes. The instructor has had thirty years' experience as Telegraph Operator, Dispatcher and Chief Dispatcher, and is admirably equipped for teaching every phase of the business."[21]

These telegraph schools (and business and liberal arts colleges with a telegraph department), with surely the exception of the Cooper Union, drew the ire of individuals who embraced the apprenticeship approach. They called such schools "ham factories" or "plug factories," and their graduates often lacked respect. "[To] teach telegraphing in one of these colleges is like teaching a boy to swim on dry-land," observed the *Telegrapher*, a trade publication. "The element is as much lacking in one as the other." An observer in the 1940s gave this assessment of telegraphic schools: "The brand of hams these schools turned out was even worse than those who came up the hard way, and the woods got full of hams." He continued, "Perhaps half of these students 'washed out' while in the school, and a good, substantial part of those who did receive a diploma never held down more than one job, and that one for only a short time. The fact is, they had to get some practical experience after their school training, and most of them got discouraged."[22]

While these for-profit schools of telegraphy had detractors much as collegiate educators today view for-profit universities, railroad-sponsored ones had a different reputation. Due to a critical shortage of qualified telegraphers that came in the wake of the federal Hours of

Service Act of 1907, several trunk roads, including the New York Central, Pennsylvania, and Southern Pacific, offered prospective recruits six- to eight-month courses on telegraphy and other essential station duties. These programs, a notable exception being the Pennsylvania's School of Telegraphy, lasted only during the immediate dearth of telegraphers. For decades, railroads in continental Europe and Great Britain, however, provided their operators with more training than those in the United States. The American home study/apprenticeship approach remained well entrenched.[23]

Most new agent-operators desired to sharpen their skills quickly and for good reason. "I lived in fear of the despatcher [sic]," remembered one such individual. "For this particular despatcher could, when he chose, send a lot of words in a minute, and it was his delight to frighten 'hams.'" The learning process became somewhat easier when instructional products appeared on the commercial market. The Instructograph is the foremost example. It was designed to increase speed and accuracy in sending and receiving the several versions of Morse code, including the one employed by railroads. Shortly after World War I, the Instructograph Company of Chicago introduced its training machine. It consisted of a set of paper tapes that contained code exercises, and these individually passed through a reading device. "If you wanted to listen to the tapes you had to hook up the sounder to the Instructograph, crank it up and then as the tape played the sounds would come through on the recorder," one user recalled. But it was hardly perfect. "With only 1 or 2 tapes a student would soon memorize the messages being sent and would then know what was coming which would not help his learning process." His expanded commentary: "[A dispatcher] had loaned me his Morse Code Instructograph machine and I took that with me to different jobs they sent me. I memorized the code pretty quick and soon learned to send pretty good, but the receiving I was never able to get very good at." He added, "I would usually have to tell the sending operator to GA SLOW (go ahead slow) and then I could get it." Later his receiving skills improved.[24]

Once individuals mastered telegraphy and other station duties, they could expect to earn a living wage. Salaries varied. Agents who worked in large stations understandably received more than those in small ones. There were regional differences too. Eastern railroads tended to pay less

Figure 2.3. The Chicago, Burlington & Quincy agent in the village of West Havana, Illinois, who stands to the left of the engineer and crew of a mixed train, likely earned only modest monthly wages. *(O. H. Means photograph; Krambles-Peterson Archive)*

than western ones. Roads in the South generally paid the least but not always. This discrepancy was especially pronounced immediately after the Civil War, when much of the former Confederacy had become an economic backwater. A majority of station agents on the North Carolina Railroad, for example, worked part time; the agent at Wilson's Mills in 1871 annually earned a paltry $100. Women employees usually (but not always) received considerably less than their male counterparts. Reasons for pay differences varied: experience and skill level, supply and demand, living costs, and the financial health of the railroad.[25]

A late-nineteenth-century snapshot of earnings for agency personnel can be found in the annual reports of the Illinois Railroad and Warehouse Commission for the 1880s. The pay scales listed for the Chicago, Milwaukee & St. Paul (Milwaukee Road) show that "station agents not telegraph operators" earned an average yearly salary of $719.48; "station agents also telegraph operators," $615.40; and "telegraph operators not station agents," $635.64. The explanation for these disparities likely means that employees in the first category were in charge of large stations and had telegraphers who worked the three daily "tricks;" the second category involved small-town agencies; and third category were telegraphers who worked in the busier stations. Monthly income of between fifty-three and sixty dollars would be adequate to keep the wolf from the door; some agency employees earned more while others less. Not so well compensated were "station agents also telegraph operators" employed by the sixty-one-mile Fulton County Narrow Gauge Railroad. Their average annual salary stood at only $420. The cost of living in rural Illinois was less than that found in most communities along the Chicago-based Milwaukee, and this short line was no money machine.[26]

In 1898, the Kansas Bureau of Labor provided this representative comparison of station agents' annual wages with those of engineers and conductors, the two highest-paid nonmanagement group of employees. Based on salaries from six railroads, station agents earned an average of $641.42 yearly; engineers, $1,079.98; and conductors, $971.68. The bureau also listed "telegraph operators and dispatchers," and their collective annual income was $706.66. There was no breakdown for these two occupations. The telegraphers included were probably those who were employed at the busiest stations and division points together with trick operators in smaller locales.[27]

Having a steady job with a living or better wage was unquestionably an attraction. There was another appeal, although seldom mentioned—that was the love of independence, an enduring American trait. The typical agent-operator worked largely in an isolated environment, meaning that he was usually free of direct managerial oversight. It was rare for a division superintendent or some other official to visit frequently or pay an unannounced call. "I never liked somebody looking over my shoulder when I was working," commented a veteran agent, "so I did not mind being out there where nobody bothered you. I always put in my 8 hours at the depot." He added, "You could always find things to do around there." For female agent-operators, however, there might be an uneasiness of working alone, especially during the night or the dark months of the year. There was that widespread belief that such an environment was unsuitable for "virtuous" women.[28]

DUTIES

In the minds of travelers, the principal duties of the station agent involved planning itineraries, selling tickets, reserving coach seat or sleeping space, and handling checked baggage. A majority of these patrons probably knew their destinations, especially for familiar or short trips, but they might require assistance when they involved longer, more complicated journeys that necessitated a change of trains or railroads. When the desired train had reserved coach seats, the agent needed to contact the company's reservation bureau to make the appropriate arrangement. If the patron sought a sleeping accommodation, he had to communicate with the Pullman Company to secure the rate and space. Most agents handled their needs with skill and confidence. They might provide a current public timetable (or ones for connecting roads), allowing travelers to find on their own arrival and departure times and any transfer points. Agents, though, might assist them in pointing out this essential information. If the precise details were not known to agents, they would consult the "timetable Bible," the *Official Railway Guide*, published by the National Railway Publication Company in New York City. This go-to reference listed up-to-date passenger train schedules, sleeping and parlor car routes, and equipment operated on named trains. It also provided maps of all major railroads along with assorted smaller ones and included a station index listing the carriers that served every city, town, and village. If there were multiple depots in a community, the *Official Railway Guide* showed distances between them. This enduring monthly publication, which first appeared in June 1868 as the 140-page *Travelers' Official Railway Guide*, could truly claim to be official. In that inaugural year, the National General Ticket Agents' Association passed this resolution: "That this Association expressly declares that the Travelers' Official Railway Guide is the only authorized source of information for the public in respect to the time-tables of the roads herein represented." There had been earlier timetable compendiums, including the popular *Distornell's Railroad, Steamboat and Telegraph Guide* launched in 1846, *Appleton's Railroad and Steam Navigation Guide* first published in 1848, and *Dinsmore's American Railroad Guide*, which appeared two years later. Some publications were notorious for blatant errors and misinformation.

Figure 2.4. LCL freight commonly included cans of milk and cream. Such shipments were heavy and needed to be kept cool during hot weather. The agent at Spring Valley, Ohio, a station on Pennsylvania affiliate Pittsburgh, Cincinnati, Chicago & St. Louis Railway, has assembled a large number of milk cans and a variety of other LCL freight. (*Author's collection*)

"I bought myself another Railway Guide," said one disgusted traveler. "I suppose it will lie to me again and get me into more trouble, but plague it, you can't travel without them!" Even after the *Official Railway Guide* began publication, other guides, perhaps annotated, continued to be launched, but they were either regional or highly specialized in coverage. The latter was represented by those issued by or for transcontinental carriers, including the Central Pacific and Union Pacific following their historic meeting at Promontory, Utah Territory. During the 1920s, the *Official Guide* reached its peak size and contained approximately 1,800 pulpy pages. It continued into the Amtrak era but at a greatly reduced page count and finally suspended publication in 2021.[29]

Women passengers could require extra assistance. It would be during the latter part of the Victorian Era when more females began to travel alone, no longer being accompanied by their husbands or other male companions. These novice riders might be perplexed about such simple matters as how to read timetables, purchase tickets, or check baggage. As more women grew accustomed to solo rail journeys, agents saw gender differences largely disappear.

Companies commonly warned agents not to sell tickets to "undesirables." The Vandalia Railroad, a Pennsylvania affiliate, had these commonsense instructions: "He must not sell tickets to persons who are not in a condition to take care of themselves, or whose conduct might endanger their lives or make them a source of annoyance to others on trains." Drunks, beware![30]

Prior to railroads establishing modern timekeeping with five standard time zones on Sunday, November 18, 1883, the day of "two noons," agents needed to make certain that the public understood that railroad time differed from solar, or "God's," time. They realized that there existed a traveler's dilemma. Railroads selected a major city, which it served, to establish its particular time, and by 1870, there were more than eighty. Although not a serious problem along a single line, it was for passengers who used multiple roads. "The traveler's watch was to him but a delusion," wrote Charles Dowd, an early advocate of standardized time, "clocks at stations staring each other in the face defiant of harmony either with one another or with surrounding local time and all wildly at variance with the traveler's watch, baffled all intelligent interpretation." Finally, the federal government during World War I officially recognized what the industry's General Time Commission had established. These zones, however, were altered; most significantly, there would be one less than in the original configuration.[31]

Nontravelers regularly consulted the station agent. They wanted to send, receive, or check on the status of carload and LCL freight or express shipments. Ideally, these individuals did not appear shortly before the arrival or departure of a passenger train or during some other busy period. Even if the station served a small community, there might be a large volume and variety of LCL freight and express. This business accelerated following the rapid growth of mail-order firms Sears, Roebuck & Company and Montgomery Ward & Company. LCL ranged from cabinets to caskets, and express included everything from corsets to clarinets. These inbound goods had to be unloaded from the baggage or express car of a passenger train or the "peddler" car or caboose of a local way freight. Usually, the agent or his young helper received assistance from the train crew or perhaps from the section gang. Occasionally, the agent might hire an unemployed man to load or unload freight and to perform other station chores. In case the customer did not come to the depot, he needed to be notified. If the arrived item was not urgent, rural patrons received notification by letter or postcard. With the widespread advent of telephones, direct contact became possible, whether in or out-side of town. In larger places, freight and express agents conducted this work, but in smaller communities, which constituted the majority of stations, the agent was in charge. If an immediate delivery were not pos-sible, the LCL and express shipments would be placed in the unheated freight room. There, however, might be an "express room" or "warm room" located between the office and the freight section. The latter space was likely found in regions that experienced severe winter temperatures. Such perishables as baby chicks, fruit, and beer needed protection. If cold weather struck and a warm room did not exist, an agent might place sensitive shipments in the office or the waiting room, perhaps to the an-noyance of passengers and others.[32]

Handling outbound LCL and express involved close attention. The agent needed to locate the appropriate tariff, complete the paperwork, and collect for prepaid shipments. Office cabinets and shelves bulged with published tariffs. "I once shipped a locomotive bell by Railway Ex-press," recalled a North Augusta, South Carolina, resident. "They had a special tariff for BELLS!" The agent, too, had to inspect the items, mak-ing certain that they were properly packed and labeled.[33]

Managing the shipping of carload freight likewise often involved considerable work. If the customer wished to send a carload of grain, fruit, livestock, or the like, he explained the contents and destination. The agent then requested that a car or cars be sent to the station. If it were a special car, for example, a "reefer," he needed to see that it was iced when delivered. Additionally, the agent had to determine the proper route, use the correct tariff, complete the waybill, and, when loaded, arrange for transportation. If the car took longer to load or unload than permitted under the waybill, he had to calculate the demurrage and any other costs and see that it was appropriately billed. In case the car required weighing, the agent arranged for that process to take place at the nearest point with track scales and incorporated that information into the billing.[34]

Agents and trick operators occasionally sent emergency telegraphic messages. These more likely covered matters other than traffic control or railroad business. They might involve a fire, robbery, or some other local crisis. Village and small-town bucket brigades commonly required assistance when conflagrations broke out in these combustible wooden communities; outside firefighters and equipment would be desperately needed. Law enforcement officials also must be warned about murders, bank heists, or similar crimes. Then there were medical emergencies. Such an event involved Louis Nickel, a Fort Pierre, South Dakota, tailor, who in 1900 homesteaded in the sparsely settled West River Country of South Dakota. With the coming of North Western affiliate Pierre, Rapid City & North Western six years later, Nickel found himself living within three miles from the depot at Wendte. In 1922, his family faced a medical crisis; daughter Frances developed severe pneumonia. Lacking a telephone, Louis rode on horseback to the Wendte depot and asked the agent to telegraph for help. This he did, contacting the Van Metre station ten miles to the west. With the dispatcher's approval, that agent notified the conductor of the eastbound *Minnesota & Black Hills Express* to stop at milepost 507 near the Nickel house. When the train reached the Fort Pierre station, a distance of less than twenty miles, the conductor notified the Pierre agent, immediately across the Missouri River, to have an ambulance ready to rush the afflicted youngster to the hospital. Frances recovered, thanks in part to the emergency message sent by the Wendte agent.[35]

The public also knew that the agent was the representative of a private telegraph firm, usually the Western Union Telegraph Company, which by the 1920s controlled 80 percent of all commercial wire traffic. Sending and receiving these messages could become a headache, being time-consuming and interfering with other railroad obligations. But for more than a century, the depot became an outpost for the "people's telegraphy."

These core agency duties made every workday different for the agent-operator; he was that highly versatile employee. Two descriptions, one from the 1870s and the other from the 1920s, exemplify the sometimes hectic nature of a station job. In what was probably commentary made by an Eastern station agent, these are the words of Joseph Taylor from his 1874 book, *A Fast Life on the Modern Highway*:

> [The agent] has to act as baggage-master, switch-tender, porter, ticket-clerk, telegraph operator, etc. Of course, the business is small, but it keeps him pretty busy, as his work comes upon him all at once, and about the time trains are due to leave or arrive.
>
> He has to make a rush at a trunk, go back to the telegraph office and send off a few clicks, sell a ticket, run outside and set up a target [switch], light a lamp and go and swing it, lay it down again and go and send off a few more clicks, fetch a baggage truck and put a few trunks on it, get his pen and make out a way-bill, put some water in the water cooler, address a few reports to the general super-intendent, and wipe his perspiring brow while answering the interrogatories of waiting passengers.
>
> Then when a train comes in, he wants to tell the engineer something, and inform the conductor, who is standing at the other end of the trains, of orders affecting him.
>
> At the same time he has to take the trunks from the train baggage-master's hands, and answer the questions of loquacious friends who recognize him from the cars—all in the space of a minute.[36]

In 1926, the Tripoli, Iowa, agent for the Great Western penned these thoughts, and they largely mirror Taylor's commentary:

> Work can be frantic, especially when you are making switch list for local due in fifteen minutes; also fifteen or twenty waybills to make; several express ship-ment to prepare for passenger train, which is due to meet local at your station, and city telephone persistently ringing, the party on the line asking a question something like this: "Did Jim or Joe get off the train or did it not arrive yet?" In all probability you do not know either of them. Turning around to the ticket window another party asks: "Is there any freight for me?" without as much as telling you his name, taking it for granted that you are the local railroad agent, you should know his name. About one minute before passenger train is due, a traveling salesman rushes up with three trunks to check, three hundred pounds excess.[37]

What might seem strange to anyone living in the twenty-first cen-tury is how active a small-town or "country" station like the one in Trip-oli had once been. A good example comes from another Hawkeye State community, Essex, with a 1900 population of 710 residents. Located on the thirty-nine-mile Red Oak–Hamburg branch of the Burlington, the agent in 1905 billed out 490 carloads of freight to Chicago alone. These included shipments of cattle, hogs, horses, corn, oats, and eggs. At the time, they had a market value of $413,391. Busy and money-generating, indeed.[38]

Receiving commercial telegraph messages could possess aggravating qualities. A fifty-year veteran of the Milwaukee Road in South Dakota and Iowa provided this illustration:

> Each half hour 9:30 AM to 2:30 PM the "bosses" of the 7 elevators and 1 flour mill [in Akron, Iowa] came to men's waiting room, lined up like a bunch of crows on the benches, and waited for the latest grain and livestock quotations, sent out of Soo City [sic] each half hour. Soo City Western Union XD [long-distance] ofs [office], interrupted all other biz. each half hour. He called no one, each opr. [operator] was expected to be at the wire to get the figures and to OK them in turn, starting with Elk Point [South Dakota] ofs. No one "broke in" on XD. If you missed a figure you got it later from a neighboring agent. How well I recall the grain men stepping out of the waiting room on winter days while I was unloading freight, covered with snow fingers so cold I couldn't write, and saying, "Hey Kid, it's time for the CND [Commercial News Department]!"

Apparently, election coverage was not always pleasant either: "Elections were bad—the office would be filled with tobacco smoke by 10 PM and by 5 AM the ol' head, or what was left of it, would be swirling. Pieces of yellow paper called 'chips,' half sheet size went into the typewriter (mill). A couple of happy fellows would stand at each shoulder and often would jerk the paper out when only a line or two had been written turning to the rest of the 'assembled mob' with, 'Hey! Listen to this "So n so wins in New York!!"'"[39]

Agent-operators might not be particularly annoyed (if compensation resulted) when they served as the news link between the outside world and their community. This generally occurred during major sporting events; boxing matches and baseball World Series are the premier examples. Recalled the same Milwaukee Road agent: "CND [Commercial News Department] offered all big events. All the local sports had to do was to pass the hat for $10.00 or so. I got 10% of it for the work. The heavyweight prize fight between Jack Johnson and 'white hope' Jess Willard [in

April 1915]. There wasn't time to copy the World Series except on Sunday PM. Far too much time would be taken from the daily routine."[40]

The son or daughter of the agent or operator might join in this form of mass communication. "On days of a World Series game, if it was Saturday or Sunday, Dad would write down the play-by-play reports as they came over the wire," remembered NBC newscaster Chet Huntley, whose father was a Northern Pacific agent-operator. "A cluster of people would gather in the waiting room, and I would bellow through the ticket window the play-by-play action of the game." The young Huntley enjoyed his first venture into broadcasting, remaining a lifelong experience.[41]

Just as residents appeared at the depot to learn the correct time or the results of important state, national, or international events, they might also inquire about weather conditions. Before more sophisticated forecasting took place, enhanced in the early 1920s by the Norwegian discovery of frontal zones, the local agent-operator received from agents and other sources telegraphic reports that indicated ground observations. Farmers, especially, often had inklings about forthcoming changes— rapidly dropping barometric readings and gathering clouds during the winter suggested a possible snowstorm or blizzard. What was occurring or had occurred elsewhere could have immediate value. Again, if the agent were not too busy, he likely shared orally what he had learned but might not take time to write out such information. A newspaper editor or reporter would also frequently inquire. "My father haunted the depot for these forecasts," recalled the daughter of an Iowa editor, "as well as important world events."[42]

All agents had to maintain station accounts and submit weekly or monthly collections and reports to various central and divisional offices. In time, these requirements became daunting, with some agents procrastinating about certain mandated duties. About 1920, an unnamed major railroad conducted a study to learn how many types of blank forms it furnished to typical stations. The total was staggering: 161, consisting of accounting, treasury, and transportation reports. In the 1940s, Northern Pacific station agents received a substantial loose-leaf binder; its title suggested coverage: *Northern Pacific Railway Company Accounting Rules and Instructions to Govern Freight and Passenger Agents*. One of its multiple sections included "Receiving Freight for Transportation," and it provided detailed instructions on "Bills of Lading" and "Waybills." Another focused on "Station Cash Book." When money was received from ticket sales, freight collections, and other sources, the agent used the station sealer and wax to make tamperproof a company mail envelope for receipts destined to the treasury department. A passenger train baggage master placed these funds in a company mailbag. In some cases, agents personally delivered monies to a local bank. Traveling auditors made certain that all such transactions were managed properly.[43]

Additional agency tasks seemed endless. One involved supervision of sidings, including the house track. An early-twentieth-century Santa Fe rule book gave these instructions to its agents: "They must know that all cars standing on side-tracks are entirely out of the way of passing trains, and in no case will they allow cars to remain on side-tracks without brakes being properly applied." There was more: "If the brakes of such cars are out of order, the wheels must be blocked. One car alone should be both braked and blocked." Agents, too, needed to compile a switch list for freight conductors, providing numbers and other information about cars to be moved. Also they were required to inspect cars to see that they were promptly loaded and unloaded. If there was a bad order car, the proper official, likely the trainmaster, required notification. Before a loaded car left the station, the agent was required to apply a car seal to the doors to protect its contents.[44]

An assignment that many agents had, but normally only for those who worked at village or small-town stations, involved managing the US mail. The principal one involved loading and unloading of mail sacks from the Railway Post Office (RPO) car. Although postal regulations varied depending on the distance between the depot and the post office (commonly eighty rods, or 1,320 feet), the agent or a helper also needed to deliver the mail to the post office, which ranged from first-class letters to newspapers and bulky catalogs. (It would not be until the Parcel Post Act of 1913 that the US Post Office handled packages, although initially they were limited to eleven pounds and width plus height of seventy-two inches.) The agent often used a two-wheel cart or wheelbarrow to make that transfer between the RPO car, which was located on the head end of the passenger train, and the post office. If the RPO clerk threw off the mailbags, they had to be retrieved. This could be a nuisance. "No matter what, if there was a mud hole anywhere near the tracks, somehow those mailbags would always land smack-dab in the middle of it." Agents were thankful when the Post Office Department replaced the bull-hide bags with canvas sacks. The former were secured with half-pound brass or iron locks. "To get one of those wrapped around an ankle meant a trip to the Doctor and a week or two off the job." Outgoing mail might be brought to the station by either the postmaster or an assistant, or all mail deliveries and pickups might be handled by a private contractor. If the train did not stop, the outgoing mail bag needed to be placed on a specially designed crane near the station platform. The North Western gave agents this instruction: "Do not hang mail pouches on mail cranes more than ten minutes before the arrival of the train." Protection of the US mail was paramount. As the train passed, perhaps at full speed, a mail hook, which an RPO clerk extended to catch the mail pouch, brought it into the car for sorting and delivery to intermediate stations, connecting RPO routes, or major post offices adjacent to or near urban terminals.[45]

Furthermore, the local agent often became the representative for an express company. Prior to World War I, four privately owned firms dominated the industry: Adams Express, American Express, Southern Express, and Wells Fargo Express. During World War I, the federal government consolidated these firms as American Railway Express, although portions of Southern Express continued to operate on the Southern Railway and the Mobile & Gulf Railroad. When the contractual arrangement expired in 1929, the assets and operations became the Railway Express Agency, collectively owned by eighty-six railroads in proportion to the express traffic on their lines. (In 1938, the remnants of Southern Express became part of this sprawling non–post office monopoly.) In the 1960s, dramatic changes occurred as railroad passenger trains dwindled. At decade's end, the company was sold to several of its officials, emerging as REA Express. Six years later, the firm entered the corporate graveyard. Generations of station agents commonly found that handling express meant extra income; it was not unknown for commissions to be greater than their monthly railroad pay.[46]

There existed additional commonsense mandates for station agents. Company rule books listed variations of these requirements: "See that their office, waiting rooms, freight houses, other station buildings and platforms are kept in a clean and orderly conditions," admonished the North Western in 1910, "that all grass, straw, or other combustible material is promptly removed from depot grounds and premises; that stock yards are kept in good order and ready for use, and that lights in their waiting rooms and on platforms are kept burning at night." A set of special rules, issued by the Spokane, Portland & Seattle Railway in 1953, emphasized matters of safety. "Station platforms must be kept free from dangerous obstructions and other hazardous conditions. Gang planks and skids, when not in use, must be kept in freight room or stood up on edge against side of building." And there was this directive: "Freight, baggage and other obstructions must be kept a sufficient distance from track edge of platform to leave a safe passage way for anyone alighting from trains."[47]

Early in the twentieth century, a good summary of the image and activities of the small-town agent appeared. "[The station agent] is the epitome of all railroad knowledge, the unfailing encyclopedia of general information, the concentration of responsibility and personification of total self-effacement," remarked J. J. Shanley, a contributor to the *Chautauquan* magazine. "He stands for all that is required from station master, agent, chief clerk, baggage master, ticket agent, express agent, telegraph operator and general factotum." Asserted Shanley: "He is at once the slave and idol of every man, woman and child for miles around."[48]

TRAIN CONTROL

With the advent of dispatching trains by telegraph, agent-operators found themselves spending considerable time (and often under pressure) in conducting train-control work. By the 1870s, telegraphic train dispatching had spread throughout the industry and, for that matter,

Facing, Figures 2.5–2.6. (1) In March 1943, the motorman of a Santa Fe "Doodlebug" with trailer car picks up his 19 train order from the agent at Isleta, New Mexico, a dozen miles south of Albuquerque. *(Jack Delano photograph; Center for Railroad Photography & Art collection)* (2) The Louisville & Nashville operator in Biloxi, Mississippi, uses a bamboo hoop in June 1956 to hand up a 19 train order to the engineer of a northbound freight. *(J. Parker Lamb photograph; Center for Railroad Photography & Art collection)*

throughout most of the developed world. For more than a century the timetable and train-order system (TT&TO) managed, with modifications, the flow of rail traffic. Dispatchers, not agents, controlled train movements. Their word was law to all operating employees. Arguably, it was the most stressful occupation in railroading. "It is similar to playing a huge game of checkers," opined a World War I–era dispatcher. (Actually, dispatchers aren't dispatching trains; they dispatch track and space and both at the same time.) Yet agents served as the eyes and ears of dispatchers. When a train passed or left a station, the agent-operator would "OS" the dispatcher's office. A dispatcher or the chief dispatcher, who toiled in company headquarters or a division point, recorded this information on a daily train sheet that ran from midnight to midnight.[49]

When the dispatcher needed to contact a train crew, he would "call" the station with messages for the conductor and engineer (C&E). There were two types of orders: the 19 and the 31.[50] Simply stated, the former conferred rights to a train, while the latter restricted its rights. The agent or operator wrote in a large, legible fashion on numbered forms the order using pen (perhaps in required India ink) or with a stylus backed by a steel plate. Later, when typewriters became available, the order appeared in all capital letters. After completing an order, the agent or operator would repeat it to the dispatcher to make certain that it had been correctly received, and an office copy would be retained. The next step involved fastening these paper tissues, or flimsies, to mousetrap-type clips on P-shaped steam-bent light wooden or bamboo train-order hoops.[51] (Thin paper made sense. Enginemen could read their orders over the light cast by the firebox, and conductors and trainmen could use their kerosene lanterns or caboose or coach lamps.) The train-order board signal, nearly always controlled from the office, would then be set ("dipping the board") to inform crew members that there were orders to be picked up on the fly. This was done by hoisting the hoop so that a member of the engine crew could stretch out his arm to retrieve the hoop and its attached order. That process of "hooping up orders" would be repeated with a crewman—usually the conductor—riding in the caboose or a passenger car. And the agent or operator had a chance to shout out a greeting and look over the train.[52]

Figure 2.7. About 1960, Great Western agent Burt Snodgrass waits in front of his Lamont, Iowa, depot for freight train No. 91. He has prepared his Y delivery fork with a 19 train order. *(Berne Ketchum photograph)*

There were drawbacks to hooping up orders. Having to stand out motionless on the platform to deliver orders in inclement weather was unpleasant, whether in blinding snow or driving rain, bitter cold or scorching heat. If it were raining, the agent or operator needed to wrap more paper around the orders so they would not get wet. "If it was windy," reflected a retired agent, "well that was a real challenge to keep everything together until the crew could grab the orders." The agent-operator then needed to place himself in the right spot—not too close and not too far from the approaching train. Being so near the locomotive meant enduring smoke and hot cinders that could land in hair, eyes, or face. Occasionally, the hoop, when being returned by a crewman, accidently struck the agent or operator. It was not unknown for an ornery engineer, who sought to scare a novice operator, to open a side valve and shoot an ear-splitting burst of steam as his locomotive passed. More likely a mischievous trainman would throw the hoop into an undesirable spot, maybe a forested area, briar patch, or watercourse some distance from the station. This forced the agent to trudge down the track to retrieve the hoop, assuming that it could be found. Since the hoops were often the same color as dead grass and weeds, an agent might paint them red and yellow to provide easier identification. It was not unknown for an engineman to throw the hoop into the firebox. A train crew, though, could be considerate. A Canadian Pacific agent in Richford, Vermont, recalled how trainmen might respond. "Sometimes both head end and rear end crews would drop off a hoop they had retained from the last train order station and keep the one just received. The hoop just received would in turn be dropped off at the next station where orders were to be picked up on the fly." He added, "Many of these men were masters at dropping the hoops onto the wooden platform so they would bounce up against the door to the telegraph office."[53]

Railroads introduced a better method for delivering train orders. By the 1920s, the Y-shaped stick, called a "delivery fork," or simply the "fork," began to replace the hoop. "It didn't take a genius several decades to invent this simple string hoop," opined a former agent. The loading

Facing top, Figure 2.8. In September 1967, the Northern Pacific agent at Hitterdal, a Norwegian-American village in Clay County, Minnesota, demonstrates how he manages a train order at night using a Y delivery folk. (Don L. Hofsommer photograph)

Facing bottom, Figure 2.9. As late as the 1970s, some railroads relied on Y forks for delivery of train orders. On July 25, 1974, the Milwaukee Road agent in Marengo, Washington, gives an order to the conductor of an eastbound freight. (John K. Bjorklund photograph; Center for Railroad Photography & Art collection)

procedure lacked complexity. "The operator tied the ends of a piece of string together with two slipknots, inserted the train order between the knots, and pulled them securely together," recalled an operator's son. "Next he attached the string to the triangle-shaped part of the hoop at the top of the Y by means of grooves at the ends of the two upper sticks and a metal clip at the point where all three sticks joined. The stock at the bottom was longer than the other two, forming a handle for the operator or agent." He continued, "Then, as the train roared past, the operator held up the hoop and the engineer's outstretched arm pulled off the piece of string with the attached train order." This left the fork remaining in the hands of the agent-operator. If it touched anything, the string would pop out, and the train would need to stop, making for a delay and an annoyed crew. There was another downside to using these forks. The agent or operator needed to cut strings and place them over two nails on the office wall. "We always had the string ready in the hoops so that if we received an order from the dispatcher to hand up to a train that might be getting close we would not have to take time to get strings in the hoops and maybe stop the train." (If there were multiple tricks, it was an expected courtesy to leave the next operator with a full complement of strings.)[54]

As with the original hoops, the agent who used the Y stick needed to place himself in the proper spot on the station platform. One railroader explained what he had been taught: "I quickly measured my distance from the rail by holding the longer train-order [Y] hoop against my hip, dropped it down level to the rail, then lifted it up for the delivery to the head end."[55]

Another alternative ultimately appeared. Some railroads made delivery much easier by installing stationary train-order stands or racks. This allowed the agent-operator to load them and then stand back to inspect the train as it passed for hot boxes, shifting loads, or other problems. These delivery processes were a familiar ritual in train operations and often caught the attention of platform loafers, railroad photographers, and others.[56]

Train-control work became highly organized for agent-operators. By the 1880s, the entire process of TT&TO had been standardized when the industry adopted *Uniform Train Rules for the Movement of Trains by Telegraphic Orders*. The dispatcher made it clear which of two train-order

Figure 2.10. The last form for manual train-order delivery came with the stationary stand. No longer was the agent or operator required to be at trackside. In April 1973, the operator for the Detroit, Toledo & Ironton in Dundee, Michigan, who has used a stand to give an order "on the fly" to a southbound freight train, waves to the crew and will check for any mechanical problems. *(John F. Bjorklund photograph; Center for Railroad Photography & Art collection)*

forms would be used. Form 19 did not require the passing train to stop, but Form 31[57] did. Engine crew members would see that if the train-order board had been set for a message but with no one (agent or operator) in sight, they knew that a stop was required. Form 31 mandated signatures from the engineer and conductor and hence forced them to detrain and enter the depot (or tower) office. By the 1930s, though, there was an increasing tendency of railroads to make greater use of 19 orders to eliminate stops. This saved time, cut fuel consumption, and reduced track wear. The introduction of automatic block signals also contributed

Figure 2.11. Not only were train orders handed up by agents, but there were also exchanges of waybills. About 1940, such an event occurred at the Chicago & North Western station in Brookings, South Dakota. *(Author's collection)*

to the demise of 31 orders. Ultimately, 19 orders disappeared as well. But before that happened, the agent needed to write in a clear hand. "It is especially important that the telegraph operator should write in a legible hand," opined an industry authority. "He should cultivate a round, plain, business hand. Avoid all eccentric forms of writing." Some took pride in their flowing, legible penmanship. When typewriters became more commonplace by World War I, legibility no longer became a concern.[58]

Nationally urgent messages occasionally passed over the wires from dispatchers to agent-operators. This information needed to be given to train crews and to inform station personnel. The deadly Japanese surprise attack on Pearl Harbor and elsewhere in the Pacific produced this response. On December 7, 1941, at 11:26 p.m., the Missouri Pacific dispatcher in Palestine, Texas, telegraphed this 19 order for "Northbound Trains." It read: "Effective At Once Have All Japanese Traveling Stopped. And Any Japanese Attempting to Buy Transportation Or Board Any Passenger or Freight Trains Have Arrested by Local Authorities With Instructions They Be Turned Over to Federal Bureau of Investigation."[59]

Agents-operators could show resourcefulness at their telegraph bench. One such case involved operator Paul Ketchum. While working the second trick in the Great Western station at Clear Lake Junction, Iowa, in the late 1930s or the early years of World War II, he responded to a dispatching emergency. A storm had disrupted the telegraph service between the dispatcher in St. Paul and Manly, Iowa, and no trains were moving, including Rock Island ones between Manly and Clear Lake Junction. So Ketchum took down a large wall calendar, drew up a train sheet on the reverse side, and started issuing train orders for southbound trains in Manly and for northbound ones in Clarion. He saved the day, and soon the company sent him a letter of commendation for restoring traffic.[60]

By the latter part of the nineteenth century, railroads sought another way to provide additional level of safety, and they did so by issuing clearance cards, known commonly as Clearance Card Form A, or simply Form A. Clearance card usage made certain that the operator had delivered *all* of the orders that were addressed to a passing train. If the crew members received a clearance card that showed that the operator had five orders, and they received only four, they needed to stop and back up to the station to get the matter corrected. The form itself was simple. The operator filled out the card to indicate the total number of orders he had for the train and then listed the number of each in the spaces provided, starting with the slow or caution orders and followed by the running orders. He then would ask the dispatcher to clear the train if there were no further orders. When the dispatcher gave approval, the operator would repeat from the clearance the total number of orders and their order numbers. If this corresponded with his record, the dispatcher would repeat the total number of orders and the numbers of each, give the operator an OK, list the time, and initial the card. A dispatcher might inform crew members, via the operator, that they had this message: "I have no orders for your train." A Baltimore & Ohio (B&O) rule book made clear that in any case, "Clearance Card Form A must be written in manifold, one copy being retained by the operator for file." As agent-operators virtually disappeared by the late 1970s and early 1980s, dispatchers used radios to contact train crews and issued track warrants that permitted trains to have running rights between designated points.[61]

Theoretically, the timetable and train-order system seemed the best way to control the movement of traffic in a safe and timely manner. Still, human errors occurred. A dispatcher might forget that he had failed to place an inferior train on a siding or permitted two passenger trains to run in opposite directions on a single track. There was always the danger of a "lap order." This involved an opposing train receiving an order to meet an approaching train at a certain siding, whereas the second train is ordered to make the meet at still another location. The result: a set of *overlapping* authorities created by a dispatcher, resulting in a potential disaster. (Train crews and agent-operators would be held blameless in this situation.) No person had the right to annul any train order issued by the dispatcher; his work must be right. Such constant pressures might cause a dispatcher to quit his job, seeking perhaps to return to the less stressful duties of a station agent, to take on the lower-pressure job of rules examiner or another white-collar position, or to retire. "Dispatching is absolutely the most hazardous job on the railroad," explained a railroader. "Just one mistake, one instant of overlooking a train, can kill people off."[62]

Yet more mistakes involved agent-operators. They could become sleepy, bored, or generally inattentive. Until work rules changed, long hours in the depot took their toll, especially for those who were assigned to the graveyard shift. One example of an operator's failure to deliver the proper order occurred on the Milwaukee Road at Minnesota Falls, Minnesota, a country station situated on the Minnesota River a few miles east of Granite Falls. What took place in October 1910 was a head-on collision between a stock train and a way freight. "Arrangement had been made for the two trains to meet at Minnesota Falls," according to a newspaper account. "The freight arrived ahead of time and the operator, instead of handing the hold order to the conductor, gave by mistake the clearance papers, and the train immediately pulled out." Disaster soon followed. The speed of the stock train, which traveled rapidly downgrade toward Minnesota Falls, resulted in a spectacular crash. Although its crew members jumped to safety, the engineer, fireman, and conductor of the freight were not so lucky; these men all perished. When railroad officials came to the Minnesota Falls depot, they discovered the undelivered order on the telegrapher's bench. Soon they learned that the operator had vanished. This badly shaken employee, perhaps a novice, refused to confront the consequences of his deadly mistake. He surely sensed that he would lose his job and maybe face criminal charges. Unfortunately, newspaper reports do not reveal if or when the runaway operator was located.[63]

Part of the evolution of train-control operations came with introduction of manual block signaling, sometimes referred to as the telegraph block system. Again, the quest for safe, efficient, and cost-effective traffic movements was on going. Prototypes appeared as early as 1863 on the Camden & Amboy and Philadelphia & Reading Railroads, and by the mid-1870s, the Pennsylvania had become an industry leader. Progress accelerated toward the end of the century, and in 1903 about thirty thousand miles of track featured manual block signaling. The concept employed was simple: prevent only a *single* train to occupy at one time a defined section of track. In 1910, it was less than five miles. But how was this accomplished? When a train entered the block, the agent-operator set a signal indicating that the track was occupied. When the train exited the block, the operator telegraphed his counterpart at the entry point to show a clear signal, permitting the next train to enter the blocked section. Railroads that had introduced manual block installations made the traveling public aware of their safety devices and other betterments. "**Block Signals–Double Track**," crowed the Chicago, St. Paul, Minneapolis & Omaha Railway (Omaha Road), a unit of the North Western, on the front of an early-twentieth-century public timetable. "As a Protection Against accidents there is nothing equal to the Block Signal System. All Trains of the North-Western Line Between Minneapolis, St. Paul and Chicago, Minneapolis and Duluth, Duluth and Chicago, and Between Minneapolis and Sioux City are protected by this Block System." The Omaha Road added: "There is also further protection between

Minneapolis, St. Paul and Chicago Because of the Many Miles of Double Track Via North-Western Line."[64]

Manual block signaling gave way to dramatic signaling improvements. Automatic block signals were the next betterment. Again the Pennsylvania blazed the way. Its first installation of its automatic block network came in 1881 in the Keystone State between Altoona and Gallitzin, and by the early twentieth century, its busy New York Division was completely protected. Under this technology, signals were operated by electricity and actuated by freight and passenger trains. As they moved, signals also moved. This replacement signaling became popular but expensive. In 1920, there were 37,969 miles of line controlled by automatic block signaling, and a decade later, coverage had soared to 60,162 miles. In the late 1920s, railroads began to install centralized traffic control (CTC). The first installation took place in 1927 on the New York Central at Fostoria, Ohio, and covered the forty miles between Berwick and Stanley, Ohio. Eventually this technology became railroading's bedrock. A CTC system allowed dispatchers to control signals (later colored lights) and switches. They could set meeting points, run faster trains around slower ones, and generally speed up traffic flow. On single-track lines, movements could be enhanced without the expense of double tracking. Contemporaries argued that progressive signaling provided fail-safe operations, yet engine crews had to observe the signals. Automatic block signaling and CTC significantly reduced the need for station and tower operators to participate in train-control work. Refinements continued.[65]

Directly related to train-control work might involve other mandatory duties. An unusual one took place shortly after the Civil War on the Nashville, Chattanooga & St. Louis Railway in southeastern Tennessee. It involved a labor-intensive way how to manage traffic on a steep grade over Cumberland Mountain. When the agent at Decherd received a telegraphic message of an oncoming freight, he mounted his horse and rode the five miles to Cowan, which lacked an operator, to tell the crew of a pusher locomotive to get up steam and assist the approaching train. Better telegraph communications ended horseback rides.[66]

Railroad companies continually altered train-order policies to enhance safety. Proposals for handling these messages might originate from agent-operators. Early in the twentieth century, the Central New

England Railroad (CNE) responded accordingly, changing station names that were similar. The Connecticut stations of Chapinsville, Clarksville, and Collinsville became Taconic and Griffins, respectively, but Collinsville, the largest of the three places, retained its historic name. So as not to be confused with Canaan, East Canaan became Allyndale. Since North Bloomfield could be mistaken for Bloomfield, CNE chose Barnards. Their two-letter station telegraphic calls were also adjusted.[67]

In 1904, railroad official Harry Forman offered these thoughts on how to protect train movements: "Perhaps the formation of *habit* is more important in railroad operation than in any other business." He continued, "A habit once formed, if a *safe* one, will be the governing impulse at all times and goes far toward insuring safety and uniformity." The Forman philosophy of making safety practices second nature found widespread acceptance in operating circles. Officials repeatedly stressed learned habits.[68]

NONTRADITIONAL OR UNUSUAL DUTIES

A wide range of nontraditional or unusual duties existed throughout the agent-operator community. Some involved specific economic and traffic needs. Southern Pacific (SP) agents stand out as having the most rigorous duties related to agriculture. This extensive railroad system, which by the 1920s exceeded eleven thousand miles and stretched between Oregon and Louisiana, allowed farmers, ranchers, researchers, and others to learn how to improve agricultural productivity. Such intelligence was expected to bolster SP car loadings, especially from growers in the Central Valley of California. SP agents periodically collected and reported information to management about soils, crop acreage, production per acre, plant diseases, and pests. They also relayed news of floods, freezes, and drought. Not to be overlooked were agents' daily reports about weather—temperatures, wind, rainfall, and snowfall. "In effect, into the early twentieth century the Southern Pacific served as the unofficial 'weather bureau' for California and much of the rest of its territory," explained historian Richard Orsi. "Its climate statistics formed the basis for early agricultural research, the siting of agricultural experiment stations, and farm planning."[69]

Figure 2.12. Some stations did not offer a positive initial view of a community. The Iowa Central station at Van Cleve, Iowa, located on a quiet branch, is an eyesore. This circa 1912 real-photo card reveals discarded crates, barrels, and other junk. *(Don L. Hofsommer collection)*

Although supported, but not required by the Southern Pacific, a related agricultural activity involved local agents encouraging crop marketing. Richard Orsi provides this commentary: "Some station agents organized farmers in their locality to market collectively." He offers this example: "In the 1870s Auburn [California] agent Clarence M. Wooster, who had established himself as an authority and unofficial adviser on orcharding, campaigned in his region for the planting of fruit varieties on the basis of their marketability and also served as the catalyst for the first cooperative out-of-state marketing of fresh fruit."[70]

Hardly as important as the Southern Pacific promoting agriculture throughout its service territory involved station beautification. "The first notion about the beautifying of stations was that of the country station agent," noted a writer for the *World's Work* in 1901. "If there was in him the slightest spark of artistic taste, he enjoyed the opportunity of improving the grounds." Beginning around the turn of the twentieth century, some railroads, including the Boston & Maine, Long Island, and Michigan Central, asked (but did not command) agents to beautify their depot grounds. In some instances, this involved elaborate depot parks, consisting of the seasonal planting and maintenance of flowers and also the planting, watering, and trimming of trees and shrubs. Division superintendents might award cash prizes or give other forms of recognition to the agent or agents who had the most attractive station gardens. This activity largely coincided with the City Beautiful Movement, which early in the twentieth century flourished nationwide, inspired by the Columbian Exposition of 1893 in Chicago and the Louisiana Purchase Exposition thirteen years later in St. Louis and, to a much lesser degree, by England's Garden City Movement. The latter turn-of-the-twentieth-century drive helps to explain why so many English stations had grounds that were things of beauty. Civic boosters loved station gardens; after all, visitors' first impressions to their community were made at this entry point. Agents, though, might not show this enthusiasm, especially those gardens with annual flowers. "The scheme of planting tender greenhouse material that has been so frequently followed in the past is neither appropriate nor satisfactory and that because it is both expensive and temporary," wrote John A. Droege, general superintendent of the New York, New Haven & Hartford Railroad, in 1916. "The beds have to be renewed each year and in a northern climate last but a few months at best, thus leaving the ground bare and unsightly from the time of the first fall of snow until the warm weather in April or May." However, he made this suggestion: "It is far better to use hardy material such as trees, shrubs and hardy herbaceous plants." Station agents likely applauded Droege's advice. Most personnel probably preferred communities to assume the design and upkeep of these public spaces.[71]

Then there were matters of public health. Agents were commonly instructed to post waiting-room notices about how to prevent communicable diseases. During the era of World War I, the public was likely to see this warning: "Spitting on the Floor Is Forbidden. All Diseases of the Air Passages Are Spread by Spitting." Some states, in fact, mandated such an edict. The Spanish influenza pandemic, which came in multiple waves between 1918 and 1920, gripped the country (and much of the world), and agents and other employees needed to be proactive. One agent posted

M. & ST. L. DEPOT, DAWSON, MINN.

L.S. & M.S. DEPOT AND PARK,
ELKHART, IND.

this ditty on the waiting-room wall to remind travelers and others of this highly communicable and deadly disease, or perhaps he sought in a humorous way to disparage the severity of the pandemic:

I had a little bird,
Its name was Enza,
I opened the window,
And in-flue-enza.

Yet meaningful enforcement might be impossible with patrons coming and going.

A decade earlier, several railroads, including the Illinois Central, Southern Pacific, and Texas & Pacific, responded to a deadly outbreak of yellow fever, or yellow jack, which began in New Orleans, a city repeatedly ravaged by this contagion. Warnings were posted in stations, and as stress, anxiety, and fear swept the region, companies directed agents not to sell tickets to anyone who sought to leave infected areas. Whether experiencing a crisis or not, railroads sent out circular notices requesting station personnel to promote sanitary behaviors and to keep drinking water sources, spittoons, toilets, and floors sanitary and to report all health concerns. The introduction of paper cups about 1910, which replaced communal ones, made self-service water coolers more hygienic.[72]

Agents occasionally faced other assorted duties. One such situation took place in Montana. Great Northern freight crews liked to rush from Havre to Zurich, leaving their trains on a siding and allowing them time to loaf about at the town's pool hall. "If a number of through [main line] trains had clearance to move eastbound, these men might spend part of the day at this popular gathering place," a local historian noted. "And when traffic changed, they needed to know. Huttinger, the station agent, hustled over to give them their orders and they'd highball for the

Facing, Figures 2.13–2.15. (1) The Dawson, Minnesota, station grounds of the Minneapolis & St. Louis reflect an agent's effort to beautify his workplace surroundings. A fence provides protection for these trees and plants. *(Don L. Hofsommer collection)* (2) Residents of Fairbury, Illinois, surely took pride in the expansive depot park located across the tracks from the Toledo, Peoria & Western station as seen in this August 8, 1915, photograph. *(C. R. Childs photograph; Krambles-Peterson Archive)* (3) A more elaborate depot park is found at the Lake Shore & Michigan Southern (New York Central system) station in Elkhart, Indiana. *(Author's collection)* division point at Bodoin, making up for lost time." In reality, this Great Northern agent served as a train-crew call boy, an individual found in terminals and division points. Another illustration involved helping passengers with special needs. Assisting the physically handicapped, elderly, or young to the train occurred from time to time. If a youngster were to travel alone, the agent might pin the ticket and itinerary to that individual's clothes and explain to the conductor or another trainman about this junior passenger. Agents, too, needed to be diligent as overseers of property and rolling stock. Martin Wells, who served as the Greenwood, South Carolina, agent for the Charleston & Western Carolina Railway (C&WC), tried to get his company to remove a "foreign" boxcar owned by Baltimore & Ohio that seemingly had been abandoned on a nearby siding. When C&WC officials failed to respond to his repeated requests for action, he did not abandon hope. Instead, Wells wrote an anonymous letter to B&O headquarters in Baltimore, and within several days the car was headed northward toward its home road.[73]

WORKPLACE

Preexisting structures continued to be used for depots. When in the early 1880s, the Louisville & Nashville (L&N) acquired the Mobile & Montgomery and the Montgomery, New Orleans & Texas Railroads, which forged a through route between the Alabama capital and the Crescent City, it operated across the Rigolets Island area of Louisiana. In this sparsely populated territory, the company maintained agencies in commercial establishments in Chef Menteur, Lake Catherine, Rigolets, and English Lookout. When business warranted, the L&N erected its own depots at these stations. Yet it was more common for short lines rather than major carriers to rely on already existing buildings. When the narrow-gauge (three-foot) Boston, Revere Beach & Lynn opened its Boston suburban service in 1875, it converted a small former furniture factory into its station at Lynn, Massachusetts. The repurposing of houses also persisted. That is what the struggling fifty-five-mile Atlantic Northern & Southern Railroad did in 1911 when it began operations at its southern terminus in Villisca, Iowa. The chronically impoverished Georgia & Florida initially converted a private dwelling in Valdosta,

Figure 2.16. In February 1959, a freight train derailed in front of the Minneapolis & St. Louis station in Morning Sun, Iowa, destroying the depot. The company quickly spotted a modified bunk car to serve as a replacement. Since passenger service had ended, there was no need to fashion a waiting room, reinstall the brick platform, and the like. *(Don L. Hofsommer collection)*

Figure 2.17. A smaller community might not have a combination-style depot but a more elaborate union depot. Such was the case in Ashland, Illinois, where the Baltimore & Ohio Southwestern (B&O system) crossed the main line of the Chicago & Alton. About 1912, the agent stands beside the baggage truck as C&A train No. 15 approaches the station en route from Bloomington, Illinois, to Kansas City, Missouri. *(Krambles-Peterson Archive)*

Georgia, into its depot, and the anemic Valdosta, Moutrie & Western occupied a storefront in the same city. At the time of construction, railroads
might temporarily employ old boxcars or passenger coaches. When the
first Santa Fe passenger train steamed into the station at Albuquerque,
New Mexico Territory, in 1880, patrons encountered an assemblage of
old boxcars. In 1906, the Pierre, Rapid City & North Western did the
same for its initial station building in Midland, South Dakota. If a depot
were destroyed by fire, windstorm, or train wreck, a boxcar, coach, or
maintenance-of-way "outfit" or "bunk" car might appear, but usually
only until a replacement structure could be constructed. Yet in some
cases the temporary became the permanent.[74]

Of the approximately seventy-five thousand depots in use at the
dawn of the twentieth century, most were railroad built and usually of
frame construction. As the nineteenth century closed, the Ohio Commissioner of Railroads and Telegraphs reported that his state had 2,199
depots: 7 stone, 85 brick, and the remainder wood. Some of the latter
were built to standard plans. This was the case throughout much of the
nation, especially in the trans-Mississippi West. These depots, most of
which shared the dreary sameness of standardized designs, were hardly
a place that celebrated architecturally the adventure of travel. Nevertheless, they were the "official" entrances to communities and served as
their nerve centers. Since the majority of these combination freight and
passenger structures were designed for a single agent-operator, anyone
who worked there immediately grasped (and probably appreciated) the
floor plan. Railroads found these tripartite structures to be practical.
They featured a waiting room, office, and baggage-freight section. Because of post–Civil War Jim Crow laws in the South, depots had a legally
mandated separate "colored" waiting area. This space might be located
between the office and the freight room and lack heating, drinking water, and adequate seating. Typical waiting rooms generally possessed a
Shaker simplicity. There were usually heavy wooden benches, perhaps
bolted to the floor, ticket counter, water dispenser, several authorized
signs and maybe a framed railroad promotional poster or photograph,
and a chalkboard showing passenger train arrival and departure times.
(It was the agent's obligation to update this information.) A potbel-
lied stove provided heat. Its location varied, and sometimes it set in a

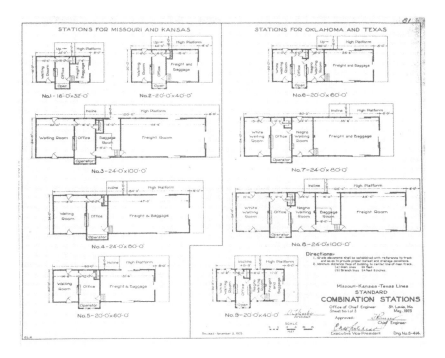

Figure 2.18. In 1925, the Missouri-Kansas-Texas developed a revised set of standardized combination depot plans. Since Oklahoma and Texas had long legalized racial segregation, railroads needed a "Negro" waiting room, something the Katy did not face in either Kansas or Missouri. *(Author's collection)*

screened aperture in the wall between the waiting room and the office. The walls themselves might feature wooden vertical or horizontal board siding, wainscoting, or beadboard. These materials could be topped off with painted plaster walls. The waiting room and office in the Elizabeth, Illinois, depot had this employment of wood coverings: "It has 3 foot vertical boards creating a 3 foot high wainscoting, which includes a 3 inch horizontal trim across the top. The same 3 inch wide wood is used horizontally for all of the walls above the wainscoting and both ceilings in both rooms [waiting room and office]. Ceiling boards run parallel to the front wall of the depot. Both ceilings are trimmed on all sides by 6 inch crown molding." Waiting rooms had multiple windows, with at least one facing trackside. There were the exterior doors, and one led to the plank or brick station platform. With the spread of public water systems, a flush toilet or toilets might be added, but outdoor privies remained common into the twentieth century. The freight room exuded an extreme starkness, but it would be cluttered with LCL freight, baggage and baggage truck, and maybe section men's tools. If the LCL business burgeoned, the Bridge & Building Department would expand the freight section to any desired length. The passenger side, too, might be lengthened or divided into separate men's ("gents'") and women's ("ladies'") waiting rooms.[75]

The office, rather than the waiting or freight rooms, served as action center. "Agents and station employes [sic] should insist upon all patrons transacting their business through the windows or over the counters provided for the purpose," noted the Station Agent's Blue Book, "and should see that only authorized persons are allowed access to the office."[76] In a typical combination depot, it was logically located in the center. The public knew the ticket window with counter, and on the agent's side, there was one of the three principal work areas: counter with a ticket dater, calendar above, and locked money drawer below. Nearby could be found a secured ticket case where a ticket punch and rubber stamps and sealers were also kept. A small safe might be in the immediate area. On the opposite side of the room stood storage cases or shelving, often for public tariffs, and the agent's wooden flat or rolltop desk. As typewriters became commonplace by the early twentieth century, one was likely on the desk. (These could be owned by the agents.) Later, an adding machine might be found there. Before the widespread use of carbon paper, there was a bulky hand-operated metal copy press. The trackside usually featured a bay window that provided a 180-degree visibility up and down the main track for the agent or operator seated at the built-in desk or telegrapher's bench or table. Here were the key and sounder and later the dispatcher's scissors telephone, which allowed the operator to pull it out to talk and push it out of the way when finished, and a commercial telephone. Nearby were levers that controlled the train-order board. Over the desk might hang the depot clock. It could be a classic Seth Thomas timepiece with its hexagon face and the lower square where the pendulum swung. Also nearby were hooks or nails to allow the customary practice of the agent hanging his pocket watch alongside his switch key.

Close by was a chair, in many cases perched on glass insulators, designed to make it easier for the operator to move about. Occasionally there was a window used to manage Form 31 train orders, although patrons might think that this was a second ticket window. A veteran agent, reflecting on his first depot assignment, carefully described this part of the office:

> The telegraph desk was in the bay window. This desk was to be kept clear of clutter as it was used for copying train orders and receiving and sending telegrams and messages. There were 3 telegraph wires coming into the office and there were 3 telegraph relays on the desk that were usually clicking away and when you heard the call [for the station][77] on one of those relays you plugged in the sounder that was mounted on a pedestal to which ever relay you were receiving the call from. The sounder had an empty Prince Albert tobacco can wedged behind the sounder to improve the sound of the dots and dashes.[78]

He continued:

> On the wall between the two front windows were the two levers to operate the train order signal. A large "N" was painted by the one for the northbound signal and a large "S" for the southbound signal. When the dispatcher called and wanted the operator to copy a train order, he would say SD [signal displayed] South if it was for a southbound train. The operator then moved the lever marked "S" to the stop position and then reported to the dispatcher SD South. There was a small compartment with 3 or 4 shelves where the train order pads were stored.[79]

Not to be overlooked would be a heating stove (wood or coal or much later maybe oil burning) and a couple of straight-backed chairs. There were doors to both the waiting and freight rooms. Coats and a uniform cap with a small nickel-plated badge indicating "Station Agent" or "Agent" might be on hangers, the latter being worn when meeting a passenger train or dealing with patrons. Hand lanterns, flags, train-order hoops or folks, boxcar seals, and other railroad paraphernalia hung on walls, often by the telegraph desk. A crowbar or additional tools were stored on the floor, as might be a box of fusees and track torpedoes. Express and other items were likely scattered about the office, making for a cluttered place.

By the post–World War II era, there were depot offices seemingly frozen in time. They were most likely found along branch lines or on shortline railroads. Lucius Beebe, who made the latter pikes famous with his 1947 book *Mixed Train Daily*, described the Cranberry, North Carolina,

Figure 2.19. The Chicago, Rock Island & Pacific depot office in Earlham, Iowa, offers a typical view of such a venue in the early-twentieth century. The ticket case, furnishings, and a large copy press are shown. *(James L. Rueber collection)*

office of the East Tennessee & Western North Carolina Railroad, known affectionately by residents and employees alike as the "Tweetsie." As he wrote, "The office of D. W. Mackie, the agent at Cranberry, would have done for a stage set of an old-time freight office, with its hand-crank telephone, cast-iron safe, antiquated correspondence files, and oddly enough, a mandolin standing in the corner beside a gigantic letter press." Beebe added that on his visit in early October, agent Mackie "maintained his premises at Turkish-bath temperature through the agency of a cannon-ball stove which glowed red all over." Beebe also discovered another antiquated depot in Baker, Oregon, on the soon-to-be-abandoned Sumpter Valley Railway, a one-time eighty-mile narrow-gauge carrier. "Inside it was warm and snug, and its properties might have served for a stage set of an old-time station agent's bay window. There were coal-oil

Figure 2.20. About 1910, a Chicago & North Western agent at an unidentified depot on the Belle Plaine, Iowa–Sanborn, Minnesota, line copies a train order at his telegrapher's table. He wears an official agent's cap and uniform jacket. *(James L. Rueber collection)*

lamps bracketed on the walls, a Franklin stove of massive proportions, two telephones of the old-fashioned, upright variety, a letter press in the corner and a vast cast-iron, key-locked safe, the twin leaves of whose doors share in equal portions a green-and-gold-painted landscape." He added to his observing eye description: "A Seth Thomas clock from Waterbury [Connecticut] and an old Oliver typewriter, a make almost coeval with the double-board L. C. Smith which now is a museum piece, completed the furniture."[80]

Artificial lighting throughout the depot was frequently poor. (Office windows usually had pull-down shades to eliminate any outside glare but often became badly tattered.) Before electrical fixtures, various types of kerosene lamps were nearly universal. Unfortunately, they did not provide good illumination. There was that "yellow gloom of the kerosene lamp in the room," remarked a writer in 1901. Other types of illumination were occasionally used. By the late nineteenth century, companies, however, frowned on or banned naphtha-fueled lamps, being dangerous and creating excess heat during the summer. Open-flame illumination of any type often cast deep, harsh shadows and could produce irritating flickering. After being wired, only a drop-cord bulb or two might individually serve the waiting room, office, and freight section. Agents were known to continue to maintain their favorite kerosene lamps until they had better lighting options.[81]

Even after World War II, lighting in country depots might not have improved dramatically. An agent recalled that in the 1950s, the initial forms of nonflame illumination continued. "Just a single cord hanging down from the ceiling in the bay window in the center above the telegraph desk. The light had either a green metal or glass shade fastened at the top of the socket that held the light bulb." He added, "This was probably to reduce glare for the operator copying train orders or telegrams." As for the rest of the depot, there was this description: "About in the center of the office part of the depot was also a long cord hanging down from the ceiling with a single bulb. I do not remember any of these having a shade. Same set up for the waiting room and out in the freight room." Fluorescent lighting for the agent's workspace might eventually appear, although this option had become commercially available during the 1930s.[82]

And there were certain office smells. Some visitors might notice the scent of sweeping compound, burning wood or coal, or cigar, cigarette, or pipe smoke,[83] but it also could be the distinct odor of ink. "Dad always smelled like a railroad depot," recalled Chet Huntley, who was born in the Northern Pacific (NP) depot in Cardwell, Montana. "The railroads of that era universally stocked their station offices with an inexpensive ink. It came to the depots along the [NP] line from the main warehouse in St. Paul in powdered form, contained in small packages. The agent or operator would frequently make up a batch of it by pouring the powder into a container and adding the required water." Huntley added, "That ink had a singular odor. It was not unpleasant but mildly pungent. I always liked the odor of Dad's clothing." Railroad enthusiast and author Ron Flanary summed up his thoughts about depot smells this way: "It seemed most every [depot] in America had the same scent—a mixture of slowly molding wood, mildewed paper and cloth, tobacco smoke, and a blend of cleaning concoctions and mysterious bacteriological material." He continued, "This was all incubated by a coal stove in winter or the natural heat of summer in subdued light for decades. It produced a singularly unique olfactory signature: 'Bouquet de Railroad.'"[84]

Visitors to an agent's office may not have been cognizant of particular odors, but they probably noticed a dog or cat. "I'm just belatedly reminded that I haven't mentioned the most important individual in our community," wrote a relief "op" to his wife about his canine friend. "He has just called to take me home. He is Buster, an elderly shepherd dog, and a very amiable gentleman. He calls at the station at one in the morning to escort Geer [another operator] home. He's at my door early in the morning, and if I don't get up when he thinks I should, he warns me." The writer added this further description of Buster's activities. "Then he takes me to work, and he stays around till he is sure everything is going nicely. So, as I call him as my best friend here." Although this lovable shepherd may not have spent long hours in the depot, a cat (or cats) might. A feline provided more than companionship, being usually a good "mouser." Rodents might be attracted to LCL freight and to discarded pieces of food scattered throughout the depot and on the station platform. A potentially uncontrolled rat and mouse problem required attention. If the agent and his family lived in the depot, the likelihood of pets, dogs, cats, or perhaps a parrot increased.[85]

There might be a roving station dog. One such canine was Roxie, who early in the twentieth century became a friend to agents and other railroad workers along the Long Island Railroad. When a puppy, she had been placed in the baggage car as her owner traveled from New York City to Roslyn. But Roxie did not like that arrangement and escaped. For more than a dozen years, she wandered up and down the line in search of her master. In the course of her wandering, this railroad dog often spent

Figure 2.21. This photograph, taken in September 1917, shows the Chicago & North Western office in Agar, South Dakota, with agent Hugh Merritt and his wife, Nellie. It also captures the depot cat. The feline appears to be comfortably at home. *(Author's collection)*

time in various stations. But one day Roxie died in her sleep at the Merrick depot and was buried on the station grounds. A tombstone, initially the pet's water bowl, marked the site.[86]

Animals in and around depots were not limited to the United States; their presence knew no geographical bounds. Great Britain stands out. "If anything surpasses the Englishman's love of steam trains, it is his love of dogs," observed the authors of a social history of world railway stations. "One feature of stations in the nineteenth century that caught

the fancy of contemporary writers was the phenomenon of station pets."
This love affair continued largely unabated.[87]

Although visitors to the freight room might detect a musty or dank
smell because the wide exterior door was usually closed or spot the depot
cat, they possibly noticed writings on the wall. In a set of instructions left
by an agent for his successor, there was this one: "First of all, let me suggest that you print your name and date on the wall of the freight house,
along with the rest of ours. It's sort of a club we have, and occasionally
some old-timer will come by and go take a look at the names on the wall.
It's nice to visit with them, if you aren't busy." This quaint agent's custom
continued sporadically into the twilight years.[88]

THREE

MATURITY: COMPLEXITIES

SIDE AND OUTSIDE BUSINESSES

The station agency job involved much more than the basic prescribed workplace duties. Although agents endured long hours on duty, some found time to engage in nonrailroad pursuits. The most common business practice involved the sale of oddments to the public, a practice generally tolerated by company officials. The mighty Pennsylvania Railroad had this rule book entry: "At less important agencies [the agent] may, when authorized by the Superintendent, engage in other business when it does not interfere with the proper discharge of his duties." These entrepreneurial activities normally took place in country depots. Agents offered an assortments of items, and ones that were usually competitively priced. Stationery, pens, and ink (with postage stamps sold at face value) were in demand. Once the picture postcard craze took hold at the turn of the twentieth century, which continued unabated until the outbreak of World War I, views of stations, towns, and local attractions became popular. These cards offered inexpensive opportunities to send brief messages—the emails and texts of that era. At the Chicago, Rock Island & Pacific (Rock Island) depot in Greensburg, Kansas, for example, postcards of the world's largest hand-dug well sold well. It was not unusual for agents to get a 100 percent markup on these postcard sales. The federal government did much to foster the popularity of picture postcards. In 1898, Congress granted privately printed postcards the same postal rate as those for government issues. A view card could go anywhere in the country for a penny. Nine years later, the Post Office Department

Figure 3.1. Ed Geerling, Great Western agent in Sheridan, Missouri, sold thread to patrons. Near the telegrapher's bench rests a six-drawer spool cabinet. Clark's, J&P Coats, and other firms provided cabinets and contents, and agents received a percentage of sales. *(James L. Rueber collection)*

allowed senders to write messages on the reverse side. Before that ruling, which created the split back with space for both address and message, it was common to find only limited blank space below or alongside the image on the front for a personal note. Another reason for the popularity of postcards was that often they could be conveniently mailed, whether in the postal box on or near the station platform or in the mail shot of an awaiting Railway Post Office car, "the Arteries of the Postal Service."[1]

Some agents offered more than stationery and postcards. They discovered that there were other possibilities for extra income. It was not unusual to find a spool cabinet in the depot office, allowing thread sales to female patrons. There were likely other notions, including pins and needles and perhaps miniature sewing kits. Far less common were agents who sold accident insurance. The Travelers Insurance Company of Hartford, Connecticut, first offered this coverage in 1864, but a growing number of firms followed suit. As with spool thread, they received a small commission for all policies sold. But agents seldom offered newspapers, magazines, and books or food, candies, and tobacco products; these could be obtained on board many trains from "news butches" or from venders in urban stations and terminals. Travelers' guidebooks, especially popular during the Gilded Age, were usually marketed along major tourist routes but available only at the largest stations.

Although it was rare for an agent to offer food, there were exceptions. In the 1870s, Charles George, the Chicago & North Western (North Western) agent in Waukegan, Illinois, took pride with his food sales. As he bragged (incorrectly), "I established what was among the first if not the first station eating-house in the United States." George explained:

> My wife, who was a thrifty New England house-keeper and noted for the excellence of her cooking, began to bake a few pies, a little cake, and some doughnuts for "the boys" who wanted some such refreshments. I had these articles set out on a little table for sale. One day Superintendent Johnson stopped at the station, and noticed this lunch-stand with its modest, yet appetizing display.
> "Who's this for?" asked Mr. Johnson.
> "For anybody who'll buy," I replied.
> "That's a good idea," he said, "a good idea. You can have one end of the station for a lunch-counter, if you want it, Charley."
> So I fitted up a neat little refectory at one end of the dingy old station, and Mr. Johnson and the trainmen soon got into the habit of lunching there every time they stopped. The superintendent had the conductors and the brakemen announce refreshments on their trains just before reaching Waukegan, and it was not long before there was a large and regular patronage. I ran the eating-house seventeen years.[2]

In an agent's spare time, he might use space in the freight room or in an auxiliary station structure for making or repairing a range of items. Radio repair is an example. When this form of home entertainment became widely popular by the 1930s, a technically inclined agent would let it be known in the community that he could replace a burned-out vacuum tube or fix some other part. Later radio repair might morph into the more complex servicing of television sets. Both activities could be more lucrative than fixing bicycle tires and chains, sharpening lawn-mowers and hand tools, or mending window and door screens. Again, these side businesses were generally overlooked at the least busy stations. This was the case for Charles Collins, longtime St. Louis-San Francisco (Frisco) agent in Bentley, Kansas. At this rural station, he convinced officials to spot a worn-out boxcar on a siding behind the depot. There Collins opened a photography galley, "[netting] him a nice profit for many years." Additional examples of company-approved sidelines include Minneapolis & St. Louis (M&StL) agent W. F. Arp, who operated an accounting service from his Victoria, Minnesota, depot, and J. A. Lillegrove, Chicago Great Western (Great Western) agent in Madison Lake, Minnesota, who owned the weekly newspaper. Yet such activities were not always approved or ignored. "Red Williams, CGW agent at Melbourne, [Iowa], was caught by an official one winter overhauling his old Chevy in the depot freight room. When discovered he was told that the car and all the straw had better be out of the depot by that night." Williams complied, saving his job.[3]

The most recalled account of an agent who engaged in nonrailroad activities was Richard Warren Sears (1863–1914), founder of the giant mail-order house of Sears, Roebuck & Company. Although details of the formative work career of this future "Barnum of merchandising" have been "lost in confusion and contradiction," it is known that as a teenager, he learned telegraphy from the Chicago, Milwaukee & St. Paul (Milwaukee Road) agent in Spring Valley, Minnesota, in exchange for doing chores at his station. After being employed by that company in several Minnesota and South Dakota communities and also by the St. Paul & Duluth in North Branch, Minnesota, Sears became relief operator for the M&StL in Lake Mills, Iowa. Soon he moved to company headquarters in Minneapolis, where he worked in the auditing department. Then at age nineteen, Sears served as the agent-operator in North Redwood Falls, Minnesota. "He was an excellent telegrapher," observed one source, "and kept his station in tip-top shape."[4]

It would be at the two-story Minneapolis & St. Louis depot in North Redwood Falls, two miles from Redwood Falls, where the young Richard Sears paved the way for his remarkable entrepreneurial career.

Figure 3.2. Eighty-seven-year-old retired agent "Charley" Macomber, who once served as a relief operator in the Lake Mills, Iowa, depot, sits at the desk used by Richard Sears who briefly worked in this office. In 1950, Minneapolis & St. Louis President Lucian Sprague learned of its existence and seized a public relations opportunity. He informed Robert Wood, chairman of the board of Sears, Roebuck & Company, about this historic artifact. "After a fitting ceremony Mr. L. C. Sprague on behalf of the Minneapolis & St. Louis Railway gave the desk to General Robert E. Wood for permanent display in the Sears, Roebeck offices in Chicago." *(Don L. Hofsommer collection)*

When employed briefly in Minneapolis, he apparently disliked receiving a straight salary. But as a small-town agent, he would have time to earn extra income from business dealings on the side, a passion (and skill) that he had shown since his early youth. It is known that in Lake Mills, Sears became involved with selling items on the side. "I know for I knew Sears," recalled Charles Macumber, the previous relief operator, "and in later years visited him and talked over old times." At North Redwood Falls, Sears became heavily involved in buying and selling. "He sold lumber, coal, and other products to the townsfolk; and from those customers he in turn purchased meat and berries, which he shipped to other localities." The pivotal event took place in 1886 when a Chicago jewelry firm sent a package of pocket watches that a local jeweler refused to accept.[5] Sears seized upon this opportunity. He arranged with the wholesaler to buy the watches for twelve dollars each. Next, he contacted other M&StL agents and offered them for fourteen dollars each, indicating that they could keep any monies over that amount. "With watches of a similar type retailing for $25 generally, the agents were able to undersell their local jewelers and make a profit for themselves." After this successful venture, Sears decided to quit station work and launch the R. W. Sears Watch Company. Soon this emerging merchandising tycoon moved to Chicago, where in partnership with watchmaker Alvah Roebuck (1864–1948), their firm of Sears, Roebuck & Company came into being, growing rapidly and prospering. A principal reason for its success was that Sears knew farmers, understood their needs and wants, and could write appealing copy for the firm's popular Wish Book catalogs. Customers could examine this "silent salesman" at their leisure and find attractively priced items. The catalog grew rapidly in size—thirty-one pages in 1891 and nearly twelve hundred pages in 1908.[6]

Much less memorable than the business career of Richard Sears involved the station agent at Hammondsport, New York. In 1875, the ten-mile narrow-gauge but later standardized Bath & Hammondsport Railroad (B&H) opened between Bath and Hammondsport, operating through the Pleasant Valley in the Finger Lakes district of western New York State. In Bath, this short line connected with the main lines of the Erie and Delaware, Lackawanna & Western (Lackawanna) Railroads. Early in the twentieth century, the Erie acquired the property, but by the time of World War I, the B&H had become a consistent money loser, a victim of "the automobile and the death of the wine industry [because of national prohibition]." In 1921, William Aber, the B&H agent at Hammondsport, joined up with the B&H's lone conductor to lease the railroad from the Erie, and these budding railroad executives planned "to operate the road upon a paying basis." They did so with limited success. Then in 1935, the Erie sold the B&H to five Hammondsport businessmen, and for decades the property operated under their management, which they promoted as "the Champagne Route," benefitting from the repeal of the Eighteenth Amendment. Later, a county development agency took control until its sale in 1996 to a short-line conglomerate.[7]

If an agent remained in a community for an extended period, he might engage in some agricultural pursuit, resembling hundreds of station masters in Great Britain and Europe. This could involve renting or buying land for field crops or vegetables. More commonly this property would be a place to raise milk cows, hogs, or poultry. Egg production was especially popular; eggs commonly served as a medium of exchange at general stores and with other local merchants. Early in the twentieth century, Hal Borland, Chicago, Burlington & Quincy (Burlington) agent at Guide Rock, Nebraska, took pride in his flock of chickens, which he raised in a fenced shelter opposite the depot. Much later, Harry Williams, Great Western agent at Stockton, Illinois, operated a small beef cattle farm. There were instances where agents, who were assigned to raw prairie communities, speculated in town lots or nearby farmlands. A few participated in the Florida land boom of the early 1920s before it went bust in 1926.[8]

There was extra income generated from the express and telegraph business. As the local representative for one of the several private express companies prior to World War I and subsequently for the consolidated American Railway Express Company and its successor Railway Express Agency, this work constituted part of an agent's duties. Compensation varied. It became standard practice for the agent to be paid a commission of 15 percent of the outgoing business and 10 percent of the incoming. By month's end, this compensation could be substantial. An alert agent might assist a local express shipper and receive additional remuneration for that service.[9]

Unlike the express business, the small-town agent frequently found that commercial telegraphic work generated only modest income and was often time-consuming and stressful. It was labor that outweighed compensation. An agent explained his thoughts about the shortcomings of this nonrailroad albeit sanctioned activity.

> Invariably, somebody would show up about 20 minutes or so before you'd go off duty with a handful of death messages. They expected you to accept them with graciousness and to get them out right away. All the operator made from a telegram was 10 percent of any money he handled. If somebody came in with 5 or 6 telegrams that were to be paid for at the other end, I wouldn't get a nickel from sending any of them. When you accepted the telegrams, you didn't know how long it was going to take to get rid of them because you had to call a relay operator. And you had to wait until he was not busy. You might sit there for 2 hours waiting for him past your time to go home. On in-bound telegrams if the telegram was paid for on the other end, you never got anything out of it. If [the message] was for out in the country, and the people had no phone, and if it was an urgent message, you felt that you almost had to deliver it. It was a fine thing for the Western Union but it was a mighty poor arrangement for the agent.[10]

NEGATIVES

It would be more than aspects of commercial messages that agents regularly detested, and these annoyances and challenges knew neither time period nor geographic region. Yet usually these headaches did not prompt the agent to quit. "He often encounters almost as great a variety of knotty problems as the [division] superintendent himself, though he has the advantage that he can generally turn them over to a superior if he feels unequal to them." Thus there existed a safety valve of sorts. In 1925, O. B. Kirkpatrick, author of *The Station Agent's Blue Book*, noted a related dimension: "It is often said that a station agent has more 'bosses' than any man in the employ of the railroad." This situation potentially could create stress and strain in the workplace.[11]

Dealing directly with the public had its displeasures. "The agent had to be ready, like the conductor to submit to some abuse from ill-bred customers," observed B. B. Adams, editor of the *Railroad Gazette*. One agent gave this advice to his son: "Whatever you do, don't ever take a job where you have to work with the damn public." In "Observations of a Country Station-Agent," which appeared in a 1917 issue of *Railroad*

Man's Magazine, J. E. Smith echoed these thoughts: "We [agents] have the arbitrary and the unreasonable, as well as the bores and the pests. We have the breed that is never satisfied, along with the breed that is so over satisfied that it camps with us and overstays our patience." For one thing, there were those aggravating questions asked by travelers. Although that harried Great Western agent at Tripoli, Iowa, noted several irritations, there were more. Agents faced the bother of explaining to passengers the difference between a.m. and p.m. or handling those who could not interpret a timetable or understand the train bulletin board. Some of these trivial questions, in fact, verged on the silly. One frustrated agent placed the following sign under the station clock: "This is a clock; it is running; it is right; it is set every day at 10 o'clock. Now keep your mouths shut." Admittedly, it was important to have an accurate and visible clock. "It has been found by experience that the passengers are very likely to become nervous if there is not a large clock in sight." This timepiece was often placed in the office and in sight of the ticket window. Having the exact standard time commonly attracted a small crowd to the station clock for a check of their timepieces. At noon eastern standard time, the US Naval Observatory in Washington, DC, sent a telegraphic signal across the country to denote the correct Greenwich mean time. These onlookers might annoy an agent if he were exceptionally busy. But as more Americans owned reliable timepieces, especially wristwatches by the 1920s, the importance of the station clock diminished. Furthermore, when passenger service dwindled after World War II, depots might no longer have clocks in public view.[12]

Waiting areas caused no end of troubles. This room (or rooms, if there was a separate women's one or a Jim Crow section) became a venue where patrons during cold weather fussed about poorly or overheated conditions, dirty floors, overflowing spittoons, and other housekeeping concerns. But they were more likely to complain about offensive people in their midst. Dissolute town idlers might harass travelers and others. Transients might sleep on waiting-room benches, take their toilet on the premises, seek handouts, steal a passenger's food basket, consume alcohol, spit tobacco randomly, and utter abusive or foul language. This description of a waiting room found on the Louisville & Nashville in the 1890s exemplified such disagreeable conditions: "Wooden benches are often used by tramps and 'bums' to sleep on at night, and are left dirty, filthy and frequently covered with vermin. Men smoke cigars and pipes and chew and spit where they please in this small waiting room." To respond to such matters, agents needed to ask or prod these offenders to behave or leave or, if needed, request assistance from local law enforcement. In 1905, an Iowa newspaper reported how one agent planned to manage unwanted individuals: "The agent has made the announcement that hereafter loafers will be compelled to keep away from the depot and that unless his orders are heeded some arrests will be made in the very near future." And legal actions were not unknown. A Burlington agent filed misdemeanor "public nuisance" charges against four young males. "It has been the custom of boys and young men who desired to sit in there [waiting room], fill the seats to the exclusion of all traveling men who desired to sit in there and wait for their train, and with their tobacco and boisterousness make things generally unpleasant for all concerned." Girls, too, could be pests. "It is not only boys who have at times proved nuisances," explained the agent, "but that some of the girls—not to give them the dignified title of young ladies—are in the same class and that the next time no distinction will be made between the sexes, but all will be compelled to answer in court." In a most unusual response to managing troublesome patrons, the Chesapeake Beach Railway, a short line that connected Washington, DC, with the summer resort community of Chesapeake Beach, Maryland, added a small jail to its District Line depot to retain temporarily unruly passengers returning from the shore.[13]

If an agent were to take action against an unwanted individual or group of individuals, he might turn to trickery or "legitimate fun." In the 1870s, a Pittsburgh, Fort Wayne & Chicago Railroad (Pennsylvania affiliate) night operator described his favorite way to evict a person who sought "free lodging at both ends of the route:"

> In the winter the favorite amusement was to roast them out. Wood was plenty, and near at hand. [I] would close the doors, heat the stove red hot, and keep it so. Soon the sleeper would begin to gasp, to turn over, and struggle for breath; then he would wipe away the perspiration, and, finally, sit up, and say: "Operator, don't you think it extremely warm in this room now?"
>
> "O, no!" says [I], "it's barely comfortable; I'm used to it. Besides, I've had the 'ager' [aging] so much that I can almost sit on a red hot stove," and [I] would move [my] chair closer to the fire.[14]

Individuals, perhaps loitering railroad workers, could become pests if they were loud and boisterous. Usually they meant no harm, but their noisemaking interfered with telegraphic work. "It always seemed that there would be a gang of people in the depot, laughing and telling jokes just about every time I had to copy train orders," recalled an agent. "It was most difficult to copy them through all the noise, and whenever I would ask the dispatcher to repeat something he would always growl and yell, often getting quite nasty, and whenever I would yell at the men to keep the noise down, some of them would get angry and leave."[15]

Business patrons likewise could be aggravating. If freight shipments, especially LCL ones, were late or damaged in transit, patrons' tempers might flare. Such occurrences for agents were time-consuming and emotionally draining. They developed, for example, a hardy dislike for the cheap dish and drinking glass business. "Always two or three 5c each type of glasses or a couple of 1c plates broken, requiring a trip to a store for inspection of packing, reason for damage, etc.," an agent remembered. "Most time consuming, when the time was so badly needed for all the other demanding work of the day. Naturally those handling such shipments felt their needs were equally as important as those of the livestock shippers." This agent was responsible and proactive. "We strived to keep them all happy. If we could get the 2c damage handled withing 72 hours, it worked out rather well. Many times I paid them out of my own pocket to save time."[16]

Where stations maintained animal pens, conflicts might arise over their operations and use. "Tension between railroad officials and shippers always characterized the livestock business," opined railroad historian Don Hofsommer. In August 1927, the agent for the Quanah, Acme & Pacific Railway (QA&P) at Roaring Springs, Texas, became the subject of a complaint registered by its largest livestock shipper, Matador Land & Cattle Company. The Matador president contacted his counterpart at QA&P headquarters to express his concern that the agent had failed at times to inform the ranch's superintendent or inspector when carloads of cattle were being loaded and shipped from nearby Russellville. (Located east of Roaring Springs, this townsite had never developed and lacked an agency.) The railroad responded by promising that its Roaring Springs agent would rectify this situation. About the same time, a dispute erupted between Matador cowboys who were branding cattle in the Russellville pens and ranchers who were anxiously awaiting to load their cattle. The agent had to help resolve the matter. Undoubtedly, both events were trying experiences.[17]

Since the agent needed to work or at least assist in handling LCL shipments, some items required time-consuming attention. An example would be protecting milk and cream cans during hot weather. Every morning, the agent needed to purchase a large block of ice. The next steps involved bringing the ice to the station, chipping it into small chunks about the size of softballs, and placing them in the sunken area of the lids. Finally, the agent might cover these cans with several water-soaked burlap bags or blankets until they could be shipped.[18]

There were also LCL shipments that became altogether unpleasant. "Did you ever wrestle a bale of wool on a hot day?" asked an agent. "The oily wool permeates the rough burlap bag. We had no hooks so it was a free for all getting the bale out of the wagon, on the [hand] truck to the scales where we weighted it and left it for the freight crew."[19]

That same agent had this encounter with four crated pianos:

> With my height I could wrestle a piano by snugging the broad bill [hand] truck to the bottom, rock the piano a few times and slip the truck bill under the case. More rocking and a little quick work to prevent the load from wrestling me I managed to get three of them under cover. Then the rains came. Not a spring shower like warm tea but a gully washer; cyclonic winds, a baby cataract and hail the size of cranberries.
>
> The truck and piano became my refuge. If I hadn't had a good hold on the truck which was tucked under the piano the wind would have blown me bye-bye.
>
> Struggling to get my back to the wind I rocked the heavy case, broke it down and slipped on the wet platform! Piano, truck and I went down in a heap and the truck handle broke. I shoved one way and the piano went the other and off the platform into the muddy mess of man made litter and horse manure.
>
> To hell with it![20]

Arguably as challenging as contending with crated pianos was this assignment performed by the night operator who in 1914 worked for the Reid Newfoundland Railway at its Bishop's Falls station. "I had to take in and deliver all the freight for the four local merchants. One of the most arduous tasks was unloading caribou carcasses which residents of the Bishop's Falls-Botwood area had shot on the Gaff Topsails." In an understatement of sorts, he added, "There are few items of freight more difficult to handle than a caribou." Perhaps the Great Western agent at Lamont, Iowa, would add to the list of strenuous tasks the handling of 120 sixty-six-pound tubs of butter, shipped twice weekly by the local creamery. Depending on the depot design and station layout, some railroads installed a barrel skid between trackside and the freight room, making movements of LCL freight somewhat less arduous.[21]

Although not involving anything of great physical weight, one female agent had a specific complaint about the LCL business. Olive K. Campbell, who began her agency career in 1898 as agent-telegrapher at Headland, Alabama, on the Atlantic Coast Line's twenty-seven-mile Grimes-Abbeville branch, detested the liquor trade. The daughter of a Southern Baptist preacher and herself an ardent prohibitionist, "'Miss Ollie' objected to being forced to handle liquor shipments that came in from the North more than the overlong [work] day." She probably breathed a sigh of relief in 1907 when Alabama lawmakers enacted a statewide prohibition measure.[22]

Hours of duty had their negative effects. For decades, the agent of a one-person station worked daily for twelve hours. If there were operators, they had a similar schedule. Early in the twentieth century, the federally mandated Hours of Service Act meant that these station employees gained a shorter workday. Following that measure, operators usually had one of three eight-hour "tricks." Those who customarily worked at night frequently found it difficult to remain awake, especially during the wee hours of the morning. "The midnight shift was pure hell, anyway you looked at it," recalled an operator. "You can sleep for twelve hours prior to going to work, but just as soon as you settled nicely into the job, the same bugaboo came around: the urge to sleep." He went on to explain. "There were so many things that lulled you to sleep. The worst one, the operators all agreed on, were the cold winter nights when there was a warm fire in the old coal stove. The figures dancing on the wall from the partially opened door would put anyone to sleep. The telegraph was also guaranteed to act as a sleeping pill." If the agent had a family, home life could be affected. When J. A. Hawkins worked the second trick (4:00 p.m. to midnight) or the third trick (midnight to 8:00 a.m.) for the Rock Island in Goodland, Kansas, he needed to sleep during part of the day,

if that were possible during a summer heat wave. "His daytime sleeping required a family policy of holding the noise down," recalled his
son. "The result was encouragement of table games and reading, and
a child's extra naps were never frowned on." Hawkins's wife was not
pleased when her husband awoke and entered the family setting. "His
sudden appearances after napping, half-dressed and his hair uncombed,
hardly befit 'the head of the family.'" Not to be overlooked is that an agent
might need to stay at his post longer, awaiting a late passenger train, for
example. Conscientious ones likely made special trips to the depot to
allow customers to receive their LCL freight or express shipments or to
send urgent telegrams.[23]

Then there was the curse of isolation. This factor explains why some
agents, particularly at the least active stations, got involved in nonrailroad activities. Ambrose Gonzales, future editor of the *State* newspaper
in Columbia, South Carolina, early on worked for the Port Royal Railroad (later Atlantic Coast Line) in Varnville, a Hampton County hamlet
forty-two miles from Port Royal, South Carolina. This settlement sprang
up around a sawmill, and there was little in the way of passenger and express business, and nearly all shipments involved the mill. His activities
largely involved traffic control between Port Royal and Augusta, Georgia. "I have plenty of telegraphing to do," wrote Gonzales to his family in
September 1875. "The more occupation the better, for I won't have time
to think of the confounded place."[24]

Agents might become dissatisfied with the local weather. Winters
in some locales were exceptionally cold, snowy, and gloomy. Although
largely confined to a heated depot, agents still had outside duties ranging
from handing up train orders to removing ice or snow from the station
platform. This explained why H. A. (Al) Stimson, an operator in De
Smet, South Dakota, decided to leave for warmer, sunnier climes. Soon
he found a job in Delray, Florida, gladly leaving the Dakota Division of
the North Western for the Florida East Coast Railway. For the remainder
of his long agency career, Stimson remained with this Sunshine State
road.[25]

Some agents complained about workplace conditions and for good
reasons. Their depots were uninsulated, and stoves failed to produce
adequate heat, making for an unpleasant environment, especially during

cold, windy weather. A former Minneapolis, St. Paul & Sault Ste. Marie (Soo Line) agent, whose depot office faced north, recalled that on some winter days, he found it impossible to work at his bay window table, and so he retreated to the stove. There were complaints about poor air ventilation, exacerbating hot and humid conditions. When only outdoor privies were available, there were additional gripes. "[The toilet] was usually an old broken down building, located as far away as possible, and once you visited this old 'two-holer' you would know why it was built in this location," explained an agent. "The smell was terrible, and especially in the summer months when the weather was good and hot." He continued, "The inside would be covered with cobwebs, bugs of all kinds, lizards and sometimes an occasional snake." Winter could be worse. "There would be snow blowing in the walls, making whatever it was you had to do an extremely cold chore."[26]

Although station work was never considered dangerous, there were instances where it was life-threatening or fatal. Fire became an ongoing concern when illumination required open flames and wood or coal stoves provided heat. Electrical storms, too, took their toll. In North Dakota, for example, flames engulfed twenty-five Soo Line depots between 1889 and 1975. In 1947, a tragic fire destroyed that company's depot in Columbus, North Dakota. The conflagration apparently started on the second floor, and relief operator J. H. Henson, who slept in the waiting room, perished when he was overcome by smoke as he searched for the fire. And there was this unusually unlucky place: Lafayette, Illinois, located in Stark County. Before World War I, the village's Rock Island depot fell victim to flames on five occasions. Most large roads annually lost or had damaged multiple station structures. Floods and tidal surges also caused havoc, but as with fires, employees nearly always escaped. Then on rare occasions, a train, likely a freight, derailed at the station with cars smashing into the depot. This was the case in 1907 when a passing Boston & Albany freight derailed in front of the two-story depot in West Brimfield, Massachusetts, causing its virtual destruction. Noted the inscription on a real-photo postcard of the wreck scene: "A narrow escape for the Agent & his family who lived upstairs over the station." Then there were freak acts of nature, including lighting strikes. In a nationally reported story, dating from September 1890, a "great ball of fire" hit an operator while at work in the Baltimore & Ohio depot in Canton Junction, Maryland. The lightning bolt knocked him out of his chair, making him briefly unconscious and paralyzed for several hours. "It was found that the lightning bolt had struck his left arm and passed all the way down below the elbow, leaving a broad crimson mark. It stopped just where his arm touched his vest pocket containing his watch, being attracted to the timepiece. The chain was melted and broken in several places. The watch was badly disfigured." The chain and timepiece probably saved his life.[27]

Agents had a greater chance of experiencing burglaries and armed robberies than fires, floods, wrecks, or violent weather. Since depots contained cash from ticket sales, express and freight collections, and telegraph messages together with other valuables, they became targets for criminal elements. Such events were far more common than highly publicized (and romanticized) train robberies. In 1892, the agent for the Old Colony Railroad in Hanover, Massachusetts, survived an exchange of gunfire during a daring burglary. A journalist provided coverage of "A Thrilling Encounter":

> At 4:30 o'clock this morning [April 2, 1892] the house [of agent Arthur Barnes] was entered, and the intruder, who must have been somewhat acquainted stole up stairs into the chamber where Mr. and Mrs. Barnes were sleeping.
>
> He found Mr. Barnes's pantaloons, and, taking the keys of the station therefrom, started to depart, but before doing this he flashed the light into Mrs. Barnes face, which caused her to awake just in time to see a man going for the stairs.
>
> She awoke her husband, who, surmising the purpose of the visitor, started for the station. The burglar had by this time got the safe unlocked, but became frightened when he saw Barnes approaching and started to escape. The latter fired a shot, but without effect, which the thief immediately returned, and with effect, the bullet striking Barnes in the right side near the lower rib. The thief escaped.
>
> Medical aid was immediately summoned and the bullet was extracted. Although Barnes is not seriously injured, he was taken to the Massachusetts General Hospital.[28]

In 1906, a more harrowing crime took place at the Chesapeake & Ohio station in the coal-mining camp of Kayford, West Virginia. Robbers bound up agent V. E. Adams, shot him in the leg, torched the depot, and absconded with $6,000 in gold. These criminals likely knew of the presence of this substantial payroll, which belonged to a railroad contractor.[29]

Then there was the case of the well-liked Charles Conklin, New York Central agent at Croton Lake, New York. In April 1911, a robber and his accomplice outlook became involved in a shoot-out with Conklin during an attempted holdup at his depot. In the exchange of gunfire, Conklin, "while defending the contents of his office," was killed and the robber wounded. Authorities soon captured the two culprits. Later, more than a thousand mourners, including representatives from the railroad, American Express, and Western Union, attended Conklin's funeral and burial in White Plains, New York.[30]

In a most unusual event, a conflict erupted between a conductor and an operator and led to murder. In 1888, James Talmage, conductor on a Wabash freight train, got involved in a heated dispute with C. P. Tidd, operator at Brunswick, Missouri, over train orders. Gunfire erupted. A jury found Talmage, the perpetrator, guilty of second-degree murder, and a judge sentenced him to twenty-one years at hard labor in the state penitentiary at Jefferson City.[31]

Other criminal acts affected station personnel. They needed to be on guard for ticket buyers who paid with counterfeit currency, a problem that was ongoing for decades. "He must detect counterfeit ten-dollar bills with the experience of a Washington treasury-clerk," opined an industry observer. Agents likewise had to be careful with personal and commercial checks. Always they had to be watchful for petty and large-scale thefts of company and individual property.[32]

From time to time, criminality might be perpetrated by an agent. There existed the temptation to falsify receipt books or to take money from the cash drawer or safe. The New Haven Railroad discovered that George Wisham, its agent at Larchmont, New York, had embezzled about $2,000 from station accounts. A much greater defalcation occurred when David Howell, Burlington agent in Colchester, Illinois, fled with $10,000 that belonged to the Quincy Coal Company. In these two cases, crime did not pay; both individuals were brought to justice. And it was not unknown for an agent to pilfer goods from boxcars, storage areas, or other places. There were instances where agents sold or gave away company coal.[33]

Another negative, although an exceptionally rare occurrence, involved an ongoing and potentially deadly event. This surely raised an agent's stress level. One can surmise that this runaway boxcar did just that. On an August morning in 1907, a freight car spotted on a siding at Northboro, Iowa, a station on the Burlington's Tarkio Valley branch between Villisca, Iowa, and St. Joseph, Missouri, broke loose during a high wind and "went whizzing south at a terrific pace." The Northboro agent sensed the likelihood of an impending disaster, knowing that No. 51, the daily northbound passenger train, was in its likely path. Moreover, the breakaway car was moving downgrade with a steady wind propelling it forward. What to do? He wired the agent in Westboro, Missouri, six miles to the south, to warn him of this rapidly traveling car. As the agent was taking the message, he broke in to report that "the car had just passed the depot at a rate in excess of sixty miles an hour." The frantic Westboro agent contacted the Tarkio, Missouri, agent, seven miles down the line, to learn if No. 51 had left. Unfortunately, it had. The inevitable collision soon happened. The engineer saw the oncoming car and applied the air; he and the fireman then leaped from the cab, landing without serious injury. "The train came to a stop almost the moment the car struck the engine, but there was a great shattering of timbers. The engine was so badly damaged the train could neither proceed nor back up. Some of the passengers were shaken up, but none dangerously injured." A scary wreck, yes, but a deadly one, no.[34]

MOBILITY

For generations, on-the-move "boomer"[35] agent-operators were ubiquitous. They, too, might not always be honest, most likely committing petty thievery. Knowing the ins and outs of station operations and being able to continue their nomadic life, often with ease, helps to explain their criminal behavior. "Their favorite trick was to sell passenger tickets out of the back of the ticket book and then pocket the money," an agent recalled. "Since the agent would usually only check the number of the first and last tickets in the book, he would not find the in between missing ones until he came to the place where they were supposed to be in the book."[36]

Why these footloose and fancy-free agent-operators? Multiple reasons explain their presence. Most boomers had that burning desire for change; they possessed that roving disposition. Railroading for them was not so much a job but an adventure. Some jumped from railroad to railroad because they had drinking problems, having been dismissed for violating "Rule G," the industry's universal antialcohol policy. Some opted for a career of mobility due to blacklisting for labor or radical political agitation (and before the Railroad Retirement Act of 1935, they could do so by working under a "flag," or assumed name). Others may have experienced unhappy domestic lives. But there could be additional explanations. In an era when paid vacations were nonexistent, these men might want periods of free time, and so they "bunched" their jobs. Closely related were those who wished to take advantage of seasonal work in places with pleasant climates—perhaps winters in Southern California or Florida and summers in the mountains of Colorado or coastal Washington State. These agent-operators were probably unattached males in their twenties and thirties. "The boomers are young single guys, who would rather boom around over the country," observed one railroader. "Where on the other hand, most of the old heads are married men with families who have settled down." Boomers grasped the presence of an expanding rail network, especially during the frenzied construction in the 1880s, when more than sixty-eight thousand miles of new track were laid and a fluid labor market existed. They knew that they had in-demand skills, which allowed them to move freely. Not to be overlooked was that "boomerism" also occurred among various portable occupations, including carpentry, medicine, and teaching. This phenomenon can also be considered a function of the male life cycle, irrespective of one's talents or economic status. Nomadism was ingrained in the culture. Historian George Pierson described this behavior as the "m-factors" in the American experience: "movement, migration, and mobility."[37]

Thousands of these independent-minded agent-operators fell into the boomer category. Arguably, they were good railroaders, or they could not have been hired or have lasted long on any job. "A rolling rock may gather no moss, but it takes on considerable polish," the thoughts of one dispatcher. There were railroaders, including "brass hats," who considered boomers to be an elite class of workers and often available when a company needed them the most, namely, during the busiest traffic season. It might be the apple, citrus, melon, sugar, or grain rush.[38]

The flavor of a boomer's career can be found in a 1952 letter to a fellow railroader from R. H. McConnell, a retired operator and agent-operator for the Rock Island. "I worked as Opr [operator] at Greene [Iowa, for Burlington, Cedar Rapids & Northern] before going to the U.P. [Union Pacific] in 1902. Before that time, I worked nights at Laporte [Iowa]; nights at Rockford [Iowa]; and at Manly [Iowa]." He continued, "I worked extra at Emmetsburg [Iowa] and Livermore [Iowa] in 1901. Returning to Iowa in 1918, during the flu epidemic I worked at Sunbury, Tipton, Bennett, Walker, Oelwein, Mediapolis, Spirit Lake [Iowa] and Lismore, Minn. Spent considerable time at Tipton [Iowa], then got Wapello station in 1919. To Webster City [either with the Illinois Central or North Western] in 1920, when I was offered a job in Colorado. from there to Thornburg [Iowa]." McConnell closed with these remarks: "I was lucky in having enough years service to my credit (33) when I retired in [19]47." Here was a work record that reveals "booming" and advancement from relief telegrapher to agent-operator.[39]

The career of R. H. McConnell shows that whether a boomer or not, job relocations were so much part of railroading. The path to dispatcher, for example, nearly always began with stints on the "extra board" as a relief operator or agent-operator, then successfully biding in on a permanent job and using seniority to advance to better assignments. Multiple movements were also pronounced among top officials. Gregory Maxwell, who worked for the New York Central, Terminal Railroad Association of St. Louis, and lastly as president of Erie Lackawanna, relocated nineteen times before his retirement. He once built a house in Albany, New York, that his family never occupied. Union Pacific president Edd Bailey recalled a similar pattern. "In a little over a ten year period Mabel, the kids and I had moved 13 times. There was no way she could have survived this period without being flexible." Bailey added, "We moved so often that we never considered buying a house." If frequent or prolonged physical separations occurred, marital tensions might develop between husband and wife. "After some time [separations] may gradually merge into desertion," observed Fred Cottrell in a classic sociological study, *The Railroaders*.[40]

ROMANCE

Boomers and those usually with the lowest seniority might developed short- or long-term relationships with the opposite sex. Perhaps these were limited or so-called one-night stands. Changing assignments frequently provided opportunities to become friendly with semipermanent residents in hotels or rooming houses and also with barmaids and waitresses. Some of the latter might be employed by the Fred Harvey Company, the celebrated restaurant chain that dotted the sprawling Santa Fe system and was known for its unmarried and perky Harvey girls. Boomers might find their true love, marry, and decide to join the home guard, thereby establishing seniority on a railroad. There were those demonstrably positive aspects of staying with one company, most of all advancement with the likelihood of better wages and working conditions. Many of these former wanderers took satisfaction in eventually sinking family roots in a community.

Occasionally, an agency job offered something else besides the romance of the rails. Orlando Pippin, who served as the Great Northern (GN) agent-operator in Russell, Minnesota, began a "telegraph key romance" with Bertha Dahl, an operator on the Sioux Falls-Yankton branch of the GN. "The ticking of the instruments was not always of business and it did not take long for the acquaintanceship to ripen into friendship," according to a syndicated newspaper story. "And later the two met at the home of the bride in Elk Point [South Dakota]. From then on it did not take Dan Cupid long to establish a new Morse code. Soon after a wedding was arranged by wire. Both agreed to meet at Sioux City and be married." In a sense, the station telegraph served as the pioneer online dating mechanism, creating weeks or months of anticipation.[41]

The public would not have been surprised by the romantic relationship between Orlando and Bertha. There were previous accounts of telegraphic romances, including fictionalized ones. Readers of the October 1876 issue of the *Atlantic Monthly* presumably enjoyed the tale of telegrapher Mary Brown and agent-operator Jahn Thor. It was not love at first sight, but a strong attraction developed. Following their involvement in averting a wreck caused by a drunken engineer, they grew closer, and then Jahn proposed to Mary. "Of course I married Mr. Thor, six months afterwards," she tersely explained. Presumably, the couple lived a conventional Victorian life.[42]

Well into the twentieth century, feature-story writers found that telegraphic romances pleased their editors. These journalists knew that readers relished human interest stories. Deborah Shouse, who contributed this piece to the *Kansas City Star Magazine*, described the love story of Bill Davis and Arlene Parker. Shortly after World War II, Bill, age twenty-five, became a telegrapher for the Rock Island in Goodland, Kansas, and Arlene, age twenty, was employed in a similar position with the Rock Island in Phillipsburg, Kansas, 140 miles to the east. "She had worked with Bill's dad [Goodland agent] and knew all about Bill." Their relationship grew. "When Bill started learning Morse code, Arlene often stayed late to help Bill practice on the wire." It did not take long for their messages to become personal. "Naturally I was interested in him. But I was working seven days a week—all different hours," explained Arlene. "I had no time to socialize." While traveling to an assignment in Fairbury, Nebraska, Bill finally got a glimpse of Arlene, and he liked what he saw. A few months later, the two met in Phillipsburg and learned that they shared much in common. Soon Bill started to visit Arlene on weekends, and their romance blossomed. In summer 1946, the couple tied the matrimonial knot.[43]

COMMUNITY INVOLVEMENT

If a station agent achieved a permanent job rather than being assigned to the extra board, he (or she) arguably became as well known as the local banker, professional, or clergy. "The agent ranked just behind a minister in terms of respect," reflected a small-town newspaper editor. His observation was hardly exaggerated. When children of an agent were asked, "What does your father do?" they proudly responded, "He's the depot agent." This was a time, too, when many adults knew the names of railroad presidents whose companies served their communities. Citizens turned to the agent for more than railroad business and those up-to-date reports about major outside events—presidential election returns, for example.[44]

In an era when many Americans lacked much formal education, especially males who had left school before they had advanced beyond the earliest primary grades or were recent arrivals from a non-English-speaking country, the agent might serve as their "reading man." Individuals who were illiterate or largely so knew that the agent was not. "If any reading matter came their way," explained a retired agent, "they usually headed for the depot to have it interpreted." If an agent were not busy, this became a community service that was not considered burdensome. Reading and interpreting legal materials were common requests. In a related form of help, an agent might provide a notary service. Rather than being a legal notary public who used an official stamp, he pressed a sealer with the imprint "For Public Use Only" into melted wax. Envelopes or packages could be formally closed.[45]

Public services that agents were far less likely to perform—but some occasionally did—involved acting as a medical practitioner. One agent who provided this assistance was S. S. McBride, who in 1882 became the Denver & Rio Grande agent in Espanola, New Mexico Territory. Described as a "jewel of a man," he was eminently resourceful. Since his community for years lacked a medical professional, McBride practiced the healing arts with apparent success and gratitude by using *Dr. Humphrey's Homeopathic Medicine Chest*. For years, the Humphrey Homeopathic Medicine Company of New York City sold this popular product.[46]

It was not unknown for established station agents to enter politics. Typically they served as mayors, councilmen, and school board members. While other railroaders held public office, agents were ones who more frequently sought elective office. They ran the gamut of political parties, more likely to be Republicans outside the South where Democrats held sway, or they aligned themselves with third parties, for example, the People's Party in the 1890s and the prolabor Progressive Party of 1924. Yet with the rise of the municipal reform following the catastrophic depression of 1893 to 1897, nonpartisan local elections became common. Examples of political involvement are widespread. "Politics in small town America was normally the province of lawyers, bankers, and businessmen, but in Santa Fe towns some offices regularly fell to railroaders," concluded historian James Ducker in his study of labor on the Atchison, Topeka & Santa Fe Railway (Santa Fe). As he observed, "Station agents in struggling young towns represented a key business link with the outside world. Consequently, they often found themselves in high local offices." In the 1920s, the Great Western agent in Stockton, Illinois, a division point, was politically active. "At the village elections in Stockton April 16th [1926] Agent S. L. Vickers, candidate for Village President [mayor], was elected with 208 more votes than his nearest competitor," reported the company magazine. "Sam has been on the Village Council for years." Somewhat later, Archie Markee, who served for thirty-five years as the Southern Pacific agent in Canby, Oregon, once performed the duties of acting mayor, and he also headed the local Chamber of Commerce.[47]

UNIONS

Just as Sam Vickers held elective offices in Stockton, Illinois, thousands of agent-operators over the years became involved in trade union politics or participated actively in union affairs. Still, it took decades before effective unionization became a reality. The Order of Railroad Telegraphers (ORT) served as that vehicle.

During the Civil War, railroad workers began their long march toward effective unionization. The Brotherhood of Locomotive Engineers (BLE) emerged as the path-breaking organization, having been launched in 1863. Conductors followed suit in 1873 with their Brotherhood of Conductors, although renamed six years later as the Order of Railway Conductors and often referred to as the "Big O." Not until the 1880s did the majority of railroad brotherhoods appear or morphed from mutual benefit societies to active trade organizations, including the Brotherhood of Locomotive Firemen, Brotherhood of Maintenance of Way Employees, and Brotherhood of Railroad Trainmen. Railroad telegraphers, however, could claim to have been in the forefront of this ongoing process. In the same year that the BLE made its debut, the poorly organized and short-lived National Telegraphic Union (NTU) appeared. Railroad telegraphers, however, shied away from the Telegraphers' Protective Union

(TPU). Launched in 1866, it was modest in size and composed mostly of employees employed by the rapidly expanding Western Union Telegraph Company. These TPU members took more aggressive workplace stances than had the NTU, but they paid the ultimate price. A failed strike in 1870 against Western Union killed off their organization.[48]

Gilded Age efforts to create a thriving railroad telegraphers' union sputtered. Attempts to advance wages, prevent wage reductions, and reduce working hours largely fizzled. Industry officials had no desire to have unionized telegraphers (or agents). Those individuals who were union ringleaders faced intimidation, dismissal, and blacklisting. This was a time of pronounced union busting campaigns. Furthermore, a potential union with commercial telegraphers never developed. This was largely explained by the dissimilarity of their office conditions; agent-operators were widely scattered and worked for multiple employers.[49]

In the early 1880s, a resurgence of union activities by railroad telegraphers occurred. The vehicle became the Knights of Labor (officially the Noble and Holy Order of the Knights of Labor), under the leadership of Grand Master Workman Terence V. Powderly, former mayor of Scranton, Pennsylvania, and crusader for the eight-hour day. In 1880, the Knights, which sprang from a Philadelphia garment-cutters union in 1869, claimed about thirty thousand members. Three years later, the Brotherhood of Telegraphers of the United States (BTUS) emerged, technically District 45 of the Knights of Labor. This body attracted an estimated eighteen thousand telegraphers out of approximately twenty-two thousand telegraphers nationally; roughly two-thirds were railroaders. Then by June 1886, the ranks of the Knights spiked to more than seven hundred thousand members, and the number of district assemblies soared from 484 in 1882 to 5,892. (The basic unit of the Knights was the district, a kind of territorial "local," to which all workers of a given area belonged.) This dramatic surge came in the wake of its unexpected victory that followed an unsanctioned strike against Jay Gould's sprawling railroad empire. His network of roads included the Iron Mountain, Missouri Pacific, Texas & Pacific, and Wabash. This event electrified workers across America, who developed the illusion of easy organizing success. These men and women joined what was a singular labor organization. The Knights' stated primary purpose: "to secure to the toilers a proper share of the wealth they create." It granted membership to any "producer" over age eighteen regardless of race, sex, or skill. Yet it barred bankers, lawyers, liquor dealers, saloonkeepers, and stockbrokers, and it shunned Asians. A year later, the movement faltered badly due to a failed (and again unsanctioned) strike against the Gould roads. The Knights' leaders embraced a no-strike philosophy, understanding that walkouts were difficult to win and fearing that they would cripple or destroy their movement. These concerns were real. Powderly and other officials, however, could not control the actions of hundreds of scattered local and often militant assemblies.[50]

With the breakdown of the Knights and the collapse of the BTUS, the organizational efforts for railroad telegraphers took a predictable direction. The fraternal rather than trade union model became the path followed. Yet there were some trappings of the bread-and-butter unionism successfully promoted by the recently formed craft-only American Federation of Labor. The golden era of fraternal organizations was at hand, whether the Ancient Order of United Workmen, Knights of Pythias, or Woodmen of the World. As many as 20 percent of all males belonged to such groups. These secret organizations with their often elaborate rituals provided mutual social and financial support, based on the belief that every member must be his brother's keeper. Such a value system dictated how they should interact with one another and also with the general population. During this heyday of fraternal organizations, they were dubbed by contemporaries as "coffin clubs," meaning that they provided death and burial insurance. This became a powerful enticement because more families had become totally dependent on the wage system for their economic well-being. Furthermore, there was an expanding gender differential in life expectancy, meaning the likelihood of more widows and orphans.

In June 1886, wire personnel from multiple railroads, but represented heavily from those who worked in the trans-Chicago West, gathered in Cedar Rapids, Iowa. These activists voted to launch a secret organization, the Order of Railroad Telegraphers of North America. (It later dropped "of North America.") Delegates agreed to limit membership to telegraphers who had been or were actively employed in railroad service. They were not about to welcome commercial operators employed by Western Union, Postal Telegraph, and the remaining small telegraph companies. As with the Knights of Labor, the Order of Railroad Telegraphers took a no-strike stance, considering its infant union "as fragile as an eggshell." Part of this reasoning was that "a non-striking organization would encounter less serious opposition from the railroad officials." The body, nevertheless, longed to increase wages and to improve working conditions. Although inadequate pay was a pressing issue, telegraphers complained about being physically and mentally overworked, often required to be at their posts seven days a week for twelve to sixteen hours. Delegates expected that their goals could be accomplished by restricting the number of telegraphers, specifically by not permitting members to teach telegraphy to anyone seeking to enter the craft. The law of supply and demand, they reasoned, would work to their advantage. There was also the expectation that management would be pleased. If the number of inexperienced telegraphers were reduced, train-control errors would presumably decline.[51]

Immediately the ORT went to work. Its leadership hired recruiters, and success followed. Membership rolls grew from 2,250 in 1887 to about 9,000 two years later. Yet the high cost of these organizational efforts stymied any immediate expansion. To worsen matters, an erosion of members occurred, caused by a lack of interest in the fraternal structure, its insurance program, and the no-strike policy. But when more rank-and-file telegraphers felt the sting of corporate discrimination, a spirit of militancy grew, leading in 1891 to a membership spike and a reorganization. The ORT became a full-fledged trade union similar to the railroad operating brotherhoods. "The members looked to the organization for protection against injustice and expected through it to gain recognition as a craft."[52]

The 1890s was a time of severe depression and labor unrest. ORT members were now willing to strike. Soon after its reorganization, it engaged in work stoppages throughout much of the country. Between 1892 and 1893, the union met with some noteworthy successes. It secured labor agreements on twenty-five roads, being concentrated in the West and highlighted by accords with the Frisco, Missouri Pacific, and Union Pacific. Yet failures occurred, including a bitter and unsuccessful strike against the Lehigh Valley.[53]

In May 1893, a national disaster began when the stock market collapsed, and almost immediately the economy plunged into a deep, multiyear depression. Scores of railroads slipped into receivership, including some of the largest, and a 10 percent wage cut became commonplace. For the immediate future, boomer telegraphers largely disappeared; those with jobs stayed put, if possible. Within two years, ORT membership dropped from approximately eighteen thousand in 1893 to about five thousand. To worsen matters, an aggressive rival labor organization emerged in 1893, the American Railway Union (ARU). This industrial union, led by former Brotherhood of Locomotive Firemen activist Eugene V. Debs, sought to include *all* railroad workers (except African Americans and Asians), regardless of their skills, under a single structural umbrella. "We are in favor of the organization of all railroad employees and when organized, we are in favor of the federation of such organizations for mutual protection," explained the charismatic Debs. This strategy, in his words, would "secure justice," and "railroad strikes would disappear from the land as if by a decree of Jehovah."[54]

The ARU enjoyed an auspicious start. Energized by a stunning victory against James J. Hill's Great Northern Railway, which followed an eighteen-day walkout over a wage cut, the Debs rank and file felt confident about its future, creating what one member called the "Dawn of a New Era." Non-ARU railroaders paid close attention, including telegraphers and agent-operators. Although the number of ORT members who abandoned their union is unknown, labor economist Archibald McIsaac speculated that "the loss of Telegraphers may have been substantial."[55]

The ARU actions caused a crisis for the ORT. Debs's 150,000-member union agreed to boycott rolling stock belonging to the Pullman Palace Car Company. The reason: four thousand Pullman workers on May 11, 1894, had gone out on strike. The ARU sought to bolster the cause of these Pullman operatives who had had their wages slashed by as much as a third to a half while their housing rents and store prices in their "model" company town of Pullman, Illinois, located just outside Chicago, were

D. G. Jeffries.   J. A. LaFont.   F. W. Bristow.
T. D. Thomas,   D. C. Bristow.
CRYSTAL CITY AND FESTUS, MO.—SOLID O. R. T. GROUP.

Figure 3.3. This circa 1910 picture postcard shows Crystal City and Festus, Missouri, agents/telegraphers, who work at Frisco Lines stations only a mile apart, proudly announcing that they are "Solid ORT." *(Dan Sabin collection)*

not reduced. Moreover, George Pullman flatly refused to arbitrate any and all grievances. When the strike came, he promptly closed the plant and waited for the workers to capitulate. ARU militancy led to scattered acts of violence and the halting of hundreds of trains. Although the ORT sympathized with the Pullman strikers, its leadership failed to endorse the ARU boycott. Much to its displeasure, hundreds of members got involved with the ARU intervention. On the Louisville & Nashville, for example, telegraphers participated in a sympathetic strike that quickly flopped and angered management. Such actions convinced ORT officials that they must institute strict organizational discipline. As for the ARU, the federal government and courts broke the boycott, causing the promising ARU and its experiment in industrial unionism to collapse and Debs to spend six months in jail. Debs, though, won widespread fame as a defender of the rights of workers and became the longtime and beloved leader of the Socialist Party of America.[56]

During the turbulent 1890s, the ORT experienced flare-ups within its leadership ranks. Policy differences, mismanagement, and personality clashes account for this strife. A major shakeup, which occurred in 1894, produced greater harmony, yet membership remained anemic. In 1901, the ORT had less than two-thirds as many members as it claimed at the start of the 1893 depression. Yet better days were in the offing.[57]

As the twentieth century progressed, union morale soared. More telegraphers and agent-operators embraced the ORT, seeking to make their railroad or division "100 Percent ORT." The union strengthened itself by providing an attractive insurance incentive, allowing nontelegraphic towermen to join, and developing stronger ties with engine and train service brotherhoods. Railroad management realized the need for competent and stable "brass pounders," and it showed a greater willingness to support a unionized workforce. By 1907, ORT membership had climbed to thirty-seven thousand. Yet dispatchers, who belonged to the ORT, a decade later launched their own union, the American Train Dispatchers Association. Some members, however, retained their ORT affiliation.[58]

A landmark event took place in 1907. While a bankers' panic that year caused temporary financial setbacks for the industry, it encountered another one. The ORT won what it termed a "great victory" when Congress passed and President Theodore Roosevelt signed the Hours of Service Act (HOSA) on March 4, 1907. This measure, which Senator Robert La Follette Sr. spearheaded, reflected the fundamental progressive impulse of protecting the public interest. In this case, the goal was to create safer railroads. La Follette and fellow reformers argued that worker fatigue frequently contributed to the high rate of railroad accidents and collisions, occurring at a time when freight and passenger traffic continued to grow by leaps and bounds. "If anything could add to the ghastliness of a railway accident," one journalist opined, "it is to be told that it might have been avoided if the operator or train-despatcher had not been asleep or otherwise incapacitated because he had been compelled to work overtime and therefore transmitted a wrong order or no order at all!"[59]

What did the Hours of Service Act involve? It prohibited carriers from requiring their employees to remain on duty for more than sixteen consecutive hours. After that time, the law mandated that employees be granted ten consecutive hours off duty. It specifically restricted telegraphers, which included dispatchers, to nine hours of work during a twenty-four-hour period in stations continuously operated or no longer than thirteen hours in daytime-only stations. An exception allowed for four additional hours in case of an emergency. The industry had one year to comply; the implementation date was set for March 4, 1908.[60]

The La Follette–inspired law angered railroad management. Complaints were filed with the Interstate Commerce Commission (ICC) and with the courts. It appeared that carriers might be able to delay implementation, perhaps for years. Yet in 1911, their quest failed; the US Supreme Court in the case of Baltimore & Ohio Railroad Company v. Interstate Commerce Commission upheld the legality of HOSA. Postponement attempts continued, however. The industry challenged procedural detail but ultimately accepted the legislation. At the time HOSA became law, Americans saw it as "humane, timely, just, and reasonable."[61]

The Hours of Service Act affected ORT membership in multiple ways. The most obvious benefits were improved daily working conditions and the need to hire more telegraphers. Because of increasing costs at a time when federal and state regulatory bodies either refused or were slow to permit freight and passenger rate hikes, various railroads closed some of their smallest stations, usually ones maintained solely for train control. At least in one case, the elimination of a night trick operator contributed to a deadly wreck. Several major carriers briefly abandoned their manual-block signals and returned to the more dangerous time-interval method of traffic control. ORT members fussed, too, about companies imposing split shifts; the mandatory nine hours would be stretched out over a longer period of the day. What the ORT did not anticipate was that the law fostered a replacement technology—dispatching via long-distance telephone.[62]

Telephone dispatching did not originate in the wake of the Hours of Service Act. Early in the history of commercial telephony, a few railroads used Alexander Graham Bell's invention to regulate train movements, but none were large carriers. It has been widely accepted that the Boston, Revere Beach & Lynn (BRB&L) was the first railroad to use the telephone (or what some contemporaries called the "acoustic telegraph") for dispatching. This narrow-gauge short line, which carried workers and shoppers to and from Boston and during the summer hauled weekending Bostonians to Revere Beach and an adjoining amusement park, never had telegraph connections. Instead management found that telephone usage, which began in 1879, worked well once initial technical problems were solved. "There never has been any [train-order] error vitally affecting the construction of the order," declared BRB&L Superintendent C. A. Hammond in 1892. No one on the railroad needed to know Morse code, reducing hiring problems and payroll expenditures. Another attractive feature was that its communications costs were manageable because the BRB&L and other short lines acquired "off-the-shelf" telephone equipment, which steadily became less expensive. By the 1890s, some major roads, including the Jersey Central, Pennsylvania, and Santa Fe, also found the telephone to be a promising communication device, including issuing and delivering train orders. It became apparent to some observers that train dispatching by telephone would become more prevalent. "The telephone has not, as yet [1904], become an important factor in the operation of trains," commented one source. "This has been probably because the telegraph is a tried and proved servant, doing the work economically and well." Yet this prophecy: "The telephone will probably appear as a rival of the telegraph in this field. When this time comes, it will be natural that the telephone should be employed in the movement of trains."[63]

The Hours of Service Act produced a sea change in dispatcher–agent-operator communications. In the year that the HOSA became law, a telephone selector device was devised that permitted the dispatcher to select any station and connect with it without signaling other stations. It also became apparent that the telephone was faster than the telegraph, increasing the volume of traffic handled, thereby reducing the number of on-duty dispatchers. In 1909, James Latimer, a signal engineer for the Burlington, offered these thoughts: "Professional telegraph operators who would accept positions as [manual] block operators at the wages which railroad could afford to pay for such service were, as a rule, beginners—young men who expected, as soon as they became proficient enough, to be able to secure better pay in other positions." Latimer continued, "The introduction of the telephone for block purposes has made it possible for railroads to use a different and more permanent class of men for this work, which is bound to result in more efficient service in the future." And there was this industry benefit: telephony would likely reduce the power of the ORT. After all, there was no need to learn Morse code, lessening the demand for skilled labor. Yet there were naysayers. A contemporary complaint went like this: "With the telegraph, when one operator reports to the dispatcher the 'arrival,' 'departing,' or 'by' time of a train at his station or tower, all other operators may be cognizant of the fact; while with the telephone it would be impossible unless the operator kept the telephone receivers or 'lugs' constantly to their ears. This would, of course, be out of the question." And this observation: "By using Morse everyone involved was kept attuned to proceedings; it was quick, and expedient, and everyone with an ear to the Morse wire was kept informed of changing circumstances." There were other perceived disadvantages. When compared with the telegraph, initial telephone installation costs were greater; two lines instead of one were required. These double wires also resulted in higher upkeep expenses. Another negative was that generally, telephone equipment was more complicated than telegraph apparatus, requiring skilled maintenance personnel. Static and loss of signal over extended distances were common early complaints.[64]

Notwithstanding any downsides, industry acceptance of telephony expanded dramatically. By mid-1909, nearly three hundred railroads were using telephones, and they covered more than twenty-six thousand miles of track. More managements, including such major roads as the Burlington, Illinois Central, and New York Central, were impressed with the effectiveness of the telephone and saw this communication tool as a practical means to manage their train operations. The Louisville & Nashville is representative of these early users. In 1910, it began installation of the two-wire sixty-system telephones manufactured by the Western Electric Company, and between 1915 and 1916, the last segments were installed on the southern portion of the railroad. Usage grew nationally. The *Monthly Labor Review* reported that "during the period from 1915 to 1921 the total number of telegraphers and telephoners was practically stabilized, though the trend toward telephony continued." In 1925, the Telephone and Telegraph Section of the American Railroad Association reported that Class I railroads had 132,850 miles of telephone lines used for the transmission of train orders along 249,398 miles of trackage. This was an increase of more than 13,000 miles since 1920. During this same period, telegraph lines used for dispatching decreased from 136,000 miles to 121,521 miles. Another result was that ORT membership started to decline. Yet the telephone did not kill off either the union or the telegraph. The telegraph remained in operation on many railroads until the 1960s, and commercial telegraph traffic continued into that same decade. The L&N, for example, kept telegraph wires on the main line of its Montgomery, New Orleans, and Pensacola Division until 1962 and retired the last ones on the division's branch lines seven years later. And into the 1970s, the key and sounder survived on a few carriers as a backup for telephone communications.[65]

As the telephone gained acceptance by the railroad industry, ORT membership felt the sting of antiunion actions during the immediate post–World War I era. Southern carriers, most notably, showed hostility to demands for increased pay. The Atlantic Coast Line (ACL) stands out as a preeminent antiunion railroad. In 1923, its telegraphers asked for a modest pay raise. Management's response? It countered with a proposal that those who worked in small stations would receive a *reduction* of 4 percent per hour. Fruitless negotiations followed. In October 1925, 1,184 telegraphers finally approved a strike. Fortunately for the railroad, it had enough employees who remained on the job, allowing it to continue essential communications. Then early in 1926, the ACL broke the walkout. "It was getting unequivocally established that the Coast Line was a railroad company that did not respond in a kindly fashion to a strike," concluded company historian Glenn Hoffman. Later on, ORT members on the ACL and other roads benefited from the prolabor policies of the

Franklin Roosevelt administration. This was reminiscent of wage hikes during wartime federalization under the US Railroad Administration when ORT membership soared from 25,000 to 48,700.[66]

Favorable New Deal legislation did not ensure the permanency of the Order of Railroad Telegraphers. In the 1960s, an altered technology and diminished membership led the organization to join the Brotherhood of Railway & Airline Clerks, Freight Handlers, Express & Station Employees (BRAC). As organized labor declined nationally, this union, with its chunky official name, also disappeared, becoming part of the Transportation Communications International Union (TCU). In 2012, the TCU merged with the International Association of Machinists and Aerospace Workers. Yet dispatchers retained their original union structure.[67]

HOUSING

No matter the occupation, especially ones with high worker mobility, railroad station agent-operators, almost without exception, faced multiple relocations during their careers. Finding suitable housing frequently became a daunting challenge. Agent-operators probably experienced a variety of living arrangements, ones encountered during their formative years of employment before obtaining greater job seniority.

What options did the agent-operator have? The easiest and possibly the first involved "batching" in the depot itself. Meals could be prepared on the wood- or coal-burning stove, likely the one in the office, and water for cooking and drinking could be taken from the station well or maybe from an indoor connection. A makeshift bed could be placed in the office. It was not unknown for an agent to sleep on a desk, table, or bench. A relief operator, who worked in the Missouri, Kansas & Texas (Katy) depot in Arcadia, Oklahoma, recalled that "at night I slept on a pallet on the telegraph table." If the community had a hotel, arrangements could usually be made for an extended stay. Meals might be taken in the hotel or at a local restaurant, or "beanery." Since hotel rates might be perceived as too pricy, an agent, living on a modest income, would seek alternatives. These normally involved a private home or a rooming house or boardinghouse.[68]

It is difficult to determine what accommodation was the most common. Such a choice often depended on availability, cost, location, clean-
liness, and friendliness of the owner or proprietor. A private home or
rooming house may have been more favored than the boardinghouse. Yet
a rooming house had a downside; meals were nearly always unavailable.
It might be possible, though, to eat with a host family.

As with any rental accommodations, experiences varied, some good
and some much less so. The best places were reasonably priced, clean,
pest free (no bedbugs), quiet, and convenient to the station. Others
might have noticeable drawbacks. In the 1930s, relief agent Dan Knight
discovered less-than-ideal housing in a private home. While working for
the M&StL in Middle Grove, Illinois, he was left unsatisfied on a variety
of accounts. The owner was Mabel, whom Knight described as a "grass
widow in her 30's," and her abode was run-down. "My first impression
of Mabel's house, which was badly in need of paint, could have been
better. Not modern in any way, it consisted of three rooms downstairs—
kitchen, living room and bedroom, and there were probably two rooms
upstairs, but I never knew for sure, never having been above the ground
floor." Knight continued, "While being shown the house, it was necessary to walk around a washing machine standing in the kitchen filled
with used wash water, as if Mabel had been interrupted in her work, a
dish pan filled with soapy water and dirty dishes on the coal range, but
as long as I stayed there, possibly six months, neither of these household
items ever looked any different—always full." A lack of privacy was more
troubling. "Taking a bath posed a problem. There being no bathroom,
the logical place for the wash tub would have been in front of the warm
kitchen range. However, there were no doors to shut the kitchen from the
rest of the house, leaving only one other place—the garage, a building
that had seen better days."[69]

Single railroaders, including agent-operators, might prefer boardinghouses that were near the railroad corridor. In fact, in some localities
a dingy collection of boardinghouses stood convenient to the depot. One
attraction was that meals could be taken and at a reasonable price; there
was no need to patronize a commercial eatery, perhaps at some distance
from a private home or rooming house and at maybe a higher cost. A
boomer brakeman, who at the turn of the twentieth century worked

for the Toledo, St. Louis & Western (Clover Leaf Route), offered this positive description of his boardinghouse in Frankfort, Indiana: "Now I remember I paid two dollars a week for my room and two bits [25 cents] a meal at the boarding house where I lived there in Frankfort and like most all boarding houses [in wet states] in those days, it had a saloon in connection with it, and the barroom was right joining the big dining room. In the dining room there were two big long tables, where the food was put on in family style, and you could help yourself and eat all you wanted." The presence of a "watering hole" might disturb teetotalers who wanted only "Adam's ale" and other nonalcoholic beverages.[70]

If an agent-operator had a wife and possibly a family, the quest often involved locating a furnished or unfurnished apartment or house. Monthly rents depended on a variety of factors, including size, condition, and amenities. Usually rates were considerably lower in smaller communities than in larger places. Clayton, Douglas, and Thomasville, Georgia, for example, were less expensive than Atlanta, Macon, and Savannah. During World War II, a Burlington agent and his family paid seven dollars a month for the unfurnished former Methodist Church parsonage in the village of Wolbach, Nebraska. They considered themselves fortunate. Not so lucky was the Union Pacific agent at Afton, California, located in the Mojave Desert, who in early 1943 successfully bid in on a better-paying job at La Habra, California. Because of severe wartime housing shortages in Southern California, the agent and his wife were forced for five years to make their primary living quarters in the depot freight room.[71]

Hundreds of agents took advantage of a welcomed living arrangement: an apartment in the depot itself. Railroads throughout scattered parts of the country provided housing, but most were concentrated in the trans-Mississippi West. In a single-story depot, for example, popular with the Union Pacific, it was space next to the office. More often living quarters would be on the upper floor of a two-story structure.[72]

Upstairs living was hardly an American innovation. Throughout Europe, two-story depots with apartments appeared almost from the dawn of railroading. The Swiss cantons stand out as good examples of where agents lived "over the shop." Canal companies, both domestic and abroad, also erected cottages for lockkeepers and their families. While they were not public buildings, they served as integral parts of waterways and were widely recognized for their practicality.[73]

Advantages existed for both employee and employer. The agent and his family had a guaranteed place to live. This was especially welcomed because of the paucity of available or suitable housing in villages and small towns, particularly on the Great Plains and throughout much of the West. It was also true elsewhere, notably in sparsely settled regions of New England, Michigan, and Wisconsin. There were these financial benefits: companies usually did not charge rent, and they provided coal, kerosene, and maintenance. Assuming a suitable rental apartment or house were present, the landlord might demand a lease. If broken because of a reassignment, there could be monetary consequences. Living in the depot also meant that an agent would be at his place of employment. This made commuting, either on foot, horseback, or by animal-drawn conveyance, and later by bicycle, motorcycle, or automobile, unnecessary. Also the agent could observe or listen to track activities.

Railroads anticipated multiple benefits as well. Foremost, the agent was essentially on duty twenty-four hours a day, seven days a week. "This would ensure the practically continuous presence of someone to receive service and emergency messages," a trade journal observed. An occupied depot also meant that an agent or family member could respond to any crisis, whether fire, storm, or intruder. Burglars might be less likely to prey on a building that they knew to be occupied. Management normally concluded that married agents were steady and reliable; company housing attracted and retained such employees. This meshed well with railway executives' corporate paternalism. If a railroad carried commercial fire insurance, it could expect lower premium rates for all inhabited structures.[74]

Undeniably there were obvious advantages to depot living from both parties' perspectives. "I am surprised that more depots with apartments were not built," reflected a former agent. "They made considerable sense no matter the housing situation, and the railroad benefited in every way." Yet from an agent's perspective, such living accommodations were not always that desirable.[75]

What did an agent and his family discover with depot living? Railroads that provided housing had their own building plans, but they

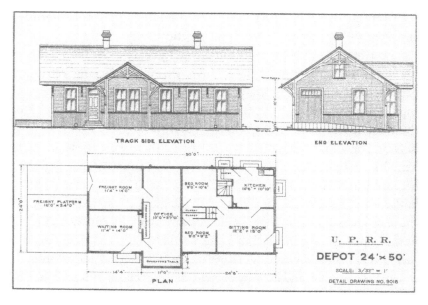

Figure 3.4. The Union Pacific preferred to provide agent housing in single-story depots. Early in the twentieth century, it erected these twenty-four-by-fifty-foot structures throughout its sprawling trans–Missouri River system. One advantage of this design was that family members did not need to negotiate a narrow, steep stairway to and from their second-story apartment. *(Author's collection)*

usually were similar and consistently utilitarian. "We gave those agents only very basic housing," remarked UP chief engineer R. M. Brown. The Burlington used a design, produced by its Lines West office in Lincoln, Nebraska, that can be considered representative. It created a standard twenty-by-forty-foot structure with upper-level living quarters. The ground floor featured the typical tripartite arrangement of waiting room, office, and freight section. The second floor contained four modest rooms: kitchen, parlor (sometimes identified as a sitting room), and two bedrooms. They collectively provided approximately 750 square feet of living space but hardly spacious when compared with houses in towns or on farms. A centrally placed stairwell led down to the office, and a private door opened to trackside. The apartment section had neither bathroom nor closets. The format for the popular Soo Line Standard Second Class depot (the company built more than two hundred of these two-story

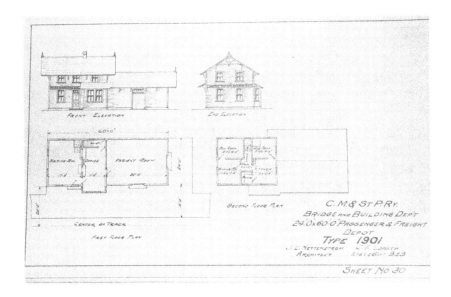

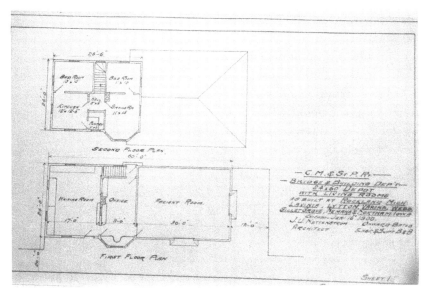

Figures 3.5–3.6. In 1901, the Milwaukee Road modified its popular twenty-four-by-sixty-foot plan of this combination-style depot. An agent and his family received basic living space over the waiting room and office. (*Author's collection*)

structures in North Dakota alone between 1891 and 1920) resembled the Burlington design. It placed a stairway at one end that connected with the ground-floor office. From the head of the stairs, a hall led to a twelve-by-seventeen-foot sitting room at one corner of the trackside front. Occupying the other front corner was a small six-foot-six-inch-by-thirteen-foot-six-inch bedroom, and the back section was split into a twelve-by-fourteen-foot kitchen and a ten-by-thirteen-foot bedroom. A four-foot-square pantry-closet opened off the kitchen. A majority of these frame depots constructed before World War I rested on wood pilings, and over time, they might settle noticeably. None had electricity until communities received such service, perhaps not until after creation of the Rural Electrification Administration during the waning New Deal. Companies commonly used their bridge & building gangs to erect these uncomplicated and rather inexpensive structures, which averaged prior to World War I about $1,500 each.[76]

Some residents who called a depot their home entertained in both the private and public sections (assuming that there were no patrons). Writer Laura Ingalls Wilder in her autobiography described a birthday party held in the upstairs living quarters of the North Western depot in De Smet, Dakota Territory. Jimmie Woodworth, the sixteen-year-old trick operator and agent's son, served as the occasion's host. "There were nine of us," she noted. "The long dining table was set and ready when we got there. It was beautiful with its silver and china and its beautiful linen tablecloth and napkins. At each place, on a pretty little plate was an orange standing on end with the peel slice in strips half way down and curled back making the orange look like a golden flower. I thought them the most beautiful thing I had ever seen, even prittier [sic] than the birthday cake in the center of the table." Wilder continued, "When supper was over we went down into the waiting room and played games. Jimmie arranged us all in a circle [in the office] holding hands and gave us a shock, that made us tingle, from his telegraph instrument. We went home early well pleased with the evening."[77]

Living in the depot did not always provide those blissful experiences for residents and guests. The list of negatives, some of which were minor, was extensive. Perhaps the most apparent was size. An apartment with such limited living and storage space might not pose a problem for a married couple, but it would be a concern if there were more than one or two children. It is hard to image how a large family could manage daily life in four small rooms.

For generations of agents and their families, living in the depot meant virtually no luxuries. Admittedly, many Americans had similar accommodations or had much less. "At Elyria [Nebraska] we lived in a 2-story depot, typical of most depots with living quarters," recalled the son of a Burlington agent. And he offered a good description of these Spartan-like conditions. "We had no electricity, used kerosene or 'aladdin' lamps. There was a hand pump in the kitchen sink. There was a wood and coal stove in the middle of the living/dining room (the only heat). There was a two-holler out back (across the side-track) with a Sears-Roebuck catalogue inside." If family members did not want to trudge to a remote outhouse during cold or inclement weather, they used bedroom chamber pots, or "vessels," requiring daily emptying and cleaning. Outdoor privies also had to be maintained, becoming a challenge to control rodents, insects, especially flies, and pungent smells. Using lime or other chemical agents helped, but this usually did not eradicate odors or pests. In desert environments, scorpions posed problems. "The outside toilet had big vinegarrons [sic] crawling around the hole, underneath the seat," recalled the Union Pacific agent-operator who once lived at the Boulder Junction, Nevada, depot.[78]

Depot residents regularly suffered from temperature extremes, too cold in the winter, too hot in the summer. The former might be considered the worse in less temperate climes with subzero days and frequently strong winds. These trackside structures nearly always lacked insulation, storm windows and doors, and central heating. Much later, cold weather protections might be installed. This could involve wrapping depots with Insulbrick panels and other types of asphalt sidings or filling hollow depot walls with newspapers or granulated rock wool. During a summer heat wave, indoor temperatures were often brutal. This was especially so because depots were often "smack in the middle of the rail yards. There was really nothing to cast a shadow." Before electricity, only open windows could provide some relief. Yet during such extreme temperatures, almost everyone in America endured similar conditions before electric-powered cooling options.[79]

Although not an inconvenience for those depots with apartments on the ground level, occupants of two-story ones had to manage steep, narrow stairways. This meant lugging pails of water from an outside pump up to the kitchen for bathing, drinking, and washing. Some railroads installed cisterns and connected them to upstairs hand pumps. This water was probably used solely for cooking and drinking. Coal, wood, and kindling also had to be carried from outside storage up to the kitchen or parlor. "There was a 'coal house' across the side-track behind the depot, where we went to get coal for the stove and coal oil for the lamps," recalled a former depot dweller. "There was a wood-pile next to the coal house, where my dad and I chopped wood." How would pieces of bulky furniture be accommodated? "One problem in those typical two-story depots was what to do with a piano. My dad played the piano. But there was no way to get one up to the second floor. Maybe Dad found a spot in the waiting room or in the freight room."[80]

The depot's proximity to the tracks caused washday worries. Soft-coal-burning locomotives repeatedly belched black, acrid smoke and occasional sparks. The practical responses? After carrying the washed clothes from the kitchen or maybe from the freight room, the drying process commonly took place out of doors. That was usually fine, but potentially risky when a train steamed through or stopped at the station. Depending on train activity and weather conditions, clothes could be hung in the freight room or in living quarters to ensure a successful washday. Baskets of laundry always needed to be lugged about the depot.

An agent never knew what the condition of a depot apartment would be. When the previous occupant left, he might have removed all or part of his improvements, for example, kitchen cabinets, ones that he paid for out of his own pocket. "You might well find a depot that was really messed up by the previous tenant tearing off the wallpaper, taking out shelves or whatever," recalled the son of a Minnesota agent. "There might have been some person who had gone wild with the paint brush, covering everything with a strange color of paint."[81]

Of greater concern was the closeness of the depot to main and side tracks. If the agent and his wife had children, there existed the danger of trackside living. "My mother hated the depot. She worried about me and my brother and sister," reflected a child of depot living. "The platform and tracks were our playground, and the trains on the main line provided a frequent, serious threat." His mother's concerns were real. "Youngsters were easily injured falling when running across the tracks. I once tripped with my toes on one rail and made a one-point landing on my jaw against the other rail. My jaw wasn't broken, but I was in pain and couldn't eat for a while." These hazards were much greater than when local children placed pennies on the tracks before oncoming trains and then attempted to find their flattened coins. No one denied that the railroad corridor always endangered children.[82]

Male youngsters of agents, whether their families lived in depots or elsewhere in the community, were known to play with potentially dangerous items found in or around stations. Lamar Robinette, son of the Frisco agent in Coy, Alabama, recalled playing with fusees and track torpedoes, which he took secretly from the depot office. His most memorable recollection was fabricating a small cannon. Robinette accomplished this with a piece of metal pipe, torpedo, and steel ball bearings. When ignited, his makeshift weapon produced impressive power, capable of piercing a fifty-five-gallon barrel.[83]

Youngsters, even ones who lived in the depot, might participate in acts of vandalism or thievery. It was known that teenagers, most likely, on occasion broke into freight rooms. They would enter an unlocked room and steal LCL items. (The agent's son might have access to a switch key.) A creative way to acquire liquor involved "drilling." The grandson of a longtime small-town agent recalled hearing this tale: "Back in the early days liquor in some form or another was shipped in wooden barrels. Some of the more enterprising lads would loosen some siding and slip under the building with a brace and bit." He further explained, "They would drill until they hit a barrel and then would fill their buckets with ill-gotten gain. They would slip out the same route as they entered and have a night full of revelry."[84]

Being on the railroad corridor posed another concern. Transients, whose numbers soared during hard times, might seek food handouts. Most were respectful, but a few posed a potential threat, becoming aggressive or hostile when their demands were not met. If the husband were absent, the wife might feel particularly vulnerable. The general wisdom of railroad employees: "If you give food to one, you'll soon have a steady

Figure 3.7. The two-story Chicago, Rock Island & Pacific (née Burlington, Cedar Rapids & Northern) depot at Titonka, Iowa, has an attached outside wooden ladder that provides an emergency escape for upstairs occupants. The BCR&N constructed multiple depots of this design. *(Dan Sabin collection)*

stream of them coming to the door." These "sidecar Pullman" travelers supported one another, marking places where handouts were likely.[85]

If the agent and his family occupied the upstairs, a potential fire was a concern. Sparks from locomotives, flames from lamps, and hot coals from stoves enhanced this danger. A wooden structure was highly combustible, and there was only that single stairway. Occupants could become trapped. To create another avenue of escape, maintenance workers or agents occasionally nailed a wooden ladder to an outside wall, placing it perhaps near a bedroom window. Or there might be a ladder anchored to the outside freight-room wall to be available in an emergency. Sometimes coiled hemp ropes were placed in bedrooms.

Although not a danger, there was the noise. The din of station happenings did not always bother an agent and his family, but for some it did. "I never really got used to all of that noise," recalled an agent's daughter.

"The piercing cry of the whistle, the clanging bell, the squeaking wheels and the monster locomotive itself would give you a good startle in the middle of the night and might keep you awake." She added, "A stopping passenger train always seemed to be especially loud, with mail, baggage and express being worked and the passengers coming and going. There weren't any 'Please Be Quiet' signs on the platform!" On the other hand, a depot resident could be affected by the *lack* of noise. "It was the silence caused by the train that did not arrive on time that was most likely to wake one up from a sound sleep," reminisced the wife of the Southern Pacific agent at Goleta, California.[86]

Everybody associated with living in the depot surely appreciated outdoor space (if possible) for gardening. Somewhere on the station grounds there might be an appropriate place for raising vegetables and flowers, with the former at times being critical. When salary cuts took place during hard times, making the agent's income dollar stretch as far as possible became mandatory. Then world wars created that national need for food conservation. "It's time now to get busy putting your victory garden in conditions for planting," the North Western told its employees and the public during World War II. "Of course you're going to have a garden—this year it's more important than ever. For, from all we can gather, vegetables for home consumption will be scarcer than ever and it is up to us to grow our own." The company added, "Next to fighting and doing essential war work, victory gardening comes first."[87]

It was not unusual for a depot family who expected to remain long term in a community to buy or build a house locally if the agent had enough seniority to protect his job. The disadvantages of depot living could be largely mitigated. That is what Gilbert and Anna Carter did in 1929. After living for fourteen years and raising three children in the North Western depot at Snyder, Nebraska, they "built the fine home on Cedar St. in the SW edge of Snyder." The Carters achieved the American Dream of an owner-occupied single-family home.[88]

AN AGENT'S WIFE

The roles wives played has been largely forgotten (or ignored) in the agent-operator experience. These women were integral parts of their husbands' workaday lives. Assisting in finding and maintaining living accommodations became a critical part of being a helpmate. Although not usually sanctioned by railroad officials, an agent's wife might assume her husband's duties if he became ill or temporarily disabled. This became more likely when the telephone became widely used. While there were unmarried agents—boomers, the youngest, the widowed, and the divorced—the majority were married. No couples shared identical experiences, but the trials and joys encountered by Genevieve Becker Hoback (1918–1993) are representative, reflecting job histories of agent-operators throughout the Railway Age.[89]

Genevieve and her husband, Glenn Hoback (1909–1976), shared much in common. Both were Nebraska natives. Genevieve hailed from Union, a farming community in Cass County south of Omaha, where her father owned a plumbing supply business and drilled agricultural water wells. Glenn grew up not far away, having been born in Tangeman, an Otoe County hamlet, where his father operated a flour mill. Later the family moved to a Cass County farm. Both were Protestants and shared similar outlooks on life.[90]

Long before Genevieve married Glenn in 1938, her future husband had abandoned agriculture. "Dad hated farming and the farm life," recalled his son Tom, "and like many boys of that age was drawn to the railroad." As a youngster, he began to stay with an aunt and uncle in Nehawka, Nebraska. Here he enjoyed watching trains on the Missouri Pacific (MP) as they ran between Union and Lincoln. Resembling many lads during the Railway Age, Glenn spent time with the Nehawka agent, who taught him telegraphy. Being bright, energetic, and loving railroads, ("Railroading became his religion"), he prepared himself for a career as an agent-operator. "Dad asked a lot of questions and absorbed everything he learned, so that by the time he graduated from high school, he became a telegrapher for the MP." In 1926 at age seventeen, he hired out as a relief telegrapher, working at nearly all of the MP stations between South Omaha and Falls City, Nebraska. But when the Great Depression struck, he found himself out of a job. Undaunted, Glenn landed a similar position with the Santa Fe, working in various places in New Mexico, Arizona, and California. Again hard times led to unemployment, and he left for a stint in Mexico before returning to Nebraska. In 1937, Glenn

Figure 3.8. Not long after Genevieve Becker married Glenn Hoback in 1938, the couple posed for this professional photograph. *(Thomas Hoback collection)*

rejoined the Santa Fe, working on its Oklahoma Division during the annual wheat harvest.[91]

Genevieve, who was deeply in love with Glenn, probably realized that being married to a relief agent-operator would be a challenge, especially as economic turmoil continued to haunt the nation. It was uncertain when railroad positions would be available. Even when short-term employment occurred, Genevieve often stayed with her family in Union. "My parents spent long periods of time separated from one another because of the uncertainty of where or when my Dad would get work." In May 1941, the couple got a fortuitous break. H. O. Wagner, superintendent of the Oklahoma Division, based in Arkansas City, Kansas, contacted Glenn about returning as a relief operator. "Assuming you can pass physical and other examinations, we shall be glad to use you during the wheat movement which starts in this territory around June 10 or possibly a little earlier. We should like to have you report about June 1." Wagner added, "It may be that we will be able to offer you permanent service following the grain rush which should last four or five weeks." This communique surely brought hope for the Hobacks. Glenn passed all requirements with flying colors: physical, visual, and the rule book examination.[92]

For the immediate future, the couple lived a nomadic life. In July 1941, while Glenn worked in Oklahoma, he received word that the Oklahoma Division had "loaned" him to the Illinois Division. This reassignment was welcomed news. Glenn and Genevieve disliked the Sooner State. "Oklahoma was more hardscrabble [than southeastern Nebraska], at least where Dad was stationed," noted his son, "and the towns did not have the commercial establishments they found in Nebraska." Their Midwestern life began with a brief stint at Medill, Missouri, situated where the Kansas City–Chicago main line of the Santa Fe crossed the Keokuk–Clarinda, Iowa, secondary line of the Burlington. What became the longest trip in Genevieve's young life had its negative and positive aspects. The initial leg of the 117-mile journey from Cushing to Arkansas City was unpleasant. "We rode in a real old fashioned train," she wrote to her mother. "It even had a stove in the car. It was not air conditioned. The windows were open. It sure was hot & dusty." Next there was an exceptionally long wait for their connecting train. "We got in Arkansas City at 4 P.M, . . . left at 4 a.[m.] sharp. That train [*The Ranger*] was sure swell to ride on, nice & cool. We rode eleven hours on that one." This journey via Kansas City totaled 451 miles.[93]

The conundrum of where to live, which would be ongoing, was readily evident in Medill, an unincorporated Clark County village of about a hundred residents. "This is a town of very few houses, no café, and very few people," explained Genevieve. "We came in at 3 o'clock this morning and had to stay in the depot until 7 because there was no hotel or anything." Fortunately, the couple found housing. "The operator called around to houses to see if we could find a Place to stay and he finally succeeded," she told her mother. "But we are on a farm. I guess it won't be so bad because we will only be here a week." Since the Hobacks lacked an automobile, they had to find a ride with either their host family or someone else or walk the several miles to Medill.[94]

Genevieve was correct; their stay in Medill was of short duration. The next place for the Hobacks would be Stronghurst, Illinois, approximately fifteen miles southeast of Burlington, Iowa, and again on the Santa Fe main line. "Stronghurst has a Population of 900 but it doesn't have as many business Places as Union." Yet as she happily noted, "They do have a dry goods store." Such access was important since the Hobacks had only what summer clothes they could pack into their several suitcases. Again, the couple encountered the housing challenge. "There are no hotels here. We stay a block from the depot. It is a widow woman, she sure is a talker." Since they could rent only a sleeping room, the Hobacks needed to take their meals in a local restaurant. "If we could get an apartment [it] would be cheaper." Largely because of eating out and living on a tight budget, Genevieve had these thoughts: "I asked Glenn the other day if he wanted me to come to Union but he said no. I should stay with him. It is best." Life in Stronghurst, though, became pleasant. "Glenn thought we would be gone from here by now [August 15], but haven't heard a thing yet. It may be tomorrow or next week." She continued, "He has worked here 13 days that is the longest he's worked in one Place since I have been with him. This is a good Place to stay, and I will hate to leave here."[95]

Although her son Tom described Genevieve as "an attractive person, sweet, thoughtful, and could adapt well to new situations," these positive qualities did not prevent repeated bouts of loneliness or perhaps depression. "Sure was glad to get your nice long letter this morning," she wrote to her mother. "Hope I receive another one." Long-distance telephone calls were out of the question; there were issues of accessibility and cost. And telegrams were impractical.[96]

Notwithstanding the Hobacks' one-month stay in Stronghurst, Genevieve developed social contacts. Most of all, she established a close relationship with the landlady, and one that lasted after she left town. "The Lady has been very good to me. She started me making a quilt. When I used her scraps up, she taught me to embroidery. I had forgotten all I knew about it. I am making a buffet set."[97]

Relocations continued. The next temporary home for the Hobacks would be Dallas City, Illinois, located on the Mississippi River sixteen miles west of Stronghurst. Once more a Santa Fe employee helped the couple locate housing. "The agent & his wife took us around to find a Place to stay. It was a hard job because we wanted a house preferring rooms. We finally succeeded," Genevieve told her folks. "It has three rooms. It is very nice [and] has hot & cold water, sink, bath room, etc. It costs $5.00 a week but is the best we could do. The depot is one block from where we stay." Again the expectation was that their time in Dallas City would be limited. "They just have one trick here, the agent. [He] & his wife are going on a vacation for about thirty days. Guess we will be here that long."[98]

By the third move since leaving Oklahoma, Genevieve had adapted to the peripatetic life of a relief operator. Her social activities are mentioned in this September 23 letter home. "The Lady where we stay entertained her club this afternoon and invited me. I had a nice time and met a lot of ladies. We played Bingo, had ice cream, cake and coffee for lunch. Afterward she brought up a big piece of cake for Glenn. It was as good as any sunshine cake could be, but I'll take chocolate any old time rather than lighter cakes."[99]

Genevieve discovered another attractive aspect of her temporary home in Dallas City. "Sunday afternoon we walked on top of the hill over looking the Mississippi river. It is one of the grandest views I have ever seen. One can see for miles around. Can see several towns in Iowa."[100]

The views provided from the Hobacks' next short stay offered less dramatic scenery. Life now centered around the prairie village of Ormonde, Illinois. This flag stop community, which had only the service of a single daily-except-Sunday motor train, was situated thirty-three miles east of Dallas City and about five miles southeast of Monmouth, Illinois. Since Ormonde lacked available housing, the couple returned to farm living.

This time Genevieve initially encountered difficulty reaching her new residence. Having come by train from her family's home in Nebraska, she found herself stranded in Galesburg, Illinois. A misunderstanding from Glenn created a momentary crisis. "Arrived in Galesburg at 6:15 [p.m.] last night [at the Burlington station.] A red cap carried my suit case to the [Santa Fe] Depot [one-half mile distant]. It cost 30 cents. No one was there to meet me so I inquired at the ticket office if there was a telegram. He sent me to the Western Union office upstairs. They called the main office in town, but there was no telegram for me." Her concerns grew. "I sat in the Depot until 7:30 debating what to do. Finally the ticket agent came out and asked me if I had found out or heard anything. I told him maybe Glenn had not received my telegram from Omaha that he was telegraph operator down here so that man got hold of Glenn on wire [and] told him I was there." Soon there was a happy ending. "Glenn sent some people after me at 9 o'clock. I had a nice long wait. Don't know what I would have done if it hadn't been for that [agent] man. He was sure swell. Glenn had tried to get the [Burlington] train to stop at Monmouth but it wouldn't. We are five miles from there and 20 from Galesburg."[101]

Genevieve and Glenn were disappointed with the Ormonde assignment. The living arrangements were strikingly different from those in Dallas City. "These people we live with are Germans. They have a large family [and] a girl and boy are staying home. The boy is 16 and a senior in High School." As she noted in a letter to her mother, father, and brother Donald, "Don't know when I will get this mailed, because I can't run to the Post Office here like I did other Places. Its [sic] to[o] far (5 miles)." This isolation meant that Glenn, whose scheduled workdays were from

Figure 3.9. Genevieve and Glenn Hoback had three children, the first was Tom, then came Mary K, and lastly Danny. In July 1964, Glenn, a train enthusiast, took them to a popular railfan destination, the Denver & Rio Grande Western narrow-gauge hub of Durango, Colorado. *(Thomas Hoback collection)*

four in the afternoon to midnight, faced a lengthy walk. Genevieve observed in an understatement: "He will have a lot exercise walking back and forth."[102]

The Hobacks' Rural Route 5, Monmouth, Illinois, address did not last long. Soon the Santa Fe sent Glenn to Edelstein, eight miles west of Chillicothe, Illinois. Living in a less isolated location allowed Genevieve access to Peoria, nineteen miles from her newest home. In late November, she reported to her mother that she enjoyed a memorable outing: "I went down [to Peoria] by myself [on a Black Hawk Motor Transit bus] at 7 o'clock and stayed till 5. Had a big day of it. I bought some Christmas Presents. Guess it is kind of early for that, but can't tell if I will get to any City again very soon." She also related a visit to nearby Dunlap to attend church. Since her family were devout Protestants, they might have been surprised, even shocked, with her comments: "I'll bet you can't guess where I went Sunday morning. To church the 'Catholic.' I enjoyed it because I had never been in one before. It was beautiful." When the couple later lived in Chillicothe, Genevieve and Glenn converted to Roman Catholicism. The explanation: close friends and work colleagues belonged to this liturgical faith.[103]

Figure 3.10. In January 1969, Glenn Hoback is at work in the Santa Fe dispatchers' office in Shoptown (Fort Madison), Iowa. *(Thomas Hoback collection)*

By early 1942, Glenn ended his career as a relief operator, finally holding a steady job. The station assignment would be McCook, Illinois, a dozen miles from the Chicago Loop, where the Santa Fe interchanged with three railroads: Baltimore & Ohio Chicago Terminal, Chicago & Illinois Western (Illinois Central), and Indiana Harbor Belt (IHB). The couple remained in Chicagoland until the closing months of World War II when they moved to Chilliocothe.[104]

Daily life for Genevieve was not that much easier than it had been previously. The Hobacks became Chicagoans, living at Sixty-Third and Central Streets near Midway Airport. Glenn toiled as a third-trick operator at McCook, and Genevieve found wartime work as a night clerk preparing yard lists at this busy freight interchange. Although her extended periods of loneliness had ended, she and Glenn endured a rigorous work routine, including a trying commute without owning an automobile. "[They] took the street car to Argo each night where they had to walk nearly two miles along the IHB to get to Santa Fe's depot at McCook," noted their son. "It was a hard slog, often in some brutal weather."[105]

Yet the Hobacks, who remained a devoted couple, were able to work together until they became residents of Chillicothe. At last they enjoyed a more normal lifestyle and could plan on starting their family. No longer employed as station agent-operator, the hardworking and capable Glenn received appointment as an assistant dispatcher. When the Santa Fe consolidated the Illinois and Missouri divisions in 1957, the Hobacks found a house near the new division headquarters in Shopton, Iowa, outside Fort Madison, where they established long-term permanency. Shortly before his death from a stroke, Glenn retired from his stress-filled job as chief dispatcher for the Illinois Division. After his passing, Genevieve continued to make Fort Madison her home.[106]

REGULATION

By the twentieth century, American businesses faced various forms of direct or indirect regulation, coming from multiple levels of government. The first public control of railroads concerned their state charters, but more involvement (some would argue intrusion) followed. In 1838, New Hampshire launched a railroad commission, becoming a regulatory template of sorts. A year later, Massachusetts followed suit. Indeed, New England states spearheaded the regulatory movement; Massachusetts, for example, had launched its regulation of the insurance industry as early as 1799. During the Gilded Age, multiple states created new or stronger regulatory bodies, especially during the Granger antirailroad agitation that swept much of the nation in the mid-1870s. Illinois, Iowa, Minnesota, and Wisconsin led with agencies designed to implement their Granger-inspired laws, focusing on long haul–short haul rate differentials.[107]

For decades, state and federal actions (the latter coming with the Interstate Commerce Act of 1887) concerned matters of rates and service. State bodies also responded to public displeasures that pertained to depots and agents, with the dominate issues involving establishing and staffing these station facilities and their proper maintenance. These complaints were nationwide and remained so until the decline of passenger service. During the Gilded Age, consumer-sensitive railroad commissioners in Illinois called attention "to the fact that at a number of stations very poor and inadequate station houses have been built, and at some stations no buildings or shelter of any kind is provided, while many

of the old depot buildings have become dilapidated and wholly insuffi-
cient to accommodate the traveling public." What did these Prairie State
regulators suggest? "It is believed that good would result by so amending
the law as to authorize the Commission to require suitable buildings to
be erected and maintained at all regular stations." Appropriate action
followed. Then take Alabama. In 1881, Cotton State lawmakers passed
a railroad commission law, and it, too, was subsequently strengthened.
A leading bone of contention involved depots. Uniontown residents, for
one, fumed about conditions in their depot, which was operated by the
East Tennessee, Virginia & Georgia Railroad. "No fires no water no Privies no Seats," charged the town in a formal complaint, "white & colored
people crowded together when it rains or is cold. Ladies have to take it as
it comes." A company representative admitted that its Uniontown depot
was not ideal. "It is a small house with two rooms, I suppose about twelve
or thirteen feet square each, with a long platform in front of it. There is
a stove in the petition thus warming the two rooms." He added, "The
office is open half an hour before the train arrives, but I am not certain
that [drinking] water is kept in it. There are benches there, and some
chairs." Remarked a student of this regulatory body, "The action of the
commission in this case, if any, is unknown." Alabama railroad regulators repeatedly showed little or no regard for people of color. In 1910, they
ordered the Alabama Great Southern "to supply said white waiting room
[at Eutaw] with a sufficient and comfortable water closet or toilet for use
by [white] lady passengers." In another Southern state, South Carolina,
its railroad commission on January 2, 1911, implemented this more progressive Jim Crow requirement about depot waiting rooms: "A separate
room for white and colored passengers, sufficient for their comfort and
convenience, shall be provided at all stations where passenger tickets are
offered for sale, and these waiting rooms shall be furnished with adequate lights, and, when the inclemency of the weather requires, with fire,
and at all times kept clean and made comfortable for passengers." While
hardly earth-shattering, a Kansas resident in 1903 complained to the state
railroad commission about "an unsanitary condition of the water-closets
[in Santa Fe depots] at Carbondale and Burlingame, Kan." A company
official responded: "Investigation develops that the water-closet at Carbondale was not in good condition, but this has been remedied." He

continued, "The one at Burlingame is and has been in good condition. These closets are unlocked [by the agent] a short time before the arrival of trains that makes stops and again locked after their departure. It would be impracticable to keep them open all of the time, because they would be misused by tramps and small boys in the towns."[108]

There was this unusual legislative proposal. In 1906, Mississippi lawmakers considered a public-spirited requirement. In a desire to promote awareness following a passenger train accident, an agent or operator needed to notify "every depot agent or telegraph operator on the line within the State of Mississippi of such accident and all details thereof." There was more. "Every agent is then required to post the fact of such accident with the names of the dead and injured, if possible, on a bulletin board in the passenger depot."[109]

Agents were not overlooked. Railroads did not want their public face besmirched by incompetent or surly employees, and they developed internal policies to combat such shortcomings. The Santa Fe included this statement in its 1909 rule book: "[Agents] must act with a view of accommodating the public and promoting the best interests of the company." Still, state railroad commissions received complaints. Usually nothing could be done in a regulatory sense, except for bodies to notify the railroad. The matter could only be remedied by exerting moral suasion. Interestingly, Oklahoma lawmakers, following statehood in 1907, passed an elaborate railroad code with a provision that required station agents to treat patrons with respect. Could it be enforced? Probably not. In all likelihood, agent-operators realized that when they took their jobs, creating good public relations were essential. The vast majority did their best to comply.[110]

On the eve of World War I, an example of how a community-spirited agent benefited his employer comes from a *Burlington* (Iowa) *Hawkeye* news story. The matter involved "an eyesore" depot in nearby Wayland. "It has caught on fire two or three times, but because Wayland folks have big hearts, they have put the blaze out," the newspaper explained. "Inside the depot is clean and neat. This is due to the agent Mr. C. B. Van Nest who has been here for ten years. The loyal spirit felt toward Agent Van Nest no doubt has saved the building, for all respect and honor him in town."[111]

The overall thoughtfulness of station agents included a range of actions. They might obtain medical assistance for ailing passengers, or they might open their depots in their off hours to allow customers to receive LCL or express shipments or to send emergency telegrams.

Two contemporary examples from the Hawkeye State reveal how the public profited from kindly, thoughtful agents. The first involves Roy Snyder, the North Western agent in Ellsworth. Although the company had discontinued passenger service at his station in June 1942, he continued to assist individuals in planning their itineraries and selling them tickets. "Ellsworth is surrounded by towns served by other C&NW stations. Three miles to the west is Jewell; four miles to the east is Radcliffe. Williams, Ia., is six miles to the north on the Illinois Central," he told a feature-story writer for the *Webster City Freeman* shortly before his sudden death in 1944. Snyder did a brisk ticket business. Here is how he accomplished that feat. "My method of selling the public train transportation is this: be a real friend to my acquaintances and treat everyone alike at the same time doing favors whenever I can." News of his services spread, and prospective travelers went out of their way to partake of his skills. "One customer drove over to my office from Williams to buy a ticket and then motored on to Iowa Falls to catch his train for Seattle," recounted Snyder. "He liked the treatment I gave him so much that he sent an air mail letter thanking me for sending him on the route I did." And in another instance, "A man living in Ames, traveled the twenty-five miles to Ellsworth to buy his ticket, then returned to Ames and boarded our *Challenger* to Los Angeles. He was a former Ellsworth resident who hadn't forgotten me." Snyder explained his core philosophy of service: "When someone from the community comes in for freight, express or a ticket, I try to find time to visit for a few minutes." He was no grumpy agent.[112]

The second illustration that reveals an agent's compassion occurred during the early months of World War II. Dan Knight, agent-operator at the joint M&StL-Wabash station in Albia, Iowa, ably assisted an elderly woman traveler who had arrived on a late M&StL train. She was headed to Kansas City on the Wabash via Moberly, Missouri. Unfortunately, she missed her Albia connection. The daily southbound M&StL train was due at 11:15 p.m. and the southbound Wabash at 12:05 a.m. The woman asked Knight what she should do. He suggested that she take a room in the Clark Hotel approximately a dozen blocks from the station and wait until the following day. Since Knight was going off duty, he volunteered to take her and her suitcase for this overnight accommodation. The woman refused, saying that it would be too expensive. This resourceful agent had another idea. He offered to drive her to Moravia, ten miles to the south, where she could get a direct connection to Kansas City on the Milwaukee Road. The *Southwestern Limited* was scheduled to make a flag stop at 3:05 a.m. and arrive in Union Station at 7:45 a.m., only fifteen minutes after her connecting Wabash train was due. The woman agreed. Knight rewrote her ticket and used his rationed gasoline to take her in his secondhand Chevrolet to the Moravia depot. The local agent did not work nights; although the waiting room was unlocked, it was unlighted. The woman complained that she would not stay alone without a light. Knight recently had bought an all-metal flashlight, having been warned by a local hardware dealer that he did not expect to acquire additional ones for the foreseeable future. War was raging, and manufacturers were making flashlights mostly from heavy cardboard. Knight gave the woman his flashlight and instructed her to leave it with the Albia agent when she made her return trip. She failed to do so.[113]

FOUR

DECLINE

INDIAN SUMMER

During the immediate post–World War II years, American railroads, which were emerging from their finest hour of service to the nation, felt optimistic about their future, anticipating a prosperous peace. Agent-operators reflected this outlook, seemingly confident about their occupation. They foresaw job security, good wages, and enhanced benefits.[1] Other improvements might be likely, including remodeled or replacement depots.[2] The industry and the economy flourished, and members of the Order of Railroad Telegraphers (ORT) continued to profit from the friendly legislation enacted by the New Deal, most of all the National Labor Relations Act (1935) and the revised Railroad Retirement Act (1937). The expectations of these agent-operators would be mostly realized; after all, from 1946 into the early 1950s, a period of "Indian summer" existed for the industry.[3] Nearly all carriers had emerged from their Depression-era bankruptcies, their treasuries were generally robust, and long-term borrowing rates remained attractive. Moreover, Americans in the late 1940s could rightly boast of the most advanced passenger trains in the world. Larger changes, however, were in the offing, including expansion of centralized traffic control, improved communications, corporate mergers, widespread line abandonments, station closings, and union setbacks. These had not been the experiences of the 1930s when installation of upgraded train-control equipment was exceptional, mergers were virtually unknown, retirement of lines (mostly hopelessly unprofitable

Figures 4.1–4.2. Through the Roarin' '20s, the Great Depression, and World War II, thousands of agents compiled years of service. Although they moved about as they gained seniority, most remained with their initial company even after it was acquired by another road. The career of Samuel F. B. Morse (a memorable name) is an example. Early in the twentieth century, he hired out with the Iowa Central, but in 1912, that railroad merged with the Minneapolis & St. Louis, and in 1960, the Chicago & North Western purchased the M&StL. (1) In 1911, Morse (*far left*) is shown in the office of the Iowa Central depot in Hampton, Iowa. (*Don L. Hofsommer collection*) (2) Decades later, he is pictured in the North Western depot in Middle Grove, Illinois, and still using his telegraphic skills. Morse possessed an unusual talent: an uncanny ability to memorize long lists of numbers. (*Don L. Hofsommer collection*)

branches and traffic-starved short lines) was modest, depot closures were limited, and labor unrest minimal.

In the 1950s, agent-operators came to realize that changes in transportation were rapidly occurring. They had only to look around their hometowns to understand why railroads faced increasing modal

competition. More of their neighbors owned automobiles both new and used. After all, the American Dream expressed itself in materialistic terms, including every family having a car. In 1950, vehicle registration stood at 40,190,632, and this number soared to 61,430,862 a decade later. Trucks, large and small, also seemed ubiquitous. Roadways were steadily improving, further encouraging people to travel in their cars on their own schedules to work, shop, or play. These infrastructure betterments included farm-to-market roads, paved, resurfaced, or widened highways, and state-owned multilane and limited-access turnpikes. The old two-lane dirt roads were disappearing. After 1956, a burgeoning toll-free interstate highway system, which federal officials projected to exceed forty thousand miles, was quickly emerging; by 1965, this interstate network reached twenty thousand miles. These roadway improvements gave trucking a competitive edge over railroads, continuing to shrink the latter's markets. This was especially so for high-revenue cargoes. If an agent-operator were to look skyward, a passing commercial airplane might be spotted, and after 1958, it could be jet powered. Unfortunately for the long-distance railroad passenger sector, airlines by the late 1950s handled roughly a third of all the commercial passenger business. This would be the golden age of commercial aviation. Essentially out of sight was the impact of the opening of the 370-mile Saint Lawrence Seaway in 1959, providing an all-water alternative to railroad freight transport between the Great Lakes and the Atlantic Ocean.[4]

These conspicuous signs of lasting changes in transportation could likewise be seen along railroad corridors. The decade saw steam in rapid retreat; the triumph of the diesel beckoned. In 1950, steam locomotives handled about 55 percent of freight work, 36 percent of passenger traffic, and 38 percent of switching assignments. But in 1960, steamers had virtually disappeared, making their final appearance on scattered branch lines, short lines, and industrial roads. With the triumph of powerful fuel-efficient and easier-to-service diesels, maintenance of these two types of motive power had become strikingly different. The result: numerous roundhouses, water tanks, and all but some of the largest coaling towers (too expensive to raze) disappeared. Steam back shops, formerly staffed by scores of blacksmiths, boilermakers, pipefitters, and other skilled workers, were either demolished or converted into diesel repair shops with a substantially reduced workforce. During the 1950s, total railroad employment dropped by 36 percent.[5]

Passenger trains were also vanishing, most noticeably on secondary and branch lines together with main line locals. And some Class I carriers had become freight-only. By way of example, the 1,127-mile Lehigh Valley Railroad operated seven pairs of passenger trains in 1954, but the last set, the *John Wilkes*, stopped running in February 1961. The passenger situation, though, was more encouraging on major intercity arteries. "By making rail travel attractive enough, we have an opportunity to enlarge our passenger business almost indefinitely," predicted Chicago, Burlington & Quincy (Burlington) President Ralph Budd in 1948. "A completed trip, if it can be looked back upon with pleasure,

should and will encourage another trip." John W. Barriger III, one of the
nation's foremost railroad executives and author of the widely acclaimed
Super-Railroads for a Dynamic American Economy (1956), likewise saw
possibilities for a profitable and traveler-supported long-distance passenger business. This would be achieved with clean trains, comfortable
cars, courteous crews, higher speeds, and customer-friendly reservations
and ticketing. Mass-circulation magazines, notably *Holiday, Life,* and
Saturday Evening Post, contained eye-catching advertisements that bal-
lyhooed the *Broadway Limited, California Zephyr, Golden State Limited,
Empire Builder, Olympian Hiawatha, Silver Meteor, Super Chief, 20th Century Limited,* and other luxury streamliners. Announced the New York
Central in a widely dissimilated marketing piece: "28 New Streamliners
for '48." The copy read in part: "Through half a million survey questions,
wartime passengers told New York Central what was wanted *first* and
most in new travel. This year you'll get the answer. And it's all written in
steel . . . the streamlined steel of 28 all-new trains. It's the largest equipment order *ever* built for *any* railroad. And it will be here *this* year." (By
1950, the Central's "Great Steel Fleet" was in full operation.) This corporate pronouncement suggested a bright future for passenger railroading
and the industry in general. It would be "All Aboard for Tomorrow!"[6]

Station agents could still be found, not just on main stems but also on
low-density lines. In spring 1959, William D. Middleton, civil engineer,
historian, and railroad enthusiast, decided to ride one of the last remaining "doodlebugs" operated by the Northern Pacific in North Dakota.
He was about to experience the end of an era. Agents, too, were part of
his journey. "The towns along the way—Woods, Coburn, Sheldon, and
Buttzville—seemed little more than a few houses and grain elevators,
and perhaps a long row or two of shiny corrugated bins for the surplus
grain, huddled close to the track," wrote Middleton. "At almost every
one a station agent, elderly and dignified in a trainman-style cap with a
metal AGENT badge on the front, waited for us in front of a weathered
yellow frame depot. The plain little train order signal above the station's
bay window was invariably set at clear, for ours was the sole train on the
line."[7]

Much also remained the same in terms of hiring, work assignments,
and agent mobility. The job history of James Bradley, who graduated

Figure 4.3. In 1970, Santa Fe operator Dayton Webb sits at his "mill" preparing a form 19 train order. At this late date, a telegraph line continues to serve this Perry, Oklahoma, depot. A Liggett and Myers Velvet tobacco can is shown, designed to enhance the sound of dots and dashes. The office also has telephone and radio connections. *(Don L. Hofsommer photograph)*

in 1959 from Buffalo High School of Wayne County in Kenova, West Virginia, is an illustration. Almost immediately after receiving his diploma, Bradley hired out on the Toledo Division of the Baltimore & Ohio (B&O). His initial job was that of student telegraph operator; the pay amounted to $1.50 per hour. "He gained most of his experience by listening and practicing—lots of practicing." It did not take long before the B&O sent Bradley to Miamisburg, Ohio, as a relief operator. Following that brief assignment, he remained on the extra board and worked at numerous stations throughout the division. By 1965, Bradley had

Figure 4.4. On December 11, 1971, Santa Fe agent Phyllis Rainbolt copies by telephone a work order for track supervisor Floyd Reisch in the Santa Fe's Kaw, Oklahoma, depot. This station still retains an active telegraph line. *(Don L. Hofsommer photograph)*

advanced to agent-operator in Bowling Green, Ohio, a county-seat town and home of Bowling Green State University. As a dedicated employee, he did his best to promote the railroad's freight and passenger business. Although the latter was in rapid decline, Bradley posted notices on the university campus to announce reduced round-trip fares that students could use to return home on weekends and holidays. His commitment to the company caught the attention of the regional sales manager. Soon Bradley received this offer: an entry position in the sales department. Although this job paid less than what he earned as the Bowling Green agent, he accepted. During his forty-two years of railroading, Bradley advanced through the ranks; promotions required his family to relocate nine times. Being an agent-operator paved the way for a rewarding career at the B&O and its later reincarnation as part of the Chessie System and CSX.[8]

Bradley, however, was part of a dying breed. In 1972, veteran railroad publisher Freeman Hubbard lamented: "No longer does the 'lonesome' steam whistle wake you up at night with a call to faraway places. No longer do boys with stars in their eyes leave factories and farms to go firin', brakin', or telegraphin', to see what lies on the other side of the mountain or beyond the prairie horizon." He continued, "No longer do telegraph operators hand up train orders written in fine flowing script to steam-engine cabs and homelike cabooses."[9]

Yet James Bradley was not alone in hiring out as a telegrapher (and later agent-operator) during the twilight years. Railroads from a struggling Georgia & Florida to a thriving Atchison, Topeka & Santa Fe continued to recruit individuals who could manage what was rapidly becoming (or had become) an obsolete technology. Take the Northern Pacific (NP). In the July 1957 issue of the ORT's monthly publication, the chief dispatcher in Tacoma, Washington, advertised: **Wanted: Telegraphers and Agent Telegraphers**. The copy ran: "Have openings for year-around employment for several men. $2.05 per hour and up. Age limit 45 years if experienced, 35 years if inexperienced. Require Morse Code 20 W.P.M. Pass visual, physical and rules exam and clear record." On the neighboring Milwaukee Road, a young "telegraph tramp," who joined the company in 1961, recalled, "Telegraph circuits were connected to all stations where operators were employed in each division, so station-to-station communications within a division were almost always done by telegraph." He added, "The Milwaukee Road was just beginning to use radio communications at that time, and it was forbidden to transmit any operating orders over the radio, as that was not considered a reliable enough mode of communication."[10]

Yet, telegraph usage was rapidly disappearing. The Akron Division of B&O provides a good example. "We had dispatcher, operator and Western Union lines," noted a veteran employee. "By 1955, however, those were all backed-up to the telephone and used by operators and dispatchers just to retain their skills and to have the fun of using Morse." Somewhat earlier, a turning point in telegraphic traffic had occurred. In 1949, the long-standing agreement between Western Union (WU) and the railroads—whereby WU used rights-of-way for its pole lines and in return provided and maintained telegraph equipment for railroad communications—was terminated. This meant that companies had to take over or contract with WU to maintain equipment, and many railroads decided that it was time to opt for replacement technologies.[11]

NORTH WESTERN V. ORT

A watershed event in the history of station personnel occurred on November 5, 1957, when the Chicago & North Western Railway (North Western) responded to what its management considered "unused, unneeded and unproductive" work, or featherbedding (a pejorative term and a dirty word among organized labor), committed by small-town agent-operators. It would be company board chairman Ben W. Heineman who spearheaded the drive to eliminate these underutilized employees. The railroad initially focused on the sixty-nine one-person stations in South Dakota where the duties of agents required no more than two hours of daily service. Some agents worked an average of only fifteen minutes a day and received as much as $91 per hour for the time they actually spent performing their assignments. They collectively squandered hundreds of thousands of dollars annually at a time when the North Western faced serious financial challenges. It and other carriers realized that without a more productive labor force, their industry would suffer enormously, leading to widespread bankruptcies, unwanted mergers, and possible liquidations.[12]

The Heineman administration predictably found itself embroiled in a battle with the Order of Railroad Telegraphers. This bitter conflict began when the North Western filed a petition with the South Dakota Public Utilities Commission to create a statewide "central agency or area headquarters setup," thus eliminating redundant agents. The company considered its agency proposal "sensible and reasonable." Times had changed. When the state's railroads were built, and stations established, explained the North Western "[they] served a farm economy geared to horse-drawn transportation. Today passenger and LCL traffic have virtually disappeared from one-man stations, but station forces have not been adjusted to modern requirements." Railroad historian John Stover agreed: "When the iron rail network was built to completion in the half-century before World War I, the nation needed every railroad that was constructed." As he explained, "In a day when the farm wagon was the main mode of transport closely spaced lines with depots located every few miles made real sense." But that was no longer the case, resembling contemporary efforts to replace one-room country schools with consolidated facilities, made possible by modern buses that operated over all-weather roads. The North Western sought to retain sixteen agents to serve multiple stations under what it called its Central Agency Plan. If that did not prove feasible, it would seek regulatory approval to padlock the lightly used depots and probably convert them into maintenance storage or have them removed.[13]

Even before the tough-minded and politically savvy Ben Heineman took the throttle, the North Western and the ORT had begun to negotiate the issue of the "quietest agencies." Starting in 1954, two years before Heineman entered the executive suite, both parties had agreed that in some cases a station might be shuttered permanently. Following that accord, the railroad averaged about two closings annually, a number that hardly solved the redundancy issue.[14]

Why did the North Western single out South Dakota? This sprawling 7,835-mile, nine-state system with 3,193 miles of branch lines had scores of stations where agents worked a minimal amount of time. "South Dakota law, as I read it, says that the state railroad commission is responsible for efficient operations of the carriers," recalled Charles Shannon, assistant to the president for operations. "So why don't we confess that we are inefficient and see what they do about it." In its formal petition to regulators, the North Western declared: "The burden of this wasteful operation, in the form of higher rates or inefficient service, must be borne by the shippers and passengers who still need and use railroad transportation." The company also argued that such salary savings "will provide funds that will help reduce deferred maintenance and maintain, rehabilitate, modernize and mechanize the railroad plant." The strategy worked. Within a short period, the North Western won approval from South Dakota authorities and from four additional state regulatory bodies to terminate these unnecessary employees.[15]

The ORT was not pleased. "We'll make a reasonable agreement with him," said its president, "but Mr. Heineman has three things to learn: Employees are human beings; they are entitled to fair and reasonable conditions; and you can't turn men off and on like you can machines." Workers in other industries shared similar attitudes. By the late 1950s, the protection of union members against displacement by automation had become a major objective in collective bargaining negotiations.[16]

Job protection was a key part of the mission of the Order of Railroad Telegraphers. Before the triumph of unionization, many agent-operators considered so-called brass hats to have wielded despotic powers. If these employees didn't like their pay or working conditions, they would quit or be dismissed. In December 1957, the ORT demanded that *no* job held by a union member could be abolished without its approval. The union sidestepped the legacy of the farm-wagon age. The Heineman road ignored the ORT, and during the next several years, it eliminated approximately five hundred positions. The union fought back, seeking to block the company by employing provisions of the National Railway Labor Act. After exhausting its legal options and disregarding the responses of two US secretaries of labor and a presidential emergency board that recommended generous allowances for displaced union members, the ORT at 7:00 a.m. on August 30, 1962, struck the North Western. The company had been repeatedly losing money: $2.8 million in 1959, $7.1 million in 1960, and $3 million in 1961. The walkout tied up the railroad until September 28, costing it approximately $600,000 a day. This strike disrupted the lives of freight customers, long-distance passengers, and thirty-five thousand Chicago-area commuters. Importantly, there existed ORT solidarity. Members knew that their union was fighting for their interests, and that included job projection. Incidentally, they paid modest monthly dues.[17]

The North Western received wide-ranging journalistic support in its battle with the ORT. "Featherbedding, already a flagrant practice in the railroad industry is no solution," editorialized the *Chicago Sun-Times*.

"But that in effect is what the North Western telegraphers are demanding. Featherbedding, along with the competition of airlines and truck transportation, has already imperiled the financial structure of most railroads." The newspaper added, "In today's economy, characterized by the profit squeeze, neither the railroads nor any other industry can afford featherbedding." The *Washington Post* echoed the *Sun-Times*. "North Western Board Chairman Ben W. Heineman cannot be blamed for taking a resolute stand of an issue which involves the survival of the road. An efficient management does everything in its power to minimize costs."[18]

Public displeasure, even anger at the strikers, pressured the ORT to accept binding arbitration. Three men hammered out a settlement: Ben Heineman; George Leighty, ORT president; and Sylvester Garrett, a Pittsburgh attorney. The swing vote would be cast by Garrett, the public representative whom President John F. Kennedy selected to reach an agreement. Garrett was no novice to the mediation process; he had previously demonstrated his negotiating skills in arbitrating disputes in the heavily unionized steel industry.[19]

Arbitration gave the Heineman administration much of what it wanted. *Time* magazine correctly assessed the final settlement: "a stunning setback for the telegraphers," and "the tide has changed." The North Western made its point that the employment of agent-operators was the prerogative of management and *not* subject to a union veto. The company did accept concessions. It agreed to provide the ORT members with ninety days' notice of discharges and to pay released employees 60 percent of their annual earnings for as long as five years. The railroad would grant agent-operators a guaranteed forty hours of pay per week, but it could determine the number of these employees. An indication that toughness worked, laid-off personnel would not be entitled to the benefits negotiated through the arbitration process. The North Western and other railroads that sought to eliminate featherbedding commonly delayed depot closings to allow veteran agents, whose retirements were imminent, opportunities to work their final days, weeks, or months. These affected agents were undoubtedly appreciative.[20]

The case can be made that when depots were shuttered, not all carriers were heartless corporations. Yet those agents who lost their jobs might experience mental stress; dismissal or reassignment could have a negative psychological impact. These individuals, after all, were important residents of a town or village. "So closing the depot meant he probably wasn't that important," reflected one railroader, "and he had to move away to follow his seniority." Furthermore, possible stress came from the fact that these agents were talented professionals—most probably considered themselves to be elite workers. Agents knew Morse code—a skill not everyone could acquire—and they had mastered the intricacies of train control and a plethora of station duties. Other railroaders might think them to be egotistical, and perhaps some were. Becoming unemployed, forced to relocate, or pushed to retire may have injured their mental or physical health.[21]

The dispute between the ORT and the North Western produced both near and long-term effects. Each side lost money, an estimated $8.5 million for agent-operators and $18 million for the railroad. There is no denying that this marked a turning point in labor relations. The company demonstrated that archaic work rules could be altered or eliminated. The outcome had been more successful than the "two per cent formula" the ORT had achieved with the Southern Pacific in fall 1961. The key provision in this case was that "abolition of positions will not exceed the rate of normal attrition (deaths, retirements, resignations, or dismissals for cause); neither will it exceed two per cent per year on a system basis." There would be no more Southern Pacific–like settlements.[22]

The matter of redundant workers in the railroad industry remained a hot-button issue during the 1960s and continued so for more than a decade. The John F. Kennedy and Lyndon B. Johnson administrations pushed Congress to address the matter. Subsequent legislation required final and binding legislation for reducing firemen on diesel locomotives and for train-crew consists. These mandates directed that other issues in dispute must be negotiated within six months between the contending parties.[23]

The railroad brotherhoods predictably opposed binding decisions reached by arbitrators. They sought redress in the courts, challenging the constitutional right of Congress to dictate required arbitration in a labor dispute. Eventually the matter reached the US Supreme Court, but as with lower court decisions, the industry consistently scored victories.

Some lonely stations had remained opened long after they should have been closed. A remarkable example took place in the Clay County, Kansas, hamlet of Oak Hill. This community, which claimed a population of sixteen and one shipper, a grain elevator, was located on the 158-mile freight-only Santa Fe branch line between Strong City, Kansas, and Superior, Nebraska. The reason the company sent a relief agent to this depot came about because the retiring agent, who had been employed there since 1935, had personal connections with members of the Kansas Corporation Commission and the state's Democratic Party. During his six-week tenure in 1968, the new agent billed out one carload of wheat and received a single LCL shipment, a stock tank. But with the departure of the veteran agent, the Santa Fe immediately pressed for a closing hearing. This action quickly led to the elimination of the Oak Hill agency.[24]

Line abandonments could make some agents' employment moot. Although the more proindustry Transportation Act of 1958 failed to grant "ICC authority over abandonment of railroad stations, depots, and other facilities," the Staggers Rail Act, signed by President Jimmy Carter on October 14, 1980, permitted extensive rail abandonments and sales. This legislation created a sea change, meaning that railroads were free from the stifling effects of excessive regulation. Prior to its enactment, attempts to shut down unprofitable trackage frequently created a storm of opposition from labor unions, shippers, communities, and local governments, and the ICC often bent to their demands. Freight business, the bread and butter of the industry, had declined most precipitously on branch lines, whether livestock, coal, or LCL shipments. A slimmed-down network became mandatory, especially as red ink and major bankruptcies mounted prior to the Staggers law. This landmark measure ultimately led to increased volumes of intermodal traffic, low-sulfur western coal, and other commodities. Class I roads thought less about feeders and more about high-speed, long-haul freight corridors. New or existing regional and short-line railroads could operate unwanted but financially viable appendages. Route miles, which stood at 223,427 in 1951, 217,552 in 1960, and 211,925 in 1965, dropped to 206,265 in 1970, plummeted to 164,822 in 1980, and totaled only 119,758 a decade later. The abandonment process was not always smooth, but massive line removals resulted in hundreds of closed agencies. No track, no depot, no agent.[25]

In 1960, the American railroad network still remained large and sprawling. The country did not experience the high percentage of line abandonments that occurred in the United Kingdom during the early 1960s. These resulted from the "Beeching cuts," or the "Beeching axe," orchestrated by British Rail head Dr. Robert Beeching. In the United States, there remained thousands of varied customers to be served profitably, including those in predominantly agricultural areas. Although livestock transport (cattle, hogs, and sheep) had declined dramatically or had already disappeared, grain and other farm products, predominately fruits and vegetables, often required long-distance rail transport. There were also inbound shipments for farmers and ranchers, including fertilizers and poultry feed.[26]

Some railroads that continued to maintain small stations into the 1960s implemented dualization. This involved an agent serving one depot in the morning and another (presumably not too distant) in the afternoon or on alternate days. These agents used their personal automobiles and received mileage allowances. In fact, the concept of dualization dated back for several decades, and there were the occasional triplized stations. Some railroad officials objected to the practice because their companies would need to maintain buildings that were staffed only part time.[27]

Mobile agencies became another response to how freight customers could be served. Railroads, which opted for this service, analyzed the workload of an agent on a proposed mobile route, which would utilize station wagons or vans, and estimated mileage from a base location. In June 1972, vans, for example, appeared on the Burlington Northern Railroad (BN) in Nebraska. "The hearse has arrived for the weathered old Burlington Northern [née Burlington] depot at Chalco," reported the *Omaha World Herald*. "It is a green van called a mobile depot and it will replace the Chalco depot." Chalco would not be the only station closed along the BN in the Cornhusker State. For the immediate future, carload freight shipments would be arranged by a company employee who operated out of these "hearses." Earlier, the BN had discontinued LCL shipments; REA Express (formerly Railway Express Agency) had dropped its association with country stations; and Western Union had terminated local telegraph service. On February 16, 1978, the railroad ended its remaining telegraph usage in the state.[28]

Nebraska could not claim the first mobile agencies. In 1966 and 1967, the Burlington had begun deploying Customer Service Offices in northern Illinois with attractive vans painted in the corporate livery and appropriately lettered. "The red, white, and black mobile units with a two-way radio and complete office furniture are fully equipped with heating and air-conditioning." And the experiment worked. "The new service has created new freight traffic, has often sped up service, and has improved the morale of the remaining agents who now feel greater job security." Also in 1966, the Missouri Pacific (MOP) launched an experimental mobile agency in the Rio Grande Valley of Texas. It subsequently expanded this service outside the Lone Star State. In Missouri, the company launched two routes in 1968. And they were successful. As with previous MOP operations, a shipper used a toll-free telephone number to call a base station, and the traveling agent, who had that assigned route, would be dispatched by radio. When the railroad sought to expand significantly its mobile operations in Missouri, a Public Service Commission hearing revealed that "some shippers had been skeptical [at first]. In all cases, these shippers admitted that the quality of service was at least as good as before and, in several instances, substantially improved."[29]

Class I railroads were not the only companies that embraced mobile agencies. Smaller carriers did too. The 246-mile Camas Prairie Railroad, headquartered in Lewiston, Idaho, and jointly owned by BN (formerly NP) and Union Pacific, is an example. Coinciding with accelerated station closings during the early 1970s, it launched mobile agencies at Craigmont and Grangeville, Idaho, to cover its Second Subdivision.[30]

In time, there was no need for these mobile agencies operated by the BN, MOP, Camas Prairie, or any other railroad. Shippers and railroads could use other ways to communicate. Later, the internet and computers effectively managed their freight business.[31]

Policy and technical changes undoubtedly annoyed some agents. There were those who disliked dualized stations or mobile agencies (but probably were happy that they still had jobs). Take this additional example. Some agents wished to keep their access to the key and sounder, but it might be for wholly nostalgic reasons. When in the early 1960s the North Western ordered the removal of the eighty-two-mile telegraph line between Tara (Fort Dodge), Iowa, and Des Moines on the former Minneapolis & St. Louis, agents in Dallas Center and Waukee convinced the dismantling crew to keep the wire connection between their two stations, a distance of six miles. The reason: "They enjoyed having personal conversations." For a time, this line remained operable.[32]

When it came to written train orders, a dramatic change took place in 1986. In a national labor agreement, dispatchers could now issue traffic instructions by radio *directly* to train crews. Carrier after carrier adopted direct train control (DTC), or what was initially called dispatcher's manual block control, allowing for verbal instructions with archived recordings. Track warrant control (TWC) also became widespread. This system used a preprinted form copied by the train crew transmitted by radio from the dispatcher. This format generally embraced guidelines contained in the General Code of Operating Rules. The multiple boxes on the warrant conveyed different aspects of authority that a train would be granted.[33]

Change remained ongoing. If there were serious problems with radio transmissions due to topography, weather, or solar conditions, the installation on locomotives in recent years of Global Positioning System (GPS) devices permitted dispatchers to learn the exact location of every piece of motive power. In certain instances, GPS offers the potential for the retirement of the traditional trackside signaling system.

By the 1960s, it is unlikely that few if anyone in America fully foresaw what would take place in a generation or two. As the twenty-first century progressed, railroaders encountered a significantly altered industry. Most observers agreed that management was no longer captive of "this is the way we have always done it" mind set. Heavy-handed federal regulation, the hallmark of progressive-era legislation, had become a thing of the past, highlighted with passage of the Staggers Act in 1980 and creation of the Surface Transportation Board sixteen years later, replacing a less-than-accommodating Interstate Commerce Commission. Furthermore, there was the dismantling of thousands of miles of track, two-person train crews (including females), longer crew districts, closure of nearly all open depots, elimination of cabooses, increased track mechanization, and disappearance of intercity passenger trains except those operated by Amtrak and commuter authorities. Now there would be the internet, fiber-optic cables and other advanced communications, computers, dispatching software, positive train control, end-of-train devices (or FREDs for flashing rear-end devices), AC and natural gas–powered locomotives, more welded rail, unit container trains, a vastly restructured and more cooperative workforce, precision scheduled railroading (PSR) schemes, and additional short-line and regional carriers. A new railway age had dawned. Agent-operators meeting the public, handling carload freight and LCL and express shipments, sending and receiving commercial telegrams, and managing train orders via the telegraph or telephone had vanished. Nevertheless, these employees would not become a totally forgotten part of America's rich railroading heritage.[34]

FIVE

LEGACY

THE JOB OF STATION AGENTS HAS LEFT MULTIPLE LEGACIES. These include published works, motion pictures, and individual artifacts preserved in museums and private collections. Moreover, there are retired personnel who have vivid memories of what has become a vanished occupation. Descendants of these employees may also recall aspects of agency life, becoming part of their family's oral traditions. Yet over time, memories fade. In 1967, the Railroad Station Historical Society emerged as a response to the rapid decline of active railroad depots, especially country ones. The focus of this small, specialized group of enthusiasts involves more than buildings; human experiences are remembered. And these interests have been reflected in its publications.

PUBLISHED WORDS

Railroads have never produced a famous literature. Compared to seafaring, they have no equivalents to Richard Henry Dana's *Two Years Before the Mast* (1840) or Herman Melville's *Moby Dick* (1851). "We need a Melville of the American rails," argued English professor William Helmer. "The opportunity, the challenge, the abundance await." Still, there exists a mostly ignored aspect of American literature, best labeled as the Railroad School. One scholar aptly called it "that thin slice of literature." There are numerous novels that include railroaders. One is *Whispering Smith* (1906), written by the prolific fiction writer Frank Hamilton Spearman (1859–1937). This work, which is an action-filled Western crime story, also appeared in two silent-screen versions and a 1948 Hollywood technicolor film. *Whispering Smith* and similar books focus on train travel, especially holdups, wrecks, and near collisions, and always reveal the excitement and glamour of railroading. The role of the station agent-operator, though, is usually negligible. These trackside railroaders achieved their acclaim mostly in articles and short stories. For decades, magazines, particularly *Railroad Man's Magazine* and its successors *Railroad Stories* and *Railroad Magazine* together with such mass-circulation ones as *American Magazine, McClure's, Muncey's, Schribner's,* and *Saturday Evening Post,* ran scores of these fictionalized stories, some in serialized form. Agent-operators may not be the main characters, but they stand out as key players and in some cases as the principals. Coverage often includes the adventurous boomers rather than the more staid home guards.[1]

One popular short story, "The Night Operator," by Frank Lucius Packard (1877–1942), epitomizes this genre. Published in 1919 in a collection of short stories bearing the same name, he relates the challenges faced by a bullied passenger-train "news butcher," dismissed by his associates because of his small stature and sharp tongue. Yet this young man desperately wants to become a "real railroader." His perseverance pays off, being taken under the wing of a kindly dispatcher who said, "I like your grit. And if you want to be a railroad man, I'll make you one—before I'm through." As a novice telegrapher, he prevents a potentially deadly head-on collision between a passenger limited and a freight train due to a lap train order. The young hero telegraphs, albeit haltingly, to the dispatcher to report that all is well. "Toddles"—he detests that nickname, demanding to be called by his legal name of Christopher Hoogan—finally gets that long-desired opportunity to become a trick operator and future agent.[2]

No matter how an agent-operator is portrayed, his daily work routine is nearly always accurately depicted. Operational details abound. The extensive writings of Harry Bedwell (1888–1955) stand out as good examples. This former boomer op, who worked for the Burlington, Rio Grande, Santa Fe, Southern Pacific, and SP's Pacific Electric subsidiary, wrote about what he knew and loved best. While more a romantic than a realist, this passage from "The Careless Road," which appeared in the February 1939 issue of *Railroad Magazine,* attests to his ability to describe one of the multitude of functions performed by an agent and trick operator.

> At the station a ham [novice] operator had broken the seal of the merchandise [LCL] car and recorded its number in his book. Then he and the rear brakeman pushed the running board from platform to car door. The ham, the clerk, the rear brakeman, and the conductor began rolling and carrying merchandise from the car to the platform. They called each piece as they took it out and the agent checked it on the waybill. . . . The agent, the clerk and the ham began checking freight to the drayman and trucking the rest into the freight room, stacking it in neat piles.[3]

Also in print are the occasional memoirs of agents. These are published by small or obscure presses or self-produced. *The Depot Agent: The History of the C.G.W. Railroad as Seen through the Eyes of an Agent* is an example. The author, Charles W. Finch, who began his railroad career in 1937, worked until the early 1970s (expect for active duty during World War II) as relief operator and agent for the Great Western in Illinois and Iowa. Written largely for fellow railroaders, enthusiasts, and his own enjoyment, coverage at times features the colorful and episodic. Still, Finch provides good commentary and insights into what it was like to work in a variety of stations.[4]

FILMS

When Americans today hear station agent, they might think of a motion picture by the same name. In 2003, Miramax Films released this comedy-drama, which stars Peter Dinklage working in a Hoboken, New Jersey, model train hobby shop owned by an elderly friend. When his employer dies suddenly, the hero inherits an abandoned small-town depot. Being an unmarried loner who is extremely conscious of his dwarfism, he moves into this building. Here he adjusts to his new venture and becomes enmeshed in the lives of his neighbors. *The Station Agent* received positive responses from critics and did well financially for a low-budget production. One reviewer captured the movie's essence: "A sweet and quirky film about a dwarf, a refreshment stand operator, and a reclusive artist connecting with one another." Railroad operations, though, are not depicted.[5]

Since the dawn of motion pictures, station agent-operators have been featured but mostly in cameo roles. In Westerns especially, they might be the ones who telegraphed urgent messages to the military or law enforcement about an Indian attack, robbery, or natural disaster. They are heroes of sorts, but they are overshadowed by the principal characters. Or these agents might be shown selling tickets, meeting passenger trains, or conducting other station chores. They are usually depicted as competent and friendly.

There are exceptions to the predictable big-screen portrayal of the agent-operator. A silent motion picture stands out, *The Lost Express*, directed by J. P. McGowan and released in 1925 by Rayart Pictures. Telegrapher Helen Martin (Helen Holmes) plays the star role in this five-reel mystery film. She is determined to find a missing train, which consists of a locomotive and business car, and to rescue baby Alice and her railroad baron grandfather. This action-packed production casts a female as the telegrapher-heroine, perhaps surprising audiences. Although Martin is shown infrequently at her telegraph table, there are scenes of her in the depot office with the young station agent. Also depicted are dispatchers at work on what presumably is the Union Pacific line between Salt Lake City and Los Angeles.

ARTIFACTS

The largest and most recognizable artifact associated with agent-operators is the depot itself. There is something special, arguably unique about this once ubiquitous right-of-way structure. In the early 1960s, artist Lloyd Foltz said it well: "The corner store and the fire station are preserved in memory, but even these lack the nostalgic aura that surrounds the long, low structure with bracketed eaves down where Main Street crosses the tracks." He continued, "Other corporate-owned properties may change in style, but the depot, even with extensive modernization, continues to look like what it is. One need not see its order board, insignia, or baggage truck to know that here is a depot. Take away even the tracks alongside and you still have a depot, however silent and forlorn."[6]

Although thousands of depots have been dismantled or destroyed by fire, storm, or neglect, some remain. Because of their adaptable floor

Figure 5.1. A railroad enthusiast constructed an exact replica of a Louisville & Nashville depot in Lynnville, Tennessee. He also assembled for his museum a variety of artifacts, including a Baldwin-built steam locomotive *(George Rieves photograph; author's collection)*

plans, availability, and cost (perhaps free if removed from trackside of an active rail line), hundreds of these structures have been recycled into a range of commercial buildings: offices, restaurants, taverns, beauty salons, barbershops, dry cleaners, or something else. That something else might be a church, the temporary fate of the ex–Grand Trunk Western depot in Pinckney, Michigan. Or it might be a bed-and-breakfast guest-house. That was the case of the one-time Nashville, Chattanooga & St. Louis depot at Centerville, Tennessee. And it could even be a winery, being the present use for the former Union Pacific depot in Gothenburg, Nebraska. Its signature wine is named for L. J. Morton, a longtime agent.

Figure 5.2. Although the author is dressed in a suit, in March 1962, he is about to explore the shuttered former Minneapolis & St. Louis depot in Sully, Iowa, located on the soon-to-be-abandoned Newton branch. *(Author's collection)*

Former depots have also become private dwellings, farm buildings, and storage sheds. Scores have been repurposed into community and visitors' centers, entertainment venues, and railroad and local museums, the latter perhaps sparked by America's extensive bicentennial celebrations in 1976. "Almost half of all surviving Indiana depots, 137 in all, are in some form of adaptive use, and this figure has increased since this survey was initiated in 1976," noted planning professor Francis Parker. More than a score were in public or museum use. Since the Parker report appeared in 1989, the Hoosier State depot census has not radically changed.[7]

Then there are the artifacts themselves. Collectors of railroadiana abound. "Steel mills don't have fans," remarked *Trains* editor David Morgan, who for decades guided this indispensable railfan publication. Railroads, however, do. By the immediate post–World War II years, this enthusiasm had been largely transformed from a solitary eccentricity (or obsession) into a well-accepted avocation. Hobbyists seek both paper and nonpaper items and flock to train shows and flea markets and spend hours on eBay and other online selling sites to find them. They are

Figure 5.3. The James H. Andrew Railroad Museum, part of the Boone Scenic Valley Railroad complex in Boone, Iowa, contains a re-created depot office, complete with an appropriately attired agent-operator mannequin. *(James L. Rueber photograph)*

particularly partial to public timetables, which once filled depot racks, and they relish copies of the *Official Railway Guide*. It is not surprising that the National Association of Timetable Collectors has flourished for decades. These "paper hounds" also like tickets, annual and trip passes, train orders, and photographs, including cabinet cards, stereo-optician views, and traditional and real-photo postcards of depots and station scenes. An impressive volume of the latter two items occurred during the Golden Age of Postcards. "Hard" artifacts are likewise eagerly sought. There are national hobby organizations that focus on these items, including the Railroadiana Collectors Association founded in 1971. Kerosene hand lanterns, especially large tin ones with blue, green, and red globes, are highly collectable. There are other items: switch keys, ticket daters and dies, brass wax sealers, brass baggage tags, agents' cap badges, telegraph keys and sounders, scissor telephones, porcelain signs, waiting-room benches, and office furniture. The latter include tariff cabinets, ticket cases, and rolltop desks. Not to be overlooked are train-order boards and baggage carts. In 1969, the Rock Island Railroad offered these signature carts for sale in a *Trains* advertisement. The copy read: "These symbols of a by-gone era in American railroading are now collectors' items. Limited supply available at $45.00 each, f.o.b. Chicago. All in good working order."[8]

Not to be forgotten are photographs. "The amount of railroad images out there has to be staggering," opined Jeff Brouws, a Center for Railroad Photography & Art director. "A recent Google search delivered in less than a minute 5.3 million results." While rail enthusiasts (and others) are attracted to locomotives and other pieces of rolling stock, they have not ignored depots and their agents and operators. The hooping up of orders has long presented opportunities for action shots.[9]

Few occupations have been honored with monuments or memorials, and the station agent-operator is no exception. Railroads, however, have spawned a limited number of monuments to commemorate their accomplishments and to memorialize their officers and high-ranking employees. A few were designed by famous architects and sculptors. Take the Ames Monument, which honored Union Pacific officials Oakes Ames (1804–1873) and his younger brother Oliver Ames (1831–1895). It was in the early 1880s that this massive sixty-five-foot granite block pyramid, the creation of architect Henry Hobson Richardson (1838–1886) and sculptor Augustus Saint-Gaudens (1848–1907), appeared along a section of the original transcontinental line between Cheyenne and Laramie, Wyoming. Perhaps this genre of remembrance supports the observation made in 1927 by Austrian philosophical novelist Robert Musil: "The most striking feature of monuments is that you do not notice them. There is nothing in the world as invisible as a monument."[10]

Although not fitting exactly into the agent-operator category is a granite monument designed by the prolific sculptor Charles Keck (1875–1951) and dedicated to Charles Minot (1810–1866), who pioneered the

Figure 5.4. Railroad modeler Robert Baudler made from scratch an agent hooping up train orders in his re-creation of the Great Western station at Moorland, Iowa. *(Robert Baudler photograph)*

employment of the telegraph for train control. On May 2, 1912, a large crowd gathered near the Erie depot in Harriman (née Turner's), New York, for the dedication of this tribute to Minot. Sponsored by the Association of Railway Telegraph Superintendents and the Old Time Telegraphers' and Historical Association, ample funds were raised. Heading the list of individual donors was Andrew Carnegie, who once worked as a telegrapher for the Pennsylvania Railroad, and Thomas Edison, who made technological improvements to the telegraph. A six-foot-tall, attached metal tablet featured a detailed inscription and came from the acclaimed Gorham Manufacturing Company. Vandals eventually damaged the monument, and about 1980, the tablet disappeared. Later it was learned that Conrail employees had taken this artifact to a New Jersey station for preservation. Although the tablet was returned to Harriman, it went missing again in the early 1990s and apparently remains so to the present.[11]

What does the future hold for perpetuating the legacy of the railroad station agent-operator? For one thing, there has been an effort to "save" American Morse code. Decades have passed since railroads used the telegraph. In May 1982, a Burlington Northern dispatcher allegedly sent the final train order in the United States to an operator in Whitehall, Montana, and three years later, the last circuit on the Milwaukee Road closed. According to one source, working wires were used by "old heads" in the Pasco, Washington, area until about 1990. Yet there is the Morse Telegraph Club, launched in 1942, which seeks to preserve the skill and pleasure of sending and receiving dots and dashes. This organization uses an internet telegraphy system called MorseKOB and maintains a website where individuals can download the client program for their personal computers. It also publishes *Dots & Dashes*, a quarterly news magazine, and operates the Antique Wireless Museum in East Bloomfield, New York.[12]

While knowledge of Morse code may eventually disappear, memories of the agent-operator occupation will probably never totally fade away. After all, railroads are the most cherished form of America's commercial land transportation. The continuing popularity of tourist railroads, especially those that operate steam locomotives and other pieces of vintage rolling stock, nearly always have at least one depot, whether original or recreated. Model railroad layouts, too, usually have a depot, maybe with a figure of an agent standing at trackside with a hand lantern or train-order hoop. Such exposures are good examples of how the public, irrespective of age, ethnicity, race, or wealth, will remember a vanished yet once vital job. Former Minneapolis & St. Louis and Chicago & North Western agent Dan Knight put it this way: "The depot agent had to be a jack of all trades and master of them all. To perform the job successfully he had to be versatile and able to adjust to all types of situations. Every day his proper performance involved matters of life and death."[13]

NOTES

1. FORMATIVE YEARS

1. *American Railroad Journal and Iron Manufacturer's and Mining Gazette* 4 (December 16, 1848): 801; L. T. C. Rolt, *The Railway Revolution: George and Robert Stephenson* (New York: St. Martin's, 1960), 83–86, 159–175, 196–202.

2. H. Roger Grant, *The Louisville, Cincinnati & Charleston Rail Road: Dreams of Linking North and South* (Bloomington: Indiana University Press, 2014), 23–26, 28–29.

3. James D. Dilts, *The Great Road: The Building of the Baltimore & Ohio, the Nation's First Railroad, 1828–1853* (Stanford, CA: Stanford University Press, 1993), 36–99.

4. Grant, *The Louisville, Cincinnati & Charleston Rail Road*, 35–37.

5. William D. Middleton, George M. Smerk, and Roberta Diehl, eds., *Encyclopedia of North American Railroads* (Bloomington: Indiana University Press, 2007), 1132.

6. Walter Licht, *Working for the Railroad: The Organization of Work in the Nineteenth Century* (Princeton, NJ: Princeton University Press, 1983), 37; *American Railroad Journal and Iron Manufacturer's and Mining Gazette* 4 (March 25, 1848): 194.

7. Licht, *Working for the Railroad*, 37; Allen W. Trelease, *The North Carolina Railroad, 1849–1871* (Chapel Hill: University of North Carolina Press, 1991), 60.

8. David St. John Thomas, *The Country Railway* (London: Book Club Associates, 1977), 58–62, 64, 67, 69.

9. Augustus J. Veenendaal Jr. to author, July 27, 2019.

10. B. A. Botkin and Alvin F. Harlow, eds. *A Treasury of Railroad Folklore* (New York: Crown, 1953), 158; *Organization and General Regulations, for Working and Conducting the Business of the Railroad & Its Branches* (New York: New-York & Erie Railroad Printing Office, 1852), 6–8.

The New-York & Erie made it clear that "Station Agents shall be subject to the general supervision and direction of the Superintendent, but more directly to the Auditor, Superintendents of Divisions, General Freight Agent, and General Ticket Agent, in all matters pertaining to *their* several Departments." (italics in the original)

11. Paul Black, "The Development of Management Personnel Policies on the Burlington Railroad, 1860–1900" (PhD diss., University of Wisconsin, 1972), 470.

12. David Lee Lightner, "Labor on the Illinois Central Railroad, 1852–1900" (PhD diss., University of Illinois, 1970), 70, 72–73, 81; Dilts, *The Great Road*, 391.

13. Charles B. George, *Forty Years on the Rail* (Chicago: R. R. Donnelley & Sons, 1887), 35.

14. Walter Arndt Lucas, *From the Hills to the Hudson: A History of the Paterson and Hudson River Rail Road and Its Associates* (New York: Railroadians of America, 1944), 128.

15. In the mid-1850s, the Ellicotts Mills freight structure began to serve passengers.

16. John F. Stover, *History of the Baltimore and Ohio Railroad* (West Lafayette, IN: Purdue University Press, 1987), 30–34; Herbert H. Harwood Jr., "History Where You Don't Expect It: Some Surprising Survivors," *Railroad History* 166 (Spring 1992): 104–107; Frederick C. Gamst, ed., *Early American Railroads: Franz Anton Ritter von Gerstner's "Die innern Communicationen," 1842–1843* (Stanford, CA: Stanford University Press, 1997), 342, 405, 676; Edward P. Alexander, *Down at the Depot: American Railroad Stations from 1831 to 1920* (New York: Bramhall House, 1970), 9; *Annual Report of the Petersburg Rail Road Company* (Petersburg, VA: Peterburg Intelligencer Job Office, 1840), 11; *American Railroad Journal and Mechanics' Magazine* 4 (April 1, 1840): 218; 10 (February 1843): 400; *American Railroad Journal and General Advertiser* 2 (July 4, 1846): 425.

17. David B. Howland, "Making Stations Attractive," *World's Work* 1 (March 1901): 517; *Galena and Chicago Union Railroad Seventh Annual Report* (Chicago: Daily Democrat Book and Job Printing, 1856), 11.

18. Botkin and Harlow, *A Treasury of Railroad Folklore*, 177.

19. H. Roger Grant, *Living in the Depot: The Two Story Railroad Station* (Iowa City: University of Iowa Press, 1993), 6–8; Paul J. Westhaeffer, *History of the Cumberland Valley Railroad, 1835–1919* (Washington, DC: Washington DC Chapter, National Railway Historical Society, 1979), 22, 58–59.

20. Interview with Louis W. Goodwin, May 16, 1992.

Another version appears in Botkin and Harlow, *A Treasury of Railroad Folklore*, 177, and parallels the one repeated by the Merwinsville Hotel Restoration Association. See also Robert F. Lord, *Country Depots in the Connecticut Hills* (New Hartford, CT: Goulet, 1996), 64–65.

21. Edward Hungerford, *The Story of the Baltimore & Ohio Railroad, 1827–1927* (New York: G. P. Putnam's Sons, 1938), 272.

22. "Spike of Gold," *Trains* 2 (May 1942): 11.

23. Boston, Clinton & Fitchburg Railroad, Mansfield & Framingham Division, Time Table No. 12, Takes Effect Monday, October 30, 1871, in possession of author.

24. Benjamin Sidney Michael Schwantes, *The Train and the Telegraph: A Revisionist History* (Baltimore, MD: Johns Hopkins University Press, 2019), 10.

25. Frank F. Hargrave, *A Pioneer Indiana Railroad: The Origins and Development of the Monon* (Indianapolis, IN: William Burford, 1932), 155.

26. Lucas, *From the Hills to the Hudson*, 251, 253–254.

27. Middleton, Smerk, and Diehl, eds., *Encyclopedia of North American Railroads*, 963; Charles E. Fisher, "Henry M. Sperry," *Bulletin of the Railway & Locomotive Historical Society* 34 (May 1934): 11; Herbert S. Balliet, "Development of Railway Signaling," *Bulletin of the Railway & Locomotive Historical Society* 37 (October 1937): 73; Robert Luther Thompson, *Wiring a Continent: The History of the Telegraph Industry in the United States, 1832–1866* (Princeton, NJ: Princeton University Press, 1947), 206; Jesse C. Burt Jr., ed., "The Savor of Old-Time Southern Railroading," *Bulletin of the Railway & Locomotive Historical Society*

84 (1951): 37; *American Railroad Journal and General Advertiser* 2 (October 17, 1846): 662; John H. White Jr., *The American Railroad Freight Car: From the Wood-Car Era to the Coming of Steel* (Baltimore, MD: Johns Hopkins University Press, 1993), 83.

During the Civil War, directional operations were used occasionally by the US Military Rail Roads (USMRR), but they were limited to a few hours at a time.

28. Erie Railway Time Table, Buffalo Division, No. 8, Takes Effect Monday, May 16, 1864, in possession of author.

29. "Railroad Accident," *Scientific American* 3 (March 25, 1848): 102.

30. JoAnne Yates, *Control through Communication: The Rise of System in American Management* (Baltimore, MD: Johns Hopkins University Press, 1989), 107; Licht, *Working for the Railroad*, 83; *Circular to all Employees of the North Missouri Railroad Company* (St. Louis, MO: M'Kee, Fishback, 1865), 8.

31. Schwantes, *The Train and the Telegraph*, 6–7; *American Railroad Journal and Mechanics' Magazine* 9 (December 15, 1842): 372; David Hochfelder, *The Telegraph in America, 1832–1920* (Baltimore, MD: Johns Hopkins University Press, 2012), 2–3; Dilts, *The Great Road*, 295; Richard R. John, *Network Nation: Inventing American Telecommunications* (Cambridge, MA: Harvard University Press, 2010), 24–89; *American Railroad Journal and General Advertiser* 2 (December 26, 1846): 827.

32. Carleton Mabee, *The American Leonardo: A Life of Samuel F. B. Morse* (New York: Alfred A. Knopf, 1943), 262–280; Richard Mowbray Haywood, *Russia Enters the Railway Age, 1842–1855* (New York: Columbia University Press, 1998), 240; Vidkunn Ulriksson, *The Telegraphers: Their Craft and Their Union* (Washington, DC: Public Affairs, 1953), 1–2; Stephen

Vail, "Early Days of the First Telegraph Line," *New England Magazine* 4 (June 1891): 458–459.

33. Advertisement in *Sam Johnson, The Experience and Observations of a Railroad Telegraph Operator* (New York: W. J. Johnston, 1878), n.p.; Marshall M. Kirkman, *Telegraph and Telephone* (New York: World Railway, 1904, Supplement to *The Science of Railways*, vol. 20), 16.

34. Edward Harold Mott, *Between the Ocean and the Lakes: The Story of Erie* (New York: John S. Collins, 1899), 415.

35. Edward Hungerford, *Men of Erie: A Story of Human Effort* (New York: Random House, 1946), 93, 210–211; Mott, *Between the Ocean and the Lakes*, 419–420; Mary Brignano and Hax McCullough, *The Search for Safety: A History of Railroad Signals and the People Who Made Them* (n.p.: Union Switch & Signal Division, American Standard, 1981), 50.

36. *Report of the Directors of the New-York and Erie Railroad Company to the Stockholders* (New York: Printed by Order of the Directors, 1853), 5, 50–51; *American Railroad Journal* 29 (April 26, 1856): 473.

37. Albert J. Churella, *The Pennsylvania Railroad: Building an Empire, 1846–1917* (Philadelphia: University of Pennsylvania Press, 2013), 600–603; *Tenth Annual Report of the Galena and Chicago Union Railroad Company* (Chicago: Daily Press Book and Job Printing House, 1856), 7; Schwantes, *The Train and the Telegraph*, x; *American Railroad Journal and Steam Navigation, Commerce, Mining, Manufacturing* 9 (September 3, 1853): 564; John O'Connell, *Railroad Album: The Story of American Railroads in Words and Pictures* (Chicago: Popular Mechanics, 1954), 26.

38. Jack Simmons, *The Victorian Railway* (New York: Thames and Hudson, 1991), 76.

39. Peter Hansen to author, January 16, 2020.

40. *American Railroad Journal and General Advertiser* 1 (October 23, 1845): 675.

41. Charles A. Beard and Mary R. Beard, *The Rise of American Civilization* (New York: Macmillan, 1930), II, 166.

42. Schwantes, *The Train and the Telegraph*, 70, 79; James A. Ward, *That Man Haupt: A Biography of Herman Haupt* (Baton Rouge: Louisiana State University Press, 1973), 118–119, 167.

43. Hargrave, *A Pioneer Indiana Railroad*, 158.

44. Maury Klein, *The Life and Legend of Jay Gould* (Baltimore, MD: Johns Hopkins University Press, 1986), 196–197; Alvin F. Harlow, *Old Wires and New Waves: The History of the Telegraph, Telephone, and Wireless* (New York: D. Appleton-Century, 1936), 213–214; Edwin Gabler, *The American Telegrapher: A Social History, 1860–1900* (New Brunswick, NJ: Rutgers University Press, 1988), 40; Hochfelder, *The Telegraph in America*, 40; Schwantes, *The Train and the Telegraph*, 148.

45. See Robert E. Conot, *Thomas A. Edison: A Streak of Luck* (New York: Da Capo, 1986).

46. Richard Reinhardt, ed., *Workin' on the Railroad: Reminiscences from the Age of Steam* (New York: Weathervane, 1970), 189.

2. MATURITY: ESSENTIALS

1. Paul V. Black, "The Development of Management Personnel Policies of the Burlington Railroad, 1860–1900" (PhD diss., University of Illinois, 1972), 204–205; Richard C. Overton, *Perkins/Budd: Railway Statesmen of the Burlington* (Westport, CT: Greenwood, 1982), 19–20.

2. Interview with John W. Barriger IV, July 2, 2019. What might be considered typical of early hiring practices took place on the Louisville & Nashville. "On the L&N there were many smaller divisions at the outset. Generally, the superintendent would make the decisions when it came to employing agents or agent-operators." Jerome Lachaussee to author, January 14, 2021.

3. The term *star agent* could have another meaning. A star agency in an ORT agreement denoted that the position did not require work with the train dispatcher and therefore was a lower-paid job. This would likely be in a custodian-type station.

4. Interview with Don L. Hofsommer, July 17, 2020; James L. Rueber to author, July 19, 2020; Dan Sabin to author, July 19, 2020.

5. H. Roger Grant, *Railroads and the American People* (Bloomington: Indiana University Press, 2012), 110; Robert C. Rowe, *It Looked Like Eden* (Victorville, CA: Mahahve Historical Society, 2009), 1; David P. Morgan, "What Do the Dots and Dashes Mean?" *Trains* 21 (July 1961): 19; Dan H. Mater, "The Development and Operation of the Railroad Seniority System," *Journal of Business of the University of Chicago* 13 (October 1940): 388; Thomas Curtis Clarke, ed., *The American Railway: Its Construction, Development, Management, and Appliances* (London: J. Murray, 1890), 412; H. Roger Grant, "The Railroad Station Agent in Small-Town Iowa," *Palimpsest* 64 (May–June 1983): 95.

The ages of newly hired agents varied, even widely. Walter Licht in *Working for the Railroad: The Organization of Work in the Nineteenth Century* (Princeton, NJ: Princeton University Press, 1983), 151, offers this striking contrast on the Illinois Central: "Charles St. John, for instance, entered the trade at the tender age of nine as a station hand. At twelve he became a telegraph operator, and just three years later received an appointment as depot master." Then there was the case of both John C. and John H. Wilson: "[They] became station agents at the age of fifty-three, after more than thirty years of service in various lesser posts."

6. *New York Times*, April 4, 1943.

7. Barbara B. Clayburn, *Prairie Stationmaster: The Story of One Man's Railroading Career in Nebraska, 1917–1963* (Detroit: Harlo, 1979), 10.

8. *Telegrapher Supplement*, November 6, 1865.

9. In 1880, on the eve of massive new construction, America's first big business employed 416,000. Fifteen percent of them (63,380) were in station service. And this number increased steadily, leveling off by the eve of World War I.

10. Thomas C. Jepsen, *My Sisters Telegraphic: Women in the Telegraph Office, 1846–1950* (Athens: Ohio University Press, 2000), 1, 6, 15; Thomas C. Jepsen, "'A Look into the Future': Women Railroad Telegraphers and Station Agents in Pennsylvania, 1855–1960," *Pennsylvania History* 76 (Spring 2009): 144–145, 153; William R. Blum, *The Military Telegraph during the Civil War in the United States* (Chicago: Jansen, McClurg, 1882, vol. 1), 346–347; *Waverly (IA) Democrat*, August 24, 1905; Thomas C. Jepsen, *Ma Kiley: The Life of a Railroad Telegrapher* (El Paso: Texas Western, 1997), 11, 15.

11. H. Roger Grant, "Kate Shelley and the Chicago & North Western Railway," *Palimpsest* 76 (Fall 1995): 138–144.

12. Patrick Irelan, *Central Standard: A Time, A Place, A Family* (Iowa City: University of Iowa Press, 2002), 29, 46.

13. There is uncertainty about the meaning of OS. Two common explanations are that these letters stand for "on-the-sheet" or "out-of-station." Neither term may be correct; the letters may not stand for anything. "These 2 letters were easy to recognize when sent on the telegraph," explained a veteran dispatcher. "'O' was a dot space dot and 'S' was 3 dots. Tap those out on the table with your finger and see if you don't think any dispatcher would recognize those letters right away." He added, "If they had any other meaning, I would guess it would be 'out of station.' I never read or head any of the old timers say it had a special meaning." James L. Rueber to author, May 22, 2020.

14. Sue R. Morehead, "Woman Op," *Railroad Magazine* (January 1944): n.p.; Elisa W. Lindenberg and Charles W. Lindenberg, "Learning the Lingo at Flagstaff," *Classic Trains* 9 (Fall 2008): 79.

15. Unlike international radio code, American landline Morse code (there is no official name) is much faster. It makes a noise upon closing an electrical contact; international radio code interrupts a constant sound, resulting in more dashes. American Morse also uses the faster system of spaced dots.

16. Marshall M. Kirkman, *Telegraph and Telephone* (New York: World Railway, Supplement to *The Science of Railways* vol. 20, 1904), 56; George Gilbert, "The Palmy Days When Ops Were Ops," *Railroad Man's Magazine* 35 (April 1918): 574; Jerome Lachaussee to author, January 15, 2021; Edmund C. Love, *The Situation in Flushing* (New York: Harper & Row, 1965), 116.

17. D. C. Sanders, *The Brasspounder* (New York: Hawthorn, 1978), 8–9.

18. Sanders, *The Brasspounder*, 10–12.

19. Grant, *Railroads and the American People*, 111–112.

20. Rossiter W. Raymond, *Peter Cooper* (New York: Houghton, Mifflin, 1901), 73; Edward C. Mack, *Peter Cooper: Citizen of New York* (New York: Duell, Sloan and Pearce, 1949), 253, 261, 328; Jepsen, *Ma Kiley*, 24.

21. *Sumner (IA) Journal*, July 27, 1905; Benjamin Sidney Michael Schwantes, *The Train and the Telegraph: A Revisionist History* (Baltimore, MD: Johns Hopkins University Press, 2019), 135; *Erie Railroad Employes Magazine* (March 1907): 43.

22. Jepsen, *Ma Kiley*, 24; O. H. Kirkpatrick, *Working on the Railroad* (Philadelphia: Dorrance, 1949), 100.

23. Schwantes, *The Train and the Telegraph*, 134; Mark Aldrich, *Safety First: Technology, Labor, and Business in the Building of American Work Safety, 1870–1939* (Baltimore, MD: Johns Hopkins University Press, 1997), 24; Albert J. Churella, *The Pennsylvania Railroad: Building an Empire, 1846–1917* (Philadelphia: University of Pennsylvania Press, 2013), 605–607.

24. Harry Bedwell, "The Mistakes of a Young Railroad Telegraph Operator," *American Magazine* 69 (November 1939): 71; James L. Rueber to author, July 16, 2019; October 28, 2019.

Although a considerable amount of an agent-operator's telegraphic work involved train orders, they were easy to copy.

Orders were brief, included a limited number of standardized forms, and words and place-names became instantly familiar. A typical one read: "Eng 758, seven five eight, displays signals and will run as First 56, fifty six. East Wayne to Bellevue Yard." Rich Melvin, *765! A Twenty-First Century Survivor* (Privately printed, 2020), 30.

25. Allen W. Trelease, *The North Carolina Railroad, 1849–1871 and the Modernization of North Carolina* (Chapel Hill: University of North Carolina Press, 1991), 229; Thomas C. Jepsen, "Two 'Lightning Slingers' from South Carolina: The Telegraphic Careers of Ambrose and Narciso Gonzales," *South Carolina Historical Magazine* 94 (October 1993): 267–268.

26. *Eighteenth Annual Report of the Railroad and Warehouse Commission of Illinois* (Springfield, IL: Springfield Printing Company, 1889), 177; *Sixteenth Annual Report of the Railroad and Warehouse Commission of Illinois* (Springfield, IL: Springfield Printing Company, 1887), 231.

27. *Fourteenth Annual Report of the Kansas Bureau of Labor and Industrial Statistics* (Topeka, KS: W. Y. Morgan, State Printer, 1899), 169.

28. Interview with E. Frank Napier, July 27, 2005; James L. Rueber to author, April 13, 2020.

29. Harold H. Baetjer, *A Book That Gathers No Dust* (New York: National Railway Publishing, 1950), 2, 5–6; B. A. Botkin and Alvin F. Harlow, eds., *A Treasury of Railroad Folklore* (New York: Crown, 1953), 518–519; Freeman Hubbard, *Encyclopedia of North American Railroads: 150 Years of Railroading in the United States and Canada* (New York: McGraw-Hill, 1981), 242.

Agents in smaller stations usually did not receive current copies of the *Official Guide*; they had hand-me-downs from larger stations. A single copy might be passed to multiple agents.

30. Vandalia Railroad Company, *Rules for the Government of the Transportation Department* (n.p., May 1, 1910), 144.

31. Ian R. Bartky, "The Invention of Railroad Time," *Railroad History* 148 (Spring 1983): 13–22.

32. Frank E. Vyzralek, H. Roger Grant, and Charles Bohi, "North Dakota's Railroad Depots: Standardization on the Soo Line," *North Dakota History* 42 (Winter 1975): 9.

The range of LCL or express shipments appears staggering but hardly surprising. "One Grand Forks [ND] laundry arranged with Great Northern station agents to ship a weekly basket to the city, and others soon created similar outposts," noted geographer John C. Hudson. "The level of business evidently was good because the North Dakota Launderers Association sought a reduction in freight rates, claiming that 'many thousands of baskets of laundered and soiled articles are shipped back and forth between local points.'" John C. Hudson, *Plains Country Towns* (Minneapolis: University of Minnesota Press, 1985), 117.

33. O. P. Kirkpatrick, *The Station Agent's Blue Book* (Chicago: Kirkpatrick,

n.d.), 43, 260; Albert M. Langley to author, December 16, 2020.

34. Albert M. Longley to author, December 16, 2020.

35. Steve Patterson, "Home on the Range," *Trains* 62 (December 2002): 68–70; Phillip L. Gerber, ed., *Bachelor Bess: The Homesteading Letters of Elizabeth Corey, 1909–1919* (Iowa City: University of Iowa Press, 1990), 440; Chicago & North Western Railway public timetable, September 2, 1923.

36. Joseph Taylor, *A Fast Life on the Modern Highway; Being a Glance into the Railway World from a New Point of View* (New York: Harper & Brothers, 1874), 108–109.

37. Grant, "The Railroad Station Agent in Small-Town Iowa," 95–96.

38. Slason Thompson, "The Railroad and the Small Town," *World To-Day* 13 (October 1907): 1035–1036.

39. H. Roger Grant and Charles W. Bohi, *The Country Railroad Station in America* (Boulder, CO: Pruett, 1978), 5, 7.

40. Grant and Bohi, *The Country Railroad Station in America*, 5, 7.

41. Chet Huntley, *The Generous Years: Remembrances of a Frontier Boyhood* (New York: Random House, 1968), 193.

42. Grant, "The Railroad Station Agent in Small-Town Iowa," 95.

43. Kirkpatrick, *The Station Agent's Blue Book*, 3; *Northern Pacific Railway Company Accounting Rules and Instructions to Govern Freight and Passenger Agents* (St. Paul, MN: Northern Pacific Railway Company, dates varied), n.p.

44. "Santa Fe." *The Atchison, Topeka & Santa Fe Railway System: Rules and Regulations of the Operating Department* (n.p., 1909), 91–92.

45. Clayburn, *Prairie Stationmaster*, 16; H. A. Stimson, *Depot Days* (Boynton Beach, FL: Star, 1972), 79; *Rules of the Operating Department Effective September 1,*

1910 (Chicago: Chicago & North Western Railway, 1910), 156.

46. Love, *The Situation in Fleming*, 19. See also Klink Garrett with Toby Smith, *Ten Turtles to Tucumcari: A Personal History of the Railway Express Agency* (Albuquerque: University of New Mexico, 2003); and V. S. Roseman, *Railway Express: An Overview* (Denver, CO: Rocky Mountain, 1992).

47. Chicago & North Western Railway, *Rules of the Operating Department Effective September 1, 1910*, 153; *Think! Is it Safe?* (Spokane, Portland & Seattle Railway, January 1, 1953), 19.

48. J. J. Shanley, "The Way Station Agent: Suggesting an Epic," *Chautauquan: A Weekly News-Magazine* 4 (January 1904): 359.

49. *Chicago Herald*, undated newspaper clipping ca. 1917 in possession of author. A former agent-operator said this about the power possessed by a dispatcher: "An operator does not interfere with a dispatcher on duty any more than a nurse with a surgeon performing an operation. It was a practice as rigid as professional or military etiquette. The penalty for breaking it was drastic." Harry Bedwell, "The Careless Road," *Railroad Magazine* 24 (February 1939): 57.

50. Mystery surrounds why train-order forms are numbered 19 and 31. A possible explanation is that they were designated as such to bring about a degree of standardization. A sampling of company rule books suggests that the numbers did not appear until the turn of the twentieth century. The forms themselves were commonly printed on different colored paper: green for 19 orders and yellow for 31 orders. This explanation is also plausible: "19 and 31 on the telegraph were quite different and would not be confusing to the receiving operator," opined a retired dispatcher. James L. Rueber to author, May 25, 2020.

51. Apparently train-order hoops appeared near the close of the nineteenth century. In 1896, an operator for the Pennsylvania Railroad made a hoop from a grapevine. "The crew man accepting it could insert an arm though it and thus the train would not have to slow down for handing up orders. The agent I worked for was so pleased that he had me make a bundle of hoops at one cent each. Years later, the Pennsy officially adopted train-order hoops." Freeman Hubbard, *The Encyclopedia of North American Railroading*, 326.

52. Dan Knight to author, n.d.

53. "Handing Up the Train Orders," *Trains* 2 (December 1941): 2; Dan Sabin, "Of Dispatcher Rosey, a Howling Snowstorm, and an Almost-Cornfield-Meet," *Classic Trains* 7 (Spring 2006): 28.

54. James L. Rueber to author, September 10, 2020; October 6, 2020; Irelan, *Central Standard*, 119.

55. Robert Jones, "Handling 'em Up," *Vintage Rails* 11 (March–April 1998): 26.

56. John E. L. Robertson, "My Life as a Telegrapher on the Kentucky Division of the Illinois Central Railroad," *Register of the Kentucky Historical Society* 98 (Summer 2000): 280–281.

57. Not every railroad referred to 31 orders as such. The Southern Pacific, for one, called these orders *restrictive*. Still, they necessitated that crews stop at the point of delivery, go into the depot, telegraph office, or tower and sign a receipt.

58. Henry Frick to author, June 8, 2020; Kirkman, *Telegraph and Telephone*, 65–66. Agent-operators issued a tremendous volume of train orders. "It is estimated that no less than 130,000 train orders are issued daily, or a total of 47,000,000 orders a year," claimed one source in 1934. "As practically all train orders are issued in duplicate, the total number delivered to trains is nearly 95,000,000 orders. This is a conservative figure as sometimes even three or more copies of an order are made."

Charles E. Fisher, "Henry M. Sperry," *Railway & Locomotive Historical Society Bulletin* 34 (May 1934): 10.

During the pretypewriter era, management considered good penmanship important, and it was not restricted to copying train orders. By way of example, Lafayette, Muncie & Bloomington Rail Road (future Nickel Plate Road) operator Ed Davis, who initially worked at Otterbein, Indiana, won promotion in 1877 to become agent at Tipton, Indiana, because "Tipton then was a grain center and the railroad wanted someone who could write waybills legibly. His penmanship had gained him this new job—with a handsome increase in wages." "Located 'em Early," *Nickel Plate Road Magazine* 4 (March 1951): 5.

59. Train Order No. 620, December 7, 1941, in possession of author.

60. Berne Ketchum to author, December 11, 2020.

61. Chicago Great Western Railway, *Rules of the Transportation Department for the Government of Locomotive Engineers and Firemen, Conductors, Brakeman, Baggagemen, Switchmen, Station Agents and Telegraph Operators, Trackman, Bridgemen and Carmen Effective April 1, 1896*, n.p; Chicago & North Western Railway, *Rules of the Operating Department Effective September 1, 1910*, 81; James L. Rueber to author, March 2, 2020; E. Ray Lichty to author, February 18, 23, 24, 2020; Baltimore & Ohio Railroad, *Rules of the Operating Department Effective April 26, 1953*, 67; interview with Don L. Hofsommer, February 26, 2020.

"There were stations at which timetable or other instructions required that a clearance be received before passing or leaving. Some of these, such as terminals, may not have had a train order signal." Chris Burger to author, March 2, 2020.

As early as 1910, railroads began to experiment with radio communications, but this work largely ended in 1930 when the federal government withdrew authorization to use certain wave bands. Then at the close of World War II, the Federal Communications Commission designated sixty channels for railroad use. In December 1945, the Missouri Pacific became one of the first companies to utilize the newly available radio resources, receiving permission from the Interstate Commerce Commission for a trial installation.

62. Fred W. Frailey, *Last Train to Texas: My Railroad Odyssey* (Bloomington: Indiana University Press, 2020), 189–190; James L. Rueber to author, January 21, 2020; *Daily Freeman-Journal* (Webster City, IA), November 10, 1909; Bill Kuebler, "This Is the Way to Run a Railroad," *Mainstreeter* 38 (Summer 2019): 39.

63. *Minneapolis Morning News*, October 10, 1910. Some of the worst railroad disasters in American history were due to operator's error, including these: May 14, 1884, on the Baltimore & Ohio at Connellsville, Pennsylvania, eight deaths; October 24, 1892, on the Reading at West Manayunk, Pennsylvania, eight deaths; August 16, 1900, on the Grand Rapids & Indiana at Pierson, Michigan, eight deaths; December, 26, 1902, on the Grand Trunk at Wanstead, Ontario, twenty-eight deaths; January 27, 1903, on the Southern Pacific at Esmond, Arizona, eight deaths; January 22, 1906, on the Seaboard Air Line at Hamlet, North Carolina, sixteen deaths; and January 2, 1907, on the Rock Island at Volland, Kansas, thirty-two deaths. See "Shaw's All-Time List of Notable Railroad Accidents, 1831–2000," *Railroad History* 184 (Spring 2001): 39–42.

64. John H. White Jr., *The American Railroad Freight Car: From the Wood-Car Era to the Coming of Steel* (Baltimore, MD: Johns Hopkins University Press, 1993), 84, 86; George H. Burgess and Miles C. Kennedy, *Centennial History of the Pennsylvania Railroad Company, 1846–1946* (Philadelphia: Pennsylvania Railroad,

1949), 494; Chicago, St. Paul, Minneapolis & Omaha Railway public timetable, February 1909.

65. Manual block and automatic block signal data compiled from Interstate Commerce Commission reports.

66. J. W. Arbuckle, *Crown Pusher District and Tunnel* (Winchester, TN: Herald-Chronicle, n.d.), 77.

67. Robert E. Ashman, *The Central New England Railroad, 1867–1967* (Salisbury, CT: Salisbury Association, 1972), 100.

68. Harry W. Forman, *Rights of Trains: A Complete Analysis of Single Track Standard Code Rules* (New York: Simmons-Boardman, 1945 ed.), 258.

69. Richard J. Orsi, *Sunset Limited: The Southern Pacific Railroad and the Development of the American West, 1850–1930* (Berkeley: University of California Press, 2005), 284–285.

70. Orsi, *Sunset Limited*, 321.

71. David B. Howland, "Making Stations Attractive," *World's Work* 1 (March 1901): 517–527; John A. Droege, *Passenger Terminals and Trains* (New York: McGraw-Hill, 1916), 266–267.

72. Jo Ann Carrigan, "The Saffron Scourge: A History of Yellow Fever in Louisiana" (PhD diss., Louisiana State University, 1961), 226–279; Fred Ash, "Yellow Fever Rides the Rails," *Railroad History* 221 (Fall–Winter 2019): 88–93.

73. Dan Cushman, *Plenty of Room & Air* (Great Falls, MT: Stay Away, Joe, 1975), 197; J. E. Smith, "Observations of a Country Station-Agent," *Railroad Man's Magazine* 32 (February 1917): 266; James H. Wade Jr., *Greenwood County and Its Railroads, 1852–1992* (Columbia, SC: R. L. Bryan, 1993), 217.

74. J. G. Lachaussee, "Rigolets, Louisiana: The Last Outpost, Part 1," *L&N Magazine* (September 2013): 12; Francis B. C. Bradlee, *The Boston, Revere Beach and Lynn: Narrow Gauge Railroad* (Salem, MA; Essex Institute, 1921), 4; Elaine Artlip

to author, March 15, 2018; Howard Bryan, *Albuquerque Remembered* (Albuquerque: University of New Mexico Press, 2006), 106–108; H. Roger Grant, *Living in the Depot: The Two-Story Railroad Station* (Iowa City: University of Iowa Press, 1993), 23.

75. James L. Rueber to author, June 18, 2020; *Mt. Pleasant (IA) Journal*, January 2, 1868; Martha Purchis to author, June 22, 2020; June 26, 2020; H. Roger Grant "Depot: Economy and Style at Trackside," *Timeline* 1 (October 1984): 57.

76. Kirkpatrick, *The Station Agent's Blue Book*, 483.

77. Each station had a two-letter code identifier. This was not unlike the three-letter identifier that airports use today. Every message to a particular station began with those two letters. D. C. McCallum, an antebellum Erie Railroad official, originated two-letter abbreviations.

78. A tobacco can placed in the resonator was a popular and long-standing trick to amplify sound.

79. James L. Rueber to author, December 14, 2019. The locked cash drawer or some other secure place might contain a loaded revolver. The express company was the usual provider.

80. Lucius Beebe, *Mixed Train Daily: A Book of Short-Line Railroads* (New York: Dutton, 1947), 83, 310.

81. Frank H. Spearman, *Held for Orders: Being Stories of Railroad Life* (New York: McClure, Phillips, 1901): 149.

82. James L. Rueber to author, February 6, 2020.

83. For decades, pipe smoking was popular among agents-operators. A pipe smoker created deliberative time by fiddling with his favorite pipe. This involved filling, tamping, lighting, relighting, knocking out ashes, and scraping the bowel. This pastime would not take place during busy periods at the station.

84. Huntley, *The Generous Years*, 22, 120–121; Ron Flanary, "'Is Anything

Close?' Locating Trains to Photograph Over 50 Years Ago Was a Lot Different Than Today," *Trains* 80 (November 2020): 45–46.

Jerome "Jerry" Lachaussee, who served as the last agent-operator at Kreole, Mississippi, on the Louisville & Nashville, made these comments about ink and related office supplies: "We still requisitioned through the stationer at Louisville needed forms and other supplies; even writing ink, which came in small cardboard boxes containing an envelope of black powder (probably some form of lampblack) which would be emptied into a quart bottle of water and mixed thoroughly." He continued, "L&N always was very frugal; you can image a station at that time (1965) doing a 6-figure business monthly [made possible by an International Paper Company plant] having recently dispensed with the assisting personnel (operator-clerk, general clerk) and having to handle business the 'old way' of typewriting, carbon copies, etc. Take it from me I had mixed emotions when they discontinued the job." Jerome Lachaussee to author, January 13, 2021.

85. Frank P. Donovan Jr., *Harry Bedwell: Last of the Great Railroad Storytellers* (Minneapolis, MN: Ross & Haines, 1959), 52.

86. Grant, *Railroads and the American People*, 162–163.

87. Jeffrey Richards and John M. MacKenzie, *The Railway Station: A Social History* (Oxford, UK: Oxford University Press, 1986), 312–313.

88. Hans Halberstadt and April Halberstadt, *The American Train Depot & Roundhouse* (Osceola, WI: Motorbooks International, 1995), 44.

3. MATURITY: ESSENTIALS

1. *Rules for the Government of the Transportation Department: Pennsylvania Lines West of Pittsburgh; Vandalia Railroad*

Company (To Take Effect May 1, 1910), 143; Grant, "The Railroad Station Agent in Small-Town Iowa," *Palimpsest* 64 (May–June 1983): 94; H. Roger Grant, *Railroad Postcards in the Age of Steam* (Iowa City: University of Iowa Press, 1994), 2–3; interview with Louis W. Goodwin, May 16, 1992; Bryant Alden Long and William Jefferson Dennis, *Mail by Rail: The Story of the Postal Transportation Service* (New York: Simmons-Boardman, 1951), 2.

2. Charles B. George, *Forty Years on the Rail* (Chicago: R. R. Donnelley & Sons, 1887), 79.

3. Interview with James L. Rueber, June 15, 2019; Rueber to the author, October 29, 2019; Bob Anderson and Sandy Schauer, eds., *I Never Worked in Pocatello: The Life and Times of Santa Fe Railroad's Paul T. Collins* (Los Lunas, NM: Montanita, 2013), 10; interview with Don L. Hofsommer, November 1, 2019.

4. Boris Emmet and John E. Jeuck, *Catalogues and Counters: A History of Sears, Roebeck and Company* (Chicago: University of Chicago Press, 1950), 23–24; Frank P. Donovan Jr., *Mileposts on the Prairie: The Story of the Minneapolis & St. Louis Railway* (New York: Simmons-Boardman, 1950), 242; Don L. Hofsommer, *The Tootin' Louis: A History of the Minneapolis & St. Louis Railway* (Minneapolis: University of Minnesota Press, 2005), 111; "Notable Americans Who Began as Railroaders," *Train Dispatcher* (December 1969): 362.

5. As the authors of *Catalogues and Counters* point out, "It was a common practice of the time for wholesalers to ship on consignment to retailers—frequently even to ship goods which had not been ordered by the retailer" (25).

6. Emmet and Jeuck, *Catalogues and Counters*, 25–26.

7. *New York Times*, December 15, 1921.

8. Barbara B. Clayburn, *Prairie Stationmaster: The Story of One Man's Railroading Career in Nebraska, 1917–1963*

(Detroit: Harlo, 1979), 13; James L. Rueber to author, October 29, 2019; interview with E. Frank Napier, July 27, 2005.

9. R. M. Neal, *High Green and the Bark Peelers: The Story of Engineman Henry A. Beaulieu and His Boston and Maine Railroad* (New York: Duell, Sloan and Pearce, 1950), 123.

10. Grant, "The Railroad Station Agent in Small-Town Iowa," 98–99.

11. Thomas C. Clarke, ed., *The American Railway: Its Construction, Management, and Appliance.* (London: J. Murry, 1890), 412; O. B. Kirkpatrick, *The Station Agent's Blue Book* (Chicago: Kirkpatrick, 1925), 3.

12. Patrick Irelan, *Central Station: A Time, A Place, A Family* (Iowa City: University of Iowa Press, 2002), 11; J. E. Smith, "Observations of a Country Station-Agent," *Railroad Man's Magazine* 32 (February 1917): 265; Grant, "The Railroad Station Agent in Small-Town Iowa," 99–100; H. Roger Grant, *Railroads and the American People* (Bloomington: Indiana University Press, 2012), 116; James L. Rueber to author, December 22, 2019.

13. Grant, *Railroads and the American People*, 116; H. Roger Grant and Charles W. Bohi, *The Country Railroad Station in America* (Boulder, CO: Pruett, 1978), 13–14; Ames W. Williams, *Otto Mears Goes East: The Chesapeake Beach Railway* (Alexandria, VA: Meridian Sun, 1975), 82.

14. John Samson, *Sam Johnson: The Experience and Observations of a Railroad Telegraph Operator* (New York: W. J. Johnston, 1878), 12.

15. C. W. Finch, *The Depot Agent: The History of the C.G. W. Railroad as Seen through the Eyes of an Agent* (Apple River, IL: North-West Associates, 1984), 77.

16. Grant, "The Railroad Agent in Small-Town Iowa," 99.

17. Don L. Hofsommer, *The Quanah Route: A History of the Quanah, Acme & Pacific Railway* (College Station: Texas A&M University Press, 1991), 30, 108; Sam

Lazarus to Charles H. Sommer, August 23, 1927; Sam Lazarus to Murdo MacKenzie, August 27, 1927, copies courtesy of Robert Edmonson.

18. *History of Transportation Henry County Iowa: Water, Railroads, Roads, Aviation* (Mt. Pleasant: Henry County Historic Preservation Commission, 2016), 107.

19. H. A. Stimson, *Depot Days* (Boynton Beach, FL: Star, 1972), 49.

20. Stimson, *Depot Days*, 70.

21. W. J. Chafe, *I've Been Working on the Railroad: Memoirs of a Railwayman, 1911–1962* (St. John's, NL: Harry Cuff, 1987), 18–19; *Oelwein (IA) Daily Register*, July 19, 1963.

22. *Dothan (AL) Eagle*, November 9, 1960.

23. Finch, *The Depot Agent*, 44; Hugh Hawkins, *Railwayman's Son: A Plains Family Memoir* (Lubbock: Texas Tech University Press, 2006), 62.

24. Thomas C. Jepsen, "Two 'Lightning Slingers' from South Carolina: The Telegraphic Careers of Ambrose and Narciso Gonzales," *South Carolina Historical Magazine* 94 (October 1993): 264, 267–268.

25. Stimson, *Depot Days*, 91.

26. Frank E. Vyzralek, H. Roger Grant, and Charles Bohi, "North Dakota Railroad Depots: Standardization on the Soo Line," *North Dakota History* 42 (Winter 1975): 15; Finch, *The Depot Agent*, 31.

27. H. Roger Grant, *Living in the Depot: The Two Story Railroad Station* (Iowa City: University of Iowa Press, 1993), 40–42; *Columbus (ND) Reporter*, September 11, 1947; *New Ulm (MN) Review*, September 10, 1890.

28. *New York Times*, April 3, 1892.

29. *New York Times*, November 26, 1906.

30. *New York Times*, April 13, 1911.

31. *Fort Worth (TX) Gazette*, November 11, 1888.

32. Clarke, *The American Railway*, 412.

33. *New York Times*, March 12, 1881; January 2, 1909.

34. *Marshalltown (IA) Times-Republican*, August 16, 1907.

35. The term *boomer* likely had its origin during the 1820s and referred to workers who followed boomtown construction camps, notably those associated with canal projects.

36. Finch, *The Depot Agent*, 78.

37. H. Roger Grant, ed., *Brownie the Boomer: The Life of Charles P. Brown, an American Railroader* (DeKalb: Northern Illinois University Press, 1991), xi–xii; George W. Pierson, "The M-Factor in American History," *American Quarterly* 14 (Summer 1962, part 2: supplement): 275, 278.

38. Anderson and Schauer, eds., *I Never Worked in Pocatello*, 31.

39. R. H. McConnell to "Friend Vick," February 11, 1952, in possession of author.

40. Interview with Gregory Maxwell, February 19, 1988; Edd H. Bailey, *A Life with the Union Pacific: The Autobiography of Edd H. Bailey* (St. Johnsbury, VT: Saltillo, 1989), 86–87; W. Fred Cottrell, *The Railroaders* (Stanford, CA: Stanford University Press, 1940), 45.

41. *Times-Republican* (Marshalltown, IA), December 18, 1907.

42. Barnet Phillips, "The Thorsdale Telegraphs," *Atlantic Monthly* (October 1876): 400–417.

43. *Kansas City Star Magazine*, October 8, 2006.

44. *Mount Ayr (IA) Record-News*, October 26, 1939.

45. Grant, "The Railroad Station Agent in Small-Town Iowa," 94.

46. Grant, *Railroads and the American People*, 121.

47. James H. Ducker, *Men of the Steel Rails: Workers on the Atchison, Topeka & Santa Fe Railroad, 1869–1900* (Lincoln: University of Nebraska Press, 1983), 86;

"Eastern Division Enters Politics," *Great Western Magazine* 8 (October 1929): n.p.; Edwin D. Culp, *Stations West: The Story of the Oregon Railways* (New York: Bonanza, 1978), 18.

48. Archibald M. McIsaac, *The Order of Railroad Telegraphers: A Study in Trade Unionism and Collective Bargaining* (Princeton, NJ: Princeton University Press, 1933), 3.

49. McIsaac, *The Order of Railroad Telegraphers*, 3. Coverage of the Knights of Labor is extensive. See, for example, Gerald N. Grob, *Workers and Utopia: A Study of Ideological Conflict in the American Labor Movement, 1865–1900* (Chicago: Quadrangle Books, 1961); Bruce Laurie, *Artisans into Workers: Labor in Nineteenth Century America* (Urbana: University of Illinois Press, 1997); and Kim Voss, *The Making of American Exceptionalism: The Knights of Labor and Class Formation in the Late Nineteenth Century* (Ithaca, NY: Cornell University Press, 1993).

50. McIsaac, *The Order of Railroad Telegraphers*, 3–4.

51. McIsaac, *The Order of Railroad Telegraphers*, 5.

52. McIsaac, *The Order of Railroad Telegraphers*, 5–7.

53. McIsaac, *The Order of Railroad Telegraphers*, 7–9.

54. Paul Michel Taillon, *Good Reliable, White Men: Railroad Brotherhoods, 1877–1917* (Urbana: University of Illinois Press, 2009), 100.

55. McIsaac, *The Order of Railroad Telegraphers*, 11; Sylvester Kiliher, "Dawn of a New Era," *Railway Carmen's Journal* 3 (May 1893): 259.

56. David Ray Papke, *The Pullman Case: The Clash of Labor and Capital in Industrial America* (Lawrence: University Press of Kansas, 1999), 20–37; Laurie, *Artisans into Workers*, 205; McIsaac, *The Order of Railroad Telegraphers*, 11.

57. McIsaac, *The Order of Railroad Telegraphers*, 12.

58. McIsaac, *The Order of Railroad Telegraphers*, 12–13; James L. Rueber to author, November 23, 2020.

59. Mark Aldrich, *Death Rode the Rails: American Railroad Accidents and Safety, 1828–1965* (Baltimore, MD: Johns Hopkins University Press, 2006), 185; "The Nine-Hour Law," *Outlook* 88 (March 14, 1908): 571–572.

60. Benjamin Sidney Michael Schwantes, *The Train and the Telegraph: A Revisionist History* (Baltimore, MD: Johns Hopkins University Press, 2019), 128–132; Aldrich, *Death Rode the Rails*, 185.

61. Schwantes, *The Train and the Telegraph*, 134; *Baltimore & Ohio Railroad, Appt. V. Interstate Commerce Commission*, 221 U.S. 612, May 29, 1911; "Nine-Hour Law," 572.

62. Aldrich, *Safety First*, 173. In the Interstate Commerce Commission investigation of the rear-end collision at Odessa, Minnesota, on the Chicago, Milwaukee & St. Paul about 4:00 a.m. on December 18, 1911, which killed two crew members and eight passengers on the *Columbian*, the absence of the third trick operator "because of economic reasons" contributed to this catastrophe. See Memorandum to Commissioner McChord relative to accident on the Chicago, Milwaukee & St. Paul Ry. Draft submitted by the Chief Commissioner of Safety Appliances as a basis for the report of the commission, February 12, 1912.

63. C. A. Hammond, "Train Orders by Telephone," *Railroad Gazette* 24 (December 30, 1892): 986; Steven W. Usselman, *Regulating Railroad Innovation: Business, Technology, and Politics in America, 1840–1920* (New York: Cambridge University Press, 2002), 306; Kirkman, *Telegraph and Telephone* (Telephone section), 23–24.

64. James Brandt Latimer, *Railway Signaling in Theory and Practice* (Chicago: Mackenzie-Klink, 1909), 354; R. H. Sawles, "Telegraph vs. Telephone for Train Dispatching," *Scientific American* 97 (November 2, 1907): 307; R. David Read, "When Trains Ran Late—and Telegraphers Earned Their Pay," *Classic Trains* 16 (Summer 2015): 55.

65. "The Telephone and the Railway," *Scientific American* 89 (October 24, 1903): 286; Schwantes, *The Train and the Telegraph*, 143–145; J. G. Lachaussee, "Train Dispatching," *Sandhouse* (November 2011): 6; "Displacement of Morse Telegraphers in Railroad Systems," *Monthly Labor Review* 34 (May 1932): 1017, 1019; "The Railroads' Nervous System: Telephone Supplanting the Telegraph as Means of Vital Communication," *Great Western Magazine* 5 (October 1926): 10.

During World War I, the 112-mile Ohio River & Western Railway, a narrow-gauge road controlled by the Pennsylvania Railroad, could no longer hire enough agents who knew Morse code, and so it replaced its telegraph with telephone lines. Edward H. Cass, *Hidden Treasurers: The Story of the Ohio River & Western Railway* (Hillsboro, OR: TimberTimes, 1997), 133.

66. Glenn Hoffman, *A History of the Atlantic Coast Line Railroad Company* (Jacksonville, FL: CSX Corporate Communications and Public Affairs, 1998), 190–191; "Trade Union Affiliation of Railroad Employees, 1915–1920," *Monthly Labor Review* 15 (July 1922): 169.

67. Gary M. Fink, "Labor Unions," *Greenwood Encyclopedia of American Institutions* (Westport, CT: Greenwood, 1977).

68. Anderson and Schauer, *I Never Worked in Pocatello*, 22.

69. "The Autobiography of Dan Knight," 256, 260, manuscript in possession of author.

70. Grant, ed., *Brownie the Boomer*, 97–98.

71. R. Dale Reeves to author, May 6, 1992, hereafter cited as Dale Reeves letter; Robert C. Rowe, *It Looked Like Eden* (Victorville, CA: Mohahve Historical Society, 2009), 4.

72. Occasionally a railroad provided an agent, with or without a family, a company bunk car. This piece of maintenance-of-way rolling stock offered limited space, yet it had cooking, eating, and sleeping areas. Bunk car housing was designed to be temporary.

73. A number of railroads, especially in the trans-Chicago West, built housing for their maintenance-of-way employees. One example involved Chicago & North Western affiliate Pierre, Rapid City & North Western, a carrier that crossed the sparsely populated West River County of South Dakota. It erected about a half-dozen standard frame houses for its "section bosses" and placed them near its depots. Interview with Charles Shannon, October 1, 1988, hereafter cited as Shannon interview.

74. Grant, *Living in the Depot*, 10.

75. H. Roger Grant, *Kansas Depots* (Topeka: Kansas State Historical Society, 1990), 16.

76. R. M. Brown to author, February 28, 1977; James J. Reisdorff and Michael M. Bartels, *Railroad Stations in Nebraska: An Era of Use and Reuse* (David City, NE: South Platte Press, 1982), 17; Vyzralek, Grant and Bohi, "North Dakota's Railroad Depots," 8.

77. Pamela Smith Hill, ed., *Pioneer Girl: The Annotated Autobiography, Laura Ingalls Wilder* (Pierre: South Dakota Historical Society, 2014), 251–252. In 1941, Wilder recast her account of the depot party in the *Little Town on the Prairie* (New York: Harper Trophy, 1971), 243–251.

78. Dale Reeves letter; Rowe, *It Looked Like Eden*, 4.

79. Shannon interview.

80. Lloyd Reeves to author, February 4, 1992.

81. Quinten L. Farmen to author, February 4, 1978.

82. Dale Reeves letter.

83. Interview with Lamar Robinette, October 23, 2020.

84. Dennis E. Holmes, "Railroad Experiences," June 2019, manuscript in possession of author.

85. Irelan, *Central Station*, 43–45.

86. Michael Bartles to author, January 31, 1992; *Daily Huronite* (Huron, SD), January 8, 1950; Gary B. Coombs, *Goleta Depot: The History of a Rural Railroad Station* (Goleta, CA: Institute for American Research, 1982), 44–45.

87. "Grow Your Own. Be Sure!," Chicago & North Western Railway (ca. 1944), poster in possession of author.

88. *Dodge (NE) Criterion*, April 29, 1993.

89. Jerome Lachaussee to author, January 14, 2021.

90. Interview with Thomas Hoback, August 8, 2019, hereafter cited as Hoback interview; Thomas Hoback to author, September 8, 2019.

91. Thomas Hoback to author, June 25, 2019; July 19, 2019. A childhood friend of Glenn Hoback told his son Tom about his father's early infatuation with trains. "Goldie told me that the teacher [of the one-room school] asked her to discreetly follow Glenn outside to see why he raised his hand to go to the outhouse at precisely the same time every day. She thought his regularity was odd. It turned out that Dad climbed a tree in the schoolyard to watch the afternoon MP [Missouri Pacific] local going from Lincoln to Union. His secret was out. Apparently the teacher never minded Dad interrupting his studies to do a little train watching!" Thomas Hobeck to author, September 8, 2019.

92. Thomas Hoback to author, August 5, 2019; H. O. Wagner to Glenn M. Hoback, May 19, 1941, letter in possession of Thomas Hoback, hereafter cited as Hoback papers.

93. Thomas Hoback to author, September 8, 2019; Genevieve Hoback to "Dear Mama," July 24, 1941, Hoback papers. Tom Hoback explained another reason by his parents were happy to leave Oklahoma: "I recall hearing my Mom mention [that] whenever she and Dad would take the train north from Oklahoma back to Nebraska, or to Illinois, how the blacks would all move to the regular passenger cars once the train crossed into Kansas. My parents did not like, nor did they feel comfortable in the highly segregated environment they found in Oklahoma. They found the 'colored' coaches offensive." Thomas Hoback to author, September 8, 2019.

94. Genevieve Hoback to "Dear Mama," July 24, 1941, Hoback papers.

95. Genevieve Hoback to "Dear Mother," August 5, 1941; August 15, 1941, Hoback papers.

96. Hoback interview; Genevieve Hoback to "Dear Mother," August 19, 1941, Hoback papers.

97. Genevieve Hoback to "Dear Mother," September 1, 1941, Hoback papers.

98. Genevieve Hoback to "Dear Mother," September 1, 1941, Hoback papers.

99. Genevieve Hoback to "Dear Mother," September 23, 1941, Hoback papers.

100. Genevieve Hoback to "Dear Mother," September 23, 1942, Hoback papers.

101. Genevieve Hoback to "Dear Mother, Dad and Donald," October 23, 1941, Hoback papers.

102. Genevieve Hoback to "Dear Mother, Dad and Donald," October 23, 1941, Hoback papers.

103. Genevieve Hoback to "Dear Mother," November 28, 1941, Hoback papers. Tom Hoback explained his parents' religious conversion. "Dad was not Roman Catholic until he moved to Chillicothe which was heavily Catholic. Most railroaders in the area were Catholic and both Mom and Dad converted to Catholicism shortly after moving to Chillicothe. The area of eastern Nebraska was heavily Protestant (mostly Baptist and Methodist) and Catholicism was viewed with healthy skepticism." Thomas Hoback to author, August 14, 2019.

104. Thomas Hoback to author, August 5, 2019.

105. Thomas Hoback to author, August 5, 2019.

106. Hoback interview.

107. The historic New Hampshire law was unique in that it initially provided for the appointment of commissioners from each county, although they had limited regulatory powers.

108. *Twelfth Annual Report of the Railroad and Warehouse Commission of Illinois* (Springfield, IL: H. W. Rokker, 1883), xvi; James F. Doster, *Alabama's First Railroad Commission, 1881–1885* (University: University of Alabama Press, 1949), 36–37, 86–87; *Annual Report Ending June 30th, 1910 Railroad Commission of Alabama* (Montgomery, AL: State Printer, 1910), 176; *Thirty-Second Annual Report of the Railroad Commission of South Carolina for the Year Ending December 31st, 1910* (Columbia: Gonzales and Bryan, State Printers, 1911), Part II, 21; *Eighteenth Report of the Board of Railroad Commissioners, State of Kansas, for the Year Ending November 30, 1904* (Topeka, KS: Geo. A. Clark, State Printer, 1904), 81.

109. *Times-Democrat* (New Orleans, LA), January 9, 1906.

110. *"Santa Fe." Rules and Regulations: Operating Department* (Atchison, Topeka & Santa Re Railway System, 1909), 91; Grant and Bohi, *The Country Railroad Station in America*, 14. An early state law, passed by Maine lawmakers in 1852, dealt with the newly introduced telegraph. "Damages for falsifying a despatch from twenty to one hundred dollars. Operators, agents, clerks and other officers are also held liable for any fraud committed or attempted by means of telegraph." *American Railroad Journal, Steam, Navigation, Commerce, Mining, Manufacturers* 8 (September 11, 1852): 586.

111. *Burlington (IA) Hawkeye*, January 16, 1916.

112. *Webster City (IA) Freeman*, July 3, 1944.

113. Dan Knight to author, n.d.

4. DECLINE

1. Returning ex-navy personnel, most notably, who had attended its renowned electronic programs, stood an excellent chance of finding employment as operators and had the likelihood of advancing to station agents. These men (and some women) had likely mastered international radio code, and it was not that difficult to pick up American Morse code. And they had acquired other technical skills along with understanding the corporate chain of commands and discipline.

2. The Missouri Pacific is an example of a railroad upgrading its depots. In the early 1950s, the company embarked on an extensive system-wide remodeling program. This often resulted in a smaller office area and a larger freight platform for LCL shipments. The emphasis focused on freight-only service. A decade later, when the Burlington replaced an eighty-year-old frame depot in Chadwick, Illinois, with a

fourteen-by-twenty-six-foot metal build-ing, an area newspaper commented, "An office and storage room for freight will be provided but there will be no passenger waiting room since passenger trains no longer stop here." Unlike most earlier postwar replacement depots, air-condi-tioning was included at Chadwick. *Free-port (IL) Journal Standard*, July 17, 1964.

3. During the immediate post–World War II era, not all railroad executives expressed an optimistic view about the future of the industry. "We expect a con-tinuation of fairly good freight traffic," opined Howard Palmer, president and receiver of the New York, New Haven & Hartford Railroad, "but passenger rev-enues undoubtedly will decline further as automobiles become more plentiful and as our highway and air competitors receive the equipment they have on order and ben-efit by the large expenditures being made by the government for their benefit." *The Official Guide of the Railways* (New York: National Railway Publishing, August 1946), 13.

4. After World War II, the American automobile culture burgeoned. In 1948, manufacturers built 3.4 million units, the first model year of full production follow-ing World War II, and volume rose steadily into the 1950s. Car factory sales in 1948 stood at 3,909,270 and soared to 7,920,186 in 1955. Registrations skyrocketed from 33,350,894 in 1948 to 52,135,583 in 1955.

5. H. Roger Grant, "For America's Railroads, the Indian Summer of the Early 1950s Gave Way to a Worsening Winter," in Robert S. McGonigal, ed., *Trains of the 1950s: Railroads Decade of Change* (Wauke-sha, WI: Kalmbach, 2013), 9.

6. "Top Passenger Officers Talk Over the Market," *Railway Age* 125 (September 15, 1948): 46–47; H. Roger Grant, "John W. Barriger's Super Railroads," *Classic Trains* 20 (Summer 2019): 47–53; Ira Silverman,

"Cutting and Pasting: In the '50s Three Roads Looked at—then Rejected—Com-bining Passenger Service," *Railroad His-tory* 223 (Fall–Winter 2020): 58, 61.

7. William D. Middleton, "A Dirge for the Doodlebug," *Trains* 21 (May 1961): 31.

8. "The Life of Jim Bradley," *RABO Club News & Notes* (October 2019): 17–19.

9. Freeman Hubbard, "The Great Days of Railroading," *Trains* 32 (March 1972): 58.

10. OTR clipping, July 1957, 47, in pos-session of author; Wade Calvert, "My Life as a Telegraph Operator at Marquette, Iowa, 1961," *Milwaukee Railroader* (Second Quarter, 2019): 44.

11. E. Ray Lichty to author, February 17, 2020.

12. "C&NW Starts Station-Closing Drive," *Railway Age* 143 (November 18, 1957): 9–10; interview with Charles C. Shannon October 1, 1988, hereafter cited as Shannon interview. John F. Stover, *The Life and Decline of the American Railroad* (New York: Oxford University Press, 1970), 239–240. The North Western was far from being alone with the scourge of rampant featherbedding. Take this example on the neighboring Minneapolis & St. Louis. Its station at Victoria, Minnesota, had a grossly underworked agent. Management considered that fifty transactions consti-tuted a normal working day, but for 1957, the count at Victoria averaged only two a day.

13. "C&NW Starts Station-Closing Drive," 9. In late 1958, the Iowa Commerce Commission expressed its happiness with the North Western's Central Agency Plan, considering it "fulfilling the needs of the shippers at all of the stations involved in the program." As a result, the commission permitted the company "to remove the depot from all its 'associate' stations—the former one-man agency stations now served by an agent based at a central

point." *Railway Age* 145 (December 15, 1958): 52.

14. Shannon interview.

15. Shannon interview. The South Dakota situation was hardly exceptional for the North Western. The company told the Wisconsin Public Service Corporation that its work-study results revealed that agents at its single-agent stations were being paid as high as $307 per hour for time actually worked. "The hours of work required to serve the public at all one-man stations throughout Wisconsin average only 26% of time for which the agent is paid." "C&NW Moves to Save $523,000," *Railway Age* 48 (April 21, 1958): 48.

16. "Kennedy Defaults on C&NW," *Trains* 23 (November 1962): 3. ORT leaders echoed sentiments of fellow railroad brotherhoods. "The viciousness of the featherbedding campaign [by the industry] is destroying employee morale and eroding employee loyalty which had been developed over a century." Redundant C&NW agents surely agreed.

17. "Kennedy Defaults on C&NW," 6; *Report to the U.S. President by the Emergency Board* (Washington, DC, June 14, 1962); *Paducah (KY) Sun*, August 30, 1962. Recalled a longtime ORT member about union dues, "[Dues] were not very much and well worth the money in case you got caught up in something that was not your fault or that you had anything to do with. The ORT would put up a good fight in your behalf." James L. Rueber to author, November 14, 2020.

18. *Chicago Sun-Times*, August 31, 1962; *Washington Post*, September 3, 1962.

19. "An End to Featherbedding," *Time* 80 (October 19, 1962): 81; *New York Times*, August 24, 1962.

20. "An End to Featherbedding," 81; *Rapid City (SD) Journal*, October 1, 1962. "It was not unusual for station agents to serve their employers for forty, fifty, or more years. There were agents who

continued to work, often at smaller agencies, for most of their careers after obtaining enough seniority to protect their jobs. At retirement, there might be a party of some sorts, but hardly a gold watch from the division superintendent. A modest celebration for a retiree might be hosted by the local chairman of the ORT or by family, friends, and coworkers. There also was likely mention of the agent's departure in the company's employee magazine and the retiree's hometown newspaper." James R. Rueber to author, July 11, 2020.

Perhaps agents simply walked out of their office on the final day of their employment. On a Friday evening in July 1968, famed railroad photographer David Plowden happened to visit the Missouri-Kansas-Texas depot in Frederick, Oklahoma. Here is what he wrote about agent R. H. Birkhead. "'I am retiring tonight after 60 years with the company,' he informed me. There was no one there, no family, no representative of the railroad, only me, a complete stranger, so I asked this 80-year-old gentleman if he would allow me to make his portrait to commemorate the occasion. He sat down on the edge of the desk and afterwards got up to take the key to the depot door off his ring and drop it in the mailbox—'for the new man on Monday morning.'" David Plowden, "Portraits of Railroaders," *Trains* 61 (October 2001): 40.

21. Interview with Don L. Hofsommer, July 17, 2020; Dan Sabin to author, July 18, 2020.

22. *Chicago & North Western Railway Company Annual Report 1962* (Chicago: Chicago & North Western Railway, 1963), 3, 6; Shannon interview.

23. Interview with Joseph D. Allen, May 10, 1989; Shannon interview.

24. Philip L. Moseley, "Oak Hill, Population 16," *Classic Trains* 19 (Winter 2018): 81–82, 84.

25. Robert W. Harheson, "The Transportation Act of 1958," *Land Economics* 35 (May 1959): 168; *Railroad Facts* (Washington, DC: Association of American Railroads, 1991), 44.

26. See T. R. Gurvish, *British Railways, 1948–73* (Cambridge: Cambridge University Press, 1986), 401–468.

27. Granger roads, which by the 1950s and 1960s were seen as having excessive branches and generally too many depots, commonly embraced dualization. In the later part of 1958, the Rock Island, for example, sought the large-scale dualization of fifty-seven one-man operations in Iowa and anticipated "substantial" savings. The Iowa Commerce Commission approved twenty-six to be dualized, twelve to be closed, and the remainder to remain open. "If agreements can't be reached with the ORT, Rock Island may close stations now tabbed for dualization." *Railway Age* 145 (September 15, 1958): 7; (December 15, 1958): 7.

28. James J. Reisdorff and Michael M. Bartels, *Railroad Stations in Nebraska: An Era of Use and Reuse* (David City, NE: South Platte Press, 1982), 47–54.

29. Stover, *The Life and Decline of the American Railroad*, 241; *Daily Standard* (Sikeston, MO), August 24, 1970; *Daily Capital News* (Jefferson City, MO), August 13, 1968.

30. Garry and Roz Miller, *The Camas Prairie: Idaho's Panhandle Railroad* (n.p.: Union Pacific Historical Society, 2020), 191.

31. Interview with Peter Hansen, April 13, 2020.

32. Interview with Don L. Hofsommer, July 28, 2020.

33. Direct traffic control (DTC) stands out as an excellent example of a rapidly changing railroad industry. "DTC is the dispatching of trains by radio using the concepts embodied in Centralized Traffic Control (CTC) rules for a piece of railroad that has not been equipped with that expensive technology," explained railroad historian Don Hofsommer in 1985 about its introduction on the Southern Pacific and affiliate St. Louis Southwestern. "In a sense, then, DTC is a 'poor man's CTC.'" Economical to install, this system is structured by dividing trackage into sections or DTC blocks and permits dispatchers to communicate orders directly with train crews and to have these radio instructions formally recognized and recorded. Don L. Hofsommer, "Direct Traffic Control: Simple and Effective," *Modern Railroads* 40 (August 1985): 24–26.

34. Not surprising is the change occurring in ticketing for commuter trains. Due to declining in-peson ticket sales at the Burlington Northern Santa Fe Railway station in Riverside, Illinois, Metra, the commuter rail division of Chicago's Regional Transportation Authority, announced in May 2016 that it would no longer staff this station with a ticket agent. Online and mobile purchasing would become the new way for passengers to pay for their Metra transportation.

5. LEGACY

1. William F. Helmer, "The Great American (Railroad) Novel," *Trains* 32 (November 1972): 58b; James D. Porterfield, ed., *The Boomer: A Story of the Rails* (Minneapolis: University of Minnesota Press, 2006), vii.

2. Frank P. Donovan Jr. and Robert Selph Henry, eds., *Headlights and Markers: An Anthology of Railroad Stories* (New York: Creative Age Press, 1946), 135–164. In 1919, the George H. Doran Company of New York published Packard's *The Night Operator*, a 320-page collection of short stories.

3. Harry Bedwell, "The Careless Road," *Railroad Magazine* 24 (February 1939): 38–39.

4. C. W. Finch, *The Depot Agent: The History of the C.G.W. Railroad as Seen through the Eyes of an Agent* (Apple River, IL: North-West Associates, 1984).

5. "The Station Agent Reviews" (http://www.metacritic.com/movie/the -station-agent).

6. Lloyd C. Foltz, "Trackside Americana," *Trains* 23 (November 1962): 39.

7. *Columbia (TN) Times*, June 26, 1991; *Gothenburg (NE) Leader*, December 12, 2020; Francis H. Parker, *Indiana Railroad Depots: A Threatened Heritage* (Muncie, IN: Ball State University, 1989), 11. The demise of a local depot elicited these sentiments from an Iola, Kansas, journalist: "The Santa Fe wants to close and sell the depot because it no longer carries its weight in the system. If the building has no value to any other business then let's shed a tear, salvage the brick and let the land be sold to some taxpaying entrepreneur with a fresh idea for its use." *Iola (KS) Register*, February 6, 1980.

8. "Sign of the Times," *Classic Trains* 3 (Spring 2002): 81.

9. Jeff Brouws to author, December 9, 2020.

10. Maury Klein, *Union Pacific: Birth of a Railroad, 1862–1893* (Garden City, NY: Doubleday, 1987), 3.

11. *New York Times*, May 5, 1912; William D. Middleton and Mark Reutter, "Railroaders in Bronze and Stone," *Railroad History* 195 (Fall–Winter 2006): 87; *Times-Record* (Middletown, NY), July 4, 1982; *AWA Journal*, October 2006. There are monuments and statues dedicated to prominent American railroad leaders. Notable is the large bust of James J. Hill, which was unveiled in 1909 at the Alaska-Yukon-Pacific Exposition held in Seattle to celebrate development of the Pacific Northwest. Today it resides on the campus of the University of Washington in Seattle. See *Seattle Times*, August 24, 2017.

12. Jim Wrinn, "Dots and Dashes Forever?," *Trains* 66 (May 2006): 76; J. Chris Hausler to author, December 12, 2020. Chris Hausler explained one possible reason a few telegraph lines remained operable until the late twentieth century for the pleasure of veteran telegraphers. "As long as there was a pole line up for signaling and phone communications, an extra wire or two wouldn't be noticed by bean counters."

13. *Wall Street Journal*, August 12, 2020; Dan Knight to author, n.d.

SELECTIVE BIBLIOGRAPHY

BOOKS

Aldrich, Mark. *Death Rode the Rails: American Railroad Accidents and Safety, 1828–1965.* Baltimore, MD: Johns Hopkins University Press, 2006.

———. *Safety First: Technology, Labor, and Business in the Building of American Work Safety, 1870–1939.* Baltimore, MD: Johns Hopkins University Press, 1997.

Alexander, Edward P. *Down at the Depot: American Railroad Stations from 1831 to 1920.* New York: Bramhall House, 1970.

Anderson, Bob, and Sandy Schauer, eds. *I Never Worked in Pocatello: The Life and Times of Santa Fe Railroad's Paul T. Collins.* Los Lunas, NM: Montanita, 2013.

Arbuckle, J. W. *Crown Pusher District and Tunnel.* Winchester, TN: Herald-Chronicle, n.d.

Ashman, Robert E. *The Central New England Railroad, 1867–1967.* Salisbury, CT: Salisbury Association, 1972.

Baetjer, Harold H. *A Book That Gathers No Dust.* New York: National Railway Publishing, 1950.

Bailey, Edd H. *A Life with the Union Pacific: The Autobiography of Edd H. Bailey.* St. Johnsbury, VT: Saltillo, 1989.

Beard, Charles A., and Mary R. Beard. *The Rise of American Civilization.* Vol. 2. New York: Macmillan, 1930.

Beebe, Lucius. *Mixed Train Daily: A Book of Short-Line Railroads.* New York: Dutton, 1947.

Blum, William R. *The Military Telegraph during the Civil War in the United States.* Vol. 1. Chicago: Jansen McClurg, 1882.

Botkin, B. A., and Alvin F. Harlow, eds. *A Treasury of Railroad Folklore.* New York: Crown, 1953.

Bradlee, Francis B. C. *The Boston, Revere Beach and Lynn: Narrow Gauge Railroad.* Salem, MA: Essex Institute, 1921.

Brignano, Mary, and Hax McCullough. *The Search for Safety: A History of Railroad Signals and the People Who Made Them.* Union Switch & Signal Division, American Standard, 1981.

Bryan, Howard. *Albuquerque Remembered.* Albuquerque: University of New Mexico Press, 2006.

Burgess, George H., and Miles C. Kennedy. *Centennial History of the Pennsylvania Railroad Company, 1846–1946.* Philadelphia: Pennsylvania Railroad Company, 1949.

Chafe, W. J. *I've Been Working on the Railroad: Memoirs of a Railwayman, 1911–1962.* St. John's, NL: Henry Cuff, 1987.

Churella, Albert J. *The Pennsylvania Railroad: Building an Empire, 1846–1917.* Philadelphia: University of Pennsylvania Press, 2013.

Clarke, Thomas Curtis, ed. *The American Railway: Its Construction, Management, and Appliances.* London: J. Murry, 1890.

Clayburn, Barbara B. *Prairie Stationmaster: The Story of One Man's Railroading Career in Nebraska, 1917–1963.* Detroit: Harlo, 1979.

Conot, Robert E. *Thomas A. Edison: A Streak of Luck.* New York: Da Capo, 1986.

Coombs, Gary B. *Goleta Depot: The History of a Rural Railroad Station.* Goleta, CA: Institute for American Research, 1982.

Cottrell, W. Fred. *The Railroaders.* Stanford, CA: Stanford University Press, 1940.

Culp, Edwin D. *Stations West: The Story of the Oregon Railways.* New York: Bonanza, 1978.

Cushman, Dan. *Plenty of Room & Air.* Great Falls, MT: Stay Away, Joe, 1975.

Dilts, James D. *The Great Road: The Building of the Baltimore & Ohio, the Nation's First Railroad, 1828–1853.* Stanford, CA: Stanford University Press, 1993.

Donovan, Frank P., Jr. *Harry Bedwell: Last of the Great Railroad Storytellers.* Minneapolis, MN: Ross & Hines, 1959.

———. *Mileposts on the Prairie: The Story of the Minneapolis & St. Louis Railway.* New York: Simmons-Boardman, 1950.

Donovan, Frank P., Jr., and Robert Selph Henry, eds. *Headlights and Markers: An Anthology of Railroad Stores.* New York: Creative Age, 1946.

Doster, James F. *Alabama's First Railroad Commission, 1881–1885.* University: University of Alabama Press, 1949.

Droege, John A. *Passenger Terminals and Trains.* New York: McGraw-Hill, 1916.

Ducker, James H. *Men of the Steel Rails: Workers on the Atchison, Topeka & Santa Fe Railroad, 1869–1900.* Lincoln: University of Nebraska Press, 1983.

Emmet, Boris, and John E. Jeuck. *Catalogues and Counters: A History of Sears, Roebeck and Company.* Chicago: University of Chicago Press, 1950.

Finch, C. W. *The Depot Agent: The History of the C.G.W. Railroad as Seen through the Eyes of an Agent.* Apple River, IL: North-West Associates, 1984.

Forman, Harry W. *Rights of Trains: A Complete Analysis of Single Track Standard Code Rules.* 3rd ed. New York: Simmons-Boardman, 1945.

Frailey, Fred W. *Last Train to Texas: My Railroad Odyssey.* Bloomington: Indiana University Press, 2020.

Gabler, Edwin. *The American Telegrapher: A Social History, 1860–1900.* New Brunswick, NJ: Rutgers University Press, 1988.

Gamst, Frederick C., ed. *Early American Railroads: Franz Ritter von Gerstner's "Die innern Communicationen," 1842–1843.* Stanford, CA: Stanford University Press, 1997.

George. Charles B. *Forty Years on the Rail.* Chicago: R. R. Donnelley & Sons, 1887.

Grant, H. Roger. *Kansas Depots.* Topeka: Kansas State Historical Society, 1990.

———. *Living in the Depot: The Two Story Railroad Station.* Iowa City: University of Iowa Press, 1993.

———. *Railroad Postcards in Age of Steam.* Iowa City: University of Iowa Press, 1994.

———. *Railroads and the American People.* Bloomington: Indiana University Press, 2012.

———. *The Louisville, Cincinnati & Charleston Rail Road: Dreams of Linking North and South.* Bloomington: Indiana University Press, 2014.

Grant, H. Roger, ed. *Brownie the Boomer: The Life of Charles P. Brown, an American Railroader.* DeKalb: Northern Illinois University Press, 1991.

Grant, H. Roger, and Charles W. Bohi. *The Country Railroad Station in America.* Boulder, CO: Pruett, 1978.

Halberstadt, Hans, and April Halberstadt. *The American Train Depot & Roundhouse.* Osceola, WI: Motorbooks International, 1995.

Hargrave, Frank F. *A Pioneer Indiana Railroad: The Origins and Development of the Monon.* Indianapolis, IN: William Burford, 1932.

Harlow, Alvin F. *Old Wires and New Waves: The History of the Telegraph, Telephone, and Wireless.* New York: D. Appleton-Century, 1936.

Hawkins, Hugh. *Railwayman's Son: A Plains Family Memoir.* Lubbock: Texas Tech University Press, 2006.

Hill, Pamela Smith, ed. *Pioneer Girl: The Annotated Autobiography, Laura Ingalls Wilder.* Pierre: South Dakota Historical Society, 2014.

Hochfelder, David. *The Telegraph in America, 1852–1920.* Baltimore, MD: Johns Hopkins University Press, 2012.

Hoffman, Glenn. *A History of the Atlantic Coast Line Railroad Company.* Jacksonville, FL: CSX Corporate Communications and Public Affairs, 1998.

Hofsommer, Don L., *The Quanah Route: A History of the Quanah, Acme & Pacific Railway.* College Station: Texas A&M University Press, 1991.

———. *The Tootin' Louie: A History of the Minneapolis & St. Louis Railway.* Minneapolis: University of Minnesota Press, 2005.

Hubbard, Freeman. *Encyclopedia of North American Railroads: 150 Years of Railroading in the United States and Canada.* New York: McGraw-Hill, 1981.

Hungerford, Edward. *Men of Erie: A Story of Human Effort.* New York: Random House, 1946.

———. *The Story of the Baltimore & Ohio Railroad, 1827–1927.* New York: G. P. Putnam's Sons, 1938.

Huntley, Chet. *The Generous Years: Remembrances of a Frontier Boyhood.* New York: Random House, 1968.

Irelan, Patrick. *Central Standard Time: A Time, a Place, a Family.* Iowa City: University of Iowa Press, 2002.

Jepsen, Thomas C. *Ma Kiley: The Life of a Railroad Telegrapher.* El Paso: Texas Western Press, 1997.

———. *My Sisters Telegraphic: Women in the Telegraph Office, 1846–1950.* Athens: Ohio University Press, 2000.

John, Richard R. *Network Nation: Inventing American Telecommunications.* Cambridge, MA: Harvard University Press, 2010.

Kirkman, Marshall M. *Supplement to the Science of Railways: Telegraph and Telephone.* New York: World Railway, 1904, vol. 20.

Kirkpatrick, O. B. *The Station Agent's Blue Book.* Chicago: Kirkpatrick, 1925.

———. *Working on the Railroad.* Philadelphia: Dorrance, 1949.

Klein, Maury. *The Life and Legend of Jay Gould.* Baltimore, MD: Johns Hopkins University Press, 1986.

———. *Union Pacific: Birth of a Railroad, 1862–1893.* Garden City, NY: Doubleday, 1987.

Latimer, James Brandt. *Railway Signaling in Theory and Practice.* Chicago: Mackenzie-Klink, 1909.

Laurie, Bruce. *Artisans into Workers: Labor in Nineteenth Century America.* Urbana: University of Illinois Press, 1997.

Licht, Walter. *Working for the Railroad: The Organization of Work in the Nineteenth Century.* Princeton, NJ: Princeton University Press, 1983.

Long, Bryant Alden, and William Jefferson Dennis. *Mail by Rail: The Story of the Postal Transportation Service.* New York: Simmons-Boardman, 1951.

Lord, Robert F. *Country Depots in the Connecticut Hills.* New Hartford, CT: Goulet Printery, 1996.

Love, Edmund C. *The Situation in Flushing.* New York: Harper & Row, 1965.

Lucas, Walter Arndt. *From the Hills to the Hudson: A History of the Paterson and Hudson River Rail Road and Its Associates.* New York: Railroadians of America, 1944.

Mabee, Carleton. *The American Leonardo: A Life of Samuel F. B. Morse.* New York: Alfred A. Knopf, 1943.

Mack, Edward C. *Peter Cooper: Citizen of New York.* New York: Duell, Sloan and Pearce, 1949.

McIsaac, Archibald M. *The Order of Railroad Telegraphers: A Study in Trade Unionism and Collective Bargaining.* Princeton, NJ: Princeton University Press, 1933.

Melvin, Rich. *759! A Twenty-First Century Survivor.* Privately Printed, 2020.

Middleton, William D., George M. Smerk, and Roberta Diehl, eds. *Encyclopedia of North American Railroads.* Bloomington: Indiana University Press, 2007.

Mott, Edward Harold. *Between the Ocean and the Lakes: The Story of the Erie.* New York: John S. Collins, 1899.

Neil, R. M. *High Green and the Bark Peelers: The Story of Engineman Henry A. Beaulieu and His Boston and Maine Railroad.* New York: Duell, Sloan and Pearce, 1950.

O'Connell, John. *Railroad Album: The Story of American Railroads in Words and Pictures.* Chicago: Popular Mechanics, 1954.

Orsi, Richard J. *Sunset Limited: The Southern Pacific Railroad and the Development of the American West, 1850–1930.* Berkeley: University of California Press, 2005.

Overton, Richard C. *Perkins/Budd: Railway Statesmen of the Burlington.* Westport, CT: Greenwood, 1982.

Papke, David Ray. *The Pullman Case: The Clash of Labor and Capital in Industrial America.* Lawrence: University Press of Kansas, 1999.

Parker, Francis H. *Indiana Railroad Depots: A Threatened Heritage.* Muncie, IN: Ball State University, 1989.

Raymond, Rossiter W. *Peter Cooper.* New York: Houghton, Mifflin, 1901.

Reinhardt, Richard, ed. *Workin' on the Railroad: Reminiscences for the Age of Steam.* New York: Weathervane, 1970.

Reisdorff, James J., and Michael M. Bartels. *Railroad Stations in Nebraska: An Era of Use and Reuse.* David City, NE: South Platte Press, 1982.

Richards, Jeffrey, and John M. MacKenzie: *The Railway Station: A Social History.* Oxford, UK: Oxford University Press, 1986.

Rolt, L. T. C. *The Railway Revolution: George and Robert Stephenson.* New York: St. Martin's, 1960.

Rowe, Robert C. *It Looked Like Eden.* Victorville, CA: Mohahve Historical Society, 2009.

Samson, John. *Sam Johnson: The Experience and Observations of a Railroad Telegraph Operator.* New York: W. J. Johnston, 1878.

Sanders, D. C. *The Brasspounder.* New York: Hawthorn, 1978.

Schwantes, Benjamin Sidney Michael. *The Train and the Telegraph: A Revisionist History.* Baltimore, MD: Johns Hopkins University, 2019.

Simmons, Jack. *The Victorian Railways.* New York: Thames and Hudson, 1991.

Spearman, Frank H. *Held for Orders: Being Stories of Railroad Life.* New York: McClure, Phillips, 1901.

Stimson, H. A. *Depot Days.* Boynton Beach, FL: Star, 1972.

Stover, John F. *History of the Baltimore and Ohio Railroad.* West Lafayette, IN: Purdue University Press, 1987.

———. *The Life and Decline of the American Railroad.* New York: Oxford University Press, 1970.

Taillon, Paul Michael. *Good Reliable, White Men: Railroad Brotherhoods,*

1877–1917. Urbana: University of Illinois Press, 2009.

Taylor, Joseph. *A Fast Life on the Modern Highway: Being a Glance into the Railroad World from a New Point of View.* New York: Harper & Brothers, 1874.

Thomas, David St. John. *The Country Railways.* London: Book Club Associates, 1977.

Thompson, Robert Luther. *Wiring a Continent: The History of the Telegraph Industry in the United States, 1832–1866.* Princeton, NJ: Princeton University Press, 1947.

Trelease, Allen W. *The North Carolina Railroad, 1849–1871.* Chapel Hill: University of North Carolina Press, 1991.

Ulriksson, Vidkunn. *The Telegraphers: Their Craft and Their Union.* Washington, DC: Public Affairs, 1953.

Usselman, Steven W. *Regulating Railroad Innovation: Business, Technology, and Politics in America, 1840–1920.* New York: Cambridge University Press, 2002.

Wade, James H., Jr. *Greenwood County and Its Railroads, 1852–1992.* Columbia, SC: R. L. Bryan, 1993.

Ward, James A. *That Man Haupt: A Biography of Herman Haupt.* Baton Rouge: Louisiana State University Press, 1973.

Westhaeffer, Paul J. *History of the Cumberland Valley Railroad, 1835–1919.* Washington, DC: National Railway Historical Society, 1979.

White, John H., Jr. *The American Railroad Freight Car: From the Wood-Car Era to the Coming of Steel.* Baltimore, MD: Johns Hopkins University Press, 1993.

Williams, Ames W. *Otto Mears Goes East: The Chesapeake Beach Railway.* Alexandria, VA: Meridian Sun, 1975.

Yates, JoAnne. *Control through Communication: The Rise of System in American Management.* Baltimore, MD: Johns Hopkins University Press, 1989.

ARTICLES

Ash, Fred. "Yellow Fever Rides the Rails." *Railroad History* 221 (Fall–Winter 2019): 88–93.

Balliet, Herbert S. "Development of Railway Signaling." *Bulletin of the Railway Historical Society* 44 (October 1937): 70–82.

Bartky, Ian R. "The Invention of Railroad Time." *Railroad History* 148 (Spring 1983): 13–22.

Bedwell, Harry. "The Careless Road." *Railroad Magazine* 24 (February 1939): 32–61.

———. "The Mistakes of a Young Railroad Telegraph Operator." *American Magazine* 69 (November 1909): 71–78.

Burt, Jesse C., Jr., ed. "The Savor of Old-Time Southern Railroading." *Bulletin of the Railway & Locomotive Historical Society* 84 (1951): 36–45.

Calvert, Wade. "My Life as a Telegraph Operator at Marquette, Iowa, 161." *Milwaukee Railroader* (Second Quarter, 2019): 35–45.

"C&NW Starts Station-Closing Drive." *Railway Age* 143 (November 19, 1957): 9–10.

"Displacement of Morse Telegraphers in Railroad Systems." *Monthly Labor Review* 34 (May 1932): 1017–28.

Fisher, Charles E. "Henry M. Sperry." *Bulletin of the Railway & Locomotive Historical Society* 34 (May 1934): 8–17.

Flanary, Ron. "'Is Anything Close?' Locating Trains to Photograph Over 50 Years Ago Was a Lot Different Than Today." *Trains* 80 (November 2020): 45–46.

Folltz, Lloyd C. "Trackside Americana." *Trains* 23 (November 1962): 39–41.

Gilbert, George. "The Palmy Days When Ops Were Ops." *Railroad Man's Magazine* 35 (April 1918): 573–75.

Grant, H. Roger. "Depot: Economy and Style at Trackside." *Timeline* 1 (October 1984): 56–70.

———. "John W. Barriger's Super-Railroads." *Classic Trains* 20 (Summer 2019): 47–53.

———. "Kate Shelley and the Chicago & North Western Railway." *Palimpsest* 76 (Fall 1995): 138–44.

———. "The Railroad Station Agent in Small-Town Iowa." *Palimpsest* 64 (May–June 1983): 93–102.

"Handing Up the Train Orders." *Trains* 2 (December 1941): 2.

Hammond, C. A. "Train Orders by Telephone." *Railroad Gazette* 24 (December 30, 1892): 986.

Harwood, Herbert H., Jr. "History Where You Don't Expect It: Some Surprising Survivors." *Railroad History* 166 (Spring 1992): 104–07.

Hofsommer, Don L. "Direct Traffic Control: Simple and Effective." *Modern Railroads* 40 (August 1985): 24–26.

Howland, David B. "Making Stations Attractive." *World's Work* 1 (March 1901): 517–27.

Jepsen, Thomas C. "'A Look into the Future': Women Railroad Telegraphers and Station Agents in Pennsylvania, 1855–1960." *Pennsylvania History* 76 (Spring 2009): 141–63.

———. "Two 'Lightning Slingers' from South Carolina: The Telegraphic Careers of Ambrose and Narciso Gonzales." *South Carolina Historical Magazine* 94 (October 1993): 264–82.

Jones, Robert. "Handling 'Em Up." *Vintage Rails* 11 (March–April 1998): 25–27.

Kiliher, Sylvester. "Dawn of a New Era." *Railway Carmen's Journal* 3 (May 1893): 259.

Kuebler, Bill. "This Is the Way to Run a Railroad." *Mainstreeter* 38 (Summer 2019): 10–14.

Lachaussee, J. G. "Rigolets, Louisiana: The Last Outpost, Part 1." *L&N Magazine* 9 (September 2013): 12–21.

———. "Train Dispatching." *Sandhouse* (November 2011): 5–30.

Lindenberg, Elisa W., and Charles W. Lindenberg. "Learning the Lingo at Flagstaff." *Classic Trains* 9 (Fall 2008): 78–81.

Mater, Dan H. "The Development and Operation of the Railroad Seniority System." *Journal of Business of the University of Chicago* 13 (October 1940): 387–419.

Middleton, William D. "A Dirge for the Doodlebug." *Trains* 21 (May 1961): 26–32.

Middleton, William D., and Mark Reutter. "Railroaders in Bronze and Stone." *Railroad History* 195 (Fall–Winter 2006): 78–87.

Morehead, Sue R. "Woman Op." *Railroad Magazine* (January 1944): 88–91.

Morgan, David P. "What Do the Dots and Dashes Mean?" *Trains* 21 (July 1961): 19.

Moseley, Philip L. "Oak Hill, Population 16." *Classic Trains* 19 (Winter 2018): 81–82, 84.

"Nine-Hour Law." *Outlook* 88 (March 14, 1908): 571–72.

Patterson, Steve. "Home on the Range." *Trains* 62 (December 2002): 68–70.

Phillips, Barnet. "The Thorsdale Telegraphs." *Atlantic Monthly* (October 1876): 400–17.

Robertson, John E. L. "My Life as a Telegrapher on the Kentucky Division of the Illinois Central Railroad." *Register of the Kentucky Historical Society* 98 (Summer 2000): 279–95.

Sabin, Dan. "Of Dispatcher Rosey, a Howling Snowstorm, and an Almost-Cornfield-Meet." *Classic Trains* 7 (Spring 2006): 22–31.

Sawles, R. H. "Telegraph vs. Telephone for Train Dispatching." *Scientific American* 97 (November 2, 1907): 307.

Shanley, J. J. "The Way Station Agent: Suggesting an Epic." *Chautauquan: A Weekly News-Magazine* 4 (January 1904): 359–60.

[Shaw, Robert]. "Shaw's All-Time List of Notable Railroad Accidents,

1891–2000." *Railroad History* 184 (Spring 2001): 37–45.

Silverman, Ira. "Cutting and Pasting: In the '50s, Three Roads Looked at—Then Rejected—Combining Passenger Service." *Railroad History* 223 (Fall–Winter 2020): 54–61.

Smith, J. E. "Observations of a Country Station-Agent." *Railroad Man's Magazine* 32 (February 1917): 263–70.

Thompson, Slason. "The Railroad and the Small Town." *World To-Day* 13 (October 1907): 1035–37.

Vail, Stephen. "Early Days of the First Telegraph Line." *New England Magazine* 4 (June 1891): 450–60.

Vyzralek, Frank E., H. Roger Grant, and Charles Bohi. "North Dakota's Railroad Depots: Standardization on the Soo Line." *North Dakota History* 42 (Winter 1975): 4–25.

Winn, Jim. "Dots and Dashes Forever?" *Trains* 66 (May 2006): 76.

DISSERTATIONS

Black, Paul. "The Development of Management Personnel Policies on the Burlington Railroad, 1860–1900." PhD diss., University of Wisconsin. 1972.

Lightner, David Lee. "Labor on the Illinois Central Railroad, 1852–1900." PhD diss., University of Illinois, 1970.

INDEX

Index pages in *italics* indicate illustrations

Aber, William, 88
Adams, V. E., 97
Adams Express Company, 5
Afton, California, 118
Agar, South Dakota, *80*
Akron, Iowa, 48
Alabama Great Southern Railroad, 137
Albany, New York, 7, 101
Albia, Iowa, 139–140
Albuquerque, New Mexico, 72
Allyndale, Connecticut, 65
American Express Company, 51, 98
American Federation of Labor, 107
American Magazine, 160
American Railroad Association, 115
American Railway Express Company, 51, 88
American Railway Union, 109–111
American Train Dispatchers Association, 111
Ames, Oakes, 166
Ames, Oliver, 166
Appleton's Railroad and Steam Navigation Guide, 42
Arcadia, Oklahoma, 116
Arp, W. F., 85
Ashland, Illinois, *71*
Association of Railway Telegraph Superintendents, 168; Atchison, Topeka & Santa Fe Railway, 35, 50, 53, 72, 102, 105, 113, 128, 130–138, 146–148, 154,190n7; Atlantic Coast Line Railroad, 94, 115.

See also Charlotte & Western Carolina Railway; Port Royal Railroad
Atlantic Northern & Southern Railroad, 70
Auburn, California, 66
automatic block signaling, 64

Bailey, Edd, 101
Baker, Oregon, 76
Baltimore, Maryland, 2
Baltimore & Ohio v. Interstate Commerce Commission (1911), 112; Baltimore & Ohio Railroad, 2, 7, 11, 17–18, 21, 62, 70, 97, 146, 148, 179n63. *See also* Baltimore & Ohio Chicago Terminal Railroad; Baltimore & Ohio Southwestern Railroad
Baltimore & Ohio Chicago Terminal Railroad, 135
Baltimore & Ohio Southwestern Railroad, *71*
Barnards, Connecticut, 65
Barriger, John W., III, 145
Bath, New York, 87
Bath & Hammondsport Railroad, 87–88
Baudler, Robert, 167
Bedwell, Harry, 160–161
Beebe, Lucius, 75
Beeching, Dr. Robert, 155
Bennet, Iowa, 101
Bentley, Kansas 85
Best Friend of Charleston (locomotive), 2

Belvidere, Illinois, 8
Benjamin, Perry, 36
Biloxi, Mississippi, 53
Birkhead, R. H., 188n20
Birmingham, Iowa, 34
Bishop's Falls, Newfoundland, 93
Borland, Hal, 88
Boston & Albany Railroad, 96
Boston & Maine Railroad, 67. *See also*
    Eastern Railroad of Massachusetts
Boston & Worcester Rail Road, 8, 15
Boston, Clinton & Fitchburg Railroad,
    12–13
Boston, Revere Beach & Lynn Railroad,
    70, 113
Boulder Junction, Nevada, 123
Bowling Green, Ohio, 147
Bowling Green State University, 147
Bracken, Rebecca, 31
Bradley, James, 145–148
British Rail, 155
Broadway Limited (passenger train), 145
Brookings, South Dakota, *60*
Brotherhood of Locomotive Engineers, 105
Brotherhood of Locomotive Firemen,
    105, 109
Brotherhood of Maintenance of Way Em-
    ployees, 105
Brotherhood of Railroad Trainmen, 105
Brotherhood of Railway Clerks, 116
Brotherhood of Telegraphers of the United
    States, 106–107
Brunswick, Missouri, 98
Burlingame, Kansas, 137–138
Burlington & Northwestern Railroad, *13*
Burlington, Cedar Rapids & Northern
    Railroad, *126*
Burlington Northern Railroad, 155–156, 168
Burlington Northern Santa Fe Railway,
    189n34
Burlington Railroad. *See* Chicago, Burl-
    ington & Quincy Railroad
Buttzville, North Dakota, 145

California Zephyr, 145
Camden & Amboy Railroad, 63
Camas Prairie Railroad, 156
Camp Hill, Pennsylvania, 21

Campbell, Olive K., 94
Canadian Pacific Railway, 56
Canby, Oregon, 105
Canton Junction, Maryland, 97
Carbondale, Kansas, 137
Cardwell, Montana, 78
Carnegie, Andrew, 168
Carter, Gilbert and Anna, 127
Centerville, Tennessee, 163
Central New England Railroad, 64–65
Central Pacific Railroad, 43
Central Railroad of New Jersey, 113
centralized traffic control, 64
Chadwick, Illinois, 186n2, 187n2
Chalco, Nebraska, 155
Challenger (passenger train), 139
Chambersburg, Pennsylvania, 10
Chapinsville, Connecticut, 65
Charleston & Western Carolina Railway, 70
Chef Menteur, Louisiana, 70
Chesapeake & Ohio Railroad, 97
Chesapeake Beach Railroad, 91
Chicago, Illinois, 87, 135
Chicago, Burlington & Quincy Railroad,
    ix, x, 5, 27, 34, *40*, 48, 88, 91, 98–99, 114,
    118, 120, 123, 130, 133, 144, 160, 186n2.
    See also Burlington & Northwestern
    Railroad; Burlington Northern & Santa
    Fe Railway; Burlington Northern Rail-
    road; Fulton County Narrow Gauge
    Railroad
Chicago, Milwaukee & St. Paul Railroad,
    40–41, 57, 62, 85, *121*, 140, 148, 168,
    183n62; Chicago, Rock Island & Pacific
    Railroad, 10, 76, 82, 94, 96, 101, 103, *126*,
    166, 179n63, 189n27. *See also* Burlington,
    Cedar Rapids & Northern Railroad
Chicago, St. Paul, Minneapolis & Omaha
    Railway, 63–64
Chicago & Alton Railroad, *71*
Chicago & Illinois Western Railroad, 135
Chicago & North Western Railway, 33,
    51–52, *60*, 77, *80*, 84, 95, 122, 127, 139, 142,
    149–153, 157, 187n13, 188n15. *See also* Chi-
    cago, St. Paul, Minneapolis & Omaha
    Railway; Galena & Chicago Union
    Railroad; Pierre, Rapid City & North
    Western Railway

Chicago Great Western Railroad, 31, 47, 55, 61, *83*, 85, 88, 94, 105, 161
Chillicothe, Illinois, 134–135
Clarion, Iowa, 61
Clarksville, Connecticut, 65
Clear Lake Junction, Iowa, 61
Clover Leaf Route. *See* Toledo, St. Louis &Western Railroad
Cogley, Elizabeth, 30–31
Colburn, North Dakota, 145
Colchester, Illinois, 98
Collins, Charles, 85
Collinsville, Connecticut, 65
Columbia & Philadelphia Railroad, 7
Columbian (passenger train), 183n62
Columbus, North Dakota, 96
Conductors, 3, 7, 41, 59, 98, 105
Conklin, Charles, 98
Connellsville, Pennsylvania, 179n63
Conzales, Ambrose, 95
Cooke, William Fothergill, 17
Cooper Union, 37
Cornell, Ezra, 19
Cowan, Tennessee, 64
Coy, Alabama, 125
Craigmont, Idaho, 156
Cranberry, North Carolina, 75–76
Croton Lake, New York, 98
Cumberland Valley Railroad, 10

Dahl, Bertha, 102
Dallas Center, Iowa 157
Dallas City, Illinois, 132
Davis, Bill, 103
Dawson, Minnesota, *68*
Debs, Eugene V., 109, 111
Decherd, Tennessee, 64
Delaware, Lackawanna & Western Railroad *9*, 87
Delaware & Hudson Canal Company, 2
Delray, Florida, 95
Denver & Rio Grande Railroad, 104, 160
Depot Agent: The History of the C.G.W. Railroad as Seen through the Eyes of an Agent (book), 161
depot parks, *67–68*
depots, 7–10, 70–72, 180n79; combination layouts and interiors, 72–77; lighting,

77–78; pets, 79–81; preserved structures, 162–264; smells, 78; state regulations, 136–138
De Smet, South Dakota, 95, 122
Des Moines, Iowa, 31
Detroit, Toledo & Ironton Railroad, 59
Dinsmore's American Railroad Guide, 42
direct-train control 157
Dr. Humphrey's Homeopathic Medicine Chest, 104
Dubuque, Iowa, 31
Dundee, Michigan, 59
Dunkirk, New York, 19

Earlham, Iowa, 76
East Canaan, Connecticut, 65
East Tennessee, Virginia & Georgia Railroad, 137
East Tennessee & Western North Carolina Railroad, 76
Eastern Railroad of Massachusetts, 22
Edelstein, Illinois, 134
Edison, Thomas, 25, 168
electric interurbans, vii
Elizabeth, Illinois, 73
Elkhart, Indiana, *68*
Elk Point, South Dakota, 102
Ellicotts Mills, Maryland, 2, 7, 172n15
Ellsworth, Iowa, 139
Elyria, Nebraska, 123
Emmetsburg, Iowa, 101
Empire Builder (passenger train), 145
English Lookout, Louisiana, 70
Erie Lackawanna Railroad, 101
Erie Railroad, 15–16, 19, 20–21, 30, 87–88, 168. *See also* New-York & Erie Railroad
Esmond, Arizona, 179n63
Espanola, New Mexico, 104
Essex, Iowa, 48
Eutaw, Alabama, 137

Fairbury, Illinois, *68*
Fast Life on the Modern Highway (book), 47
Finch, Charles W., 161
Florida East Coast Railway, 95
Fort Madison, Iowa, 136
Fort Wayne & Northern Indiana Traction Company, *x*

Fostoria, Ohio, 64
Framingham, Massachusetts, 8, 15
Frankfort, Indiana, 118
Fred Harvey Company, 102
Frederick, Oklahoma, 188n20
Fredonia, New York, 19
Frisco Railway. *See* St. Louis–San Francisco Railway
Fulton County Narrow Gauge Railroad, 41

Galena & Chicago Union Railroad, 8, 21
Galesburg, Illinois, 133
Garrett, Sylvester, 152
Gaylordsville, Connecticut, 10
Geerling, Ed, *83*
George, Charles, 84
Georgia & Florida Railroad, 70, 148
global positioning system, 157
Golden State Limited (passenger train), 145
Goleta, California, 127
Goodland, Kansas, 94, 103
Gorham Manufacturing Company, 168
Goshen, New York, 20
Gothenburg, Nebraska, 163
Gould, Jay, 106–107
Grand Rapids & Indiana Railroad, 179n63
Grand Trunk Western Railway, 36, 163, 179n63
Grangeville, Idaho, 156
Great Northern Railway, 69–70, 102, 109
Great Western Railroad. *See* Chicago Great Western Railroad
Greene, Iowa, 101
Greensburg, Kansas, 82
Greenwood, South Carolina, 70
Griffins, Connecticut, 65
Guide Rock, Nebraska, 88

Hamlet, North Carolina, 179n63
Hammondsport, New York, 87–88
Hampton, Iowa, *142*
Hanover, Massachusetts, 97
Harriman, New York. *See also* Turner's, New York
Haupt, Herman, 24
Hawkings, J. A. 94–95
Headland, Alabama, 94
Heineman, Ben W., 149–152

Hemlock, Ohio, 36
Henson, J. H., 96
Hill, Cassie, 31
Hill, James J., 190n11
Hitterdal, Minnesota, 57
Hoback, Genevieve Becker, 128, *129*, 130–136, 185n93, 186n103
Hoback, Glenn, 128, *129*, 130–133, *134–135*, 185n91, 185n93, 186n103
Hoback children, *134*
Holiday (magazine), 145
Holland Railway, 4
Hours of Service Act (1907), 38–39, 94, 111–113
Housatonic Rail Road, 10
Howell, David, 98
Humphrey Homeopathic Medicine Company, 104
Huntley, Chet, 49, 78–79

Illinois Central Railroad, 6, 16, 69, 114
Illinois Railroad and Warehouse Commission, 40
Indiana Harbor Belt Railroad, 135
International Association of Machinists and Aerospace Workers, 116
Interstate Commerce Commission, 112, 154, 157
Intructograph Company, 39
Iola, Kansas, 190n7
Iowa Central Railway, *66*, *142*
Iowa Commerce Commission, 187n13, 189n27
Irelan, Gerata (Jerry), 34
Iron Mountain Railroad. *See* St. Louis, Iron Mountain & Southern Railroad
Isleta, New Mexico, 53

Jersey Central Railroad. *See* Central Railroad of New Jersey
Jersey City, New Jersey, 14
John Wilkes (passenger train), 144

Kansas Bureau of Labor, 41
Kansas Corporation Commission, 154
Katy Railway. *See* Missouri-Kansas-Texas Railway
Kayford, West Virginia, 97–98

Keck, Charles, 166
Kenova, West Virginia, 146
Ketchum, Paul, 61
Knight, Dan, 114, 139–140, 169
Knights of Labor, 106–107
Kreole, Mississippi, 180n84

Lachaussee, Jerome, 180n84
Lafayette, Illinois, 96
Lafayette, Muncie & Bloomington Rail
    Road, 178n58
La Follette, Robert Sr., 111
La Habra, California, 118
Lake Catherine, Louisiana, 70
Lake Mills, Iowa, 85–87
Lake Shore & Michigan Southern Rail-
    road, 68
Lamont, Iowa, 55, 94
lap train orders, 62
Laporte, Iowa, 101
Larchmont, New York, 98
Lehigh Valley Railroad, 109, 144
Leighty, George, 152
Lewiston, Idaho, 156
Lewistown, Pennsylvania, 30–31
Life (magazine), 145
Lillegrove, J. A., 85
Lindenberg, Elisa Ward, 35
Lismore, Minnesota, 101
Livermore, Iowa, 101
Liverpool & Manchester Railway, 1
Locomotion (locomotive), 1
locomotive engineers, 3, 41, 59
Long Island Railroad, 67, 79
Lost Express (film), 162; Louisville &
    Nashville Railroad, 53, 70, 90–91, 110,
    114–115, 163, 180n84. See also Mobile &
    Montgomery Railroad; Montgomery,
    New Orleans & Texas Railroad
Lynn, Massachusetts, 70
Lynnville, Tennessee, 163

Mackie, D. W., 76
Macomber, Charles, 86–87
Madison Lake, Minnesota, 85
McBride, S. S., 104
McCallum, D. C., 19, 21, 24, 180n77
McClure's (magazine), 160

McConnell, R. H., 101
McCook, Illinois, 135
Magnetic Telegraph Company, 18
Manly, Iowa, 6, 101
manual block signaling, 63–64, 112
Marengo, Washington, 67
Markee, Archie, 105
Matador Land & Cattle Company, 92–93
Maxwell, Gregory, 101
Mediapolis, Iowa, 101
Medill, Missouri, 130–131
Melbourne, Iowa, 85
Merrick, New York, 80
Miamisburg, Ohio, 146
Michigan Central Railroad, 31, 67
Middle Grove, Illinois, 117, 143
Middleton, William D., 145
Middletown, New York, 20
Midland, South Dakota, 72
Milwaukee Road. See Chicago, Milwaukee
    & St. Paul Railroad
Mineral Point, Missouri, 31
Minneapolis, Minnesota, 85–86; Min-
    neapolis & St. Louis Railroad, 68, 71, 85,
    86, 87, 117, 138, 139, 142, 187n12. See also
    Iowa Central Railway
Minneapolis, St. Paul & Sault Ste. Marie
    Railroad, 96, 120, 122
Minnesota Falls, Minnesota, 62–63
Minot, Charles, 19–21, 166, 168
Missouri-Kansas-Texas Railway, 73, 116,
    188n20
Missouri Pacific Railroad, 61, 106, 109, 128,
    156, 179n61, 186n2
Mobile & Gulf Railroad, 51
Mobile & Montgomery Railroad, 70
modal competition, 142–144, 187n4; diesel
    revolution, 144; line abandonments,
    154–155; mobile agencies, 155–156; sta-
    tion consolidations, 155; technology
    advances, 157–158
Mohawk & Hudson Rail Road, 7
Moingona, Iowa, 32
Monroeville, Ohio, 7
Monroeville & Sandusky City Railroad, 7
Montgomery, New Orleans & Texas Rail-
    road, 70
Montgomery Ward & Company, 44

Monuments, 166, 168
Moorland, Iowa, 167
Moravia, Iowa, 140
Morehead, Sue, 34–35
Morning Sun, Iowa, 71
Morse, Samuel F. B. (agent), 142–143
Morse, Samuel F. B. (investor), 17–19
Morse School of Telegraphy, 37–38
Morse Telegraph Club, 168
Moscow, Idaho, *xi*
Muncy's (magazine), 160
Murphy, Nebraska, 34

Nashville, Chattanooga & St. Louis Railway, 64, 163
Nashville & Chattanooga Railroad, 15
National Association of Timetable Collectors, 165
National General Ticket Agents' Association, 42
National Labor Relations Act (1935), 141, 151
National Telegraphic Union, 105
Naviska, Arizona, 34
Nehawha, Nebraska, 128
New Albany & Salem Railroad, 13–14, 25
New Castle & Frenchtown Rail Road, 14
New Haven Railroad. *See* New York, New Haven & Hartford Railroad
New Orleans, Louisiana, 69
New-York & Erie Railroad, 5, *11*; New York Central Railroad, 39, 64, 98, 101, 114, 145. *See also* Lake Shore & Michigan Southern Railroad; Michigan Central Railroad; Mohawk & Hudson Rail Road; New York, New Haven & Hartford Railroad, 98, 187n3; Schenectady & Troy Railroad. *See also* Housatonic Rail Road; Old Colony Railroad
Newell, Medora Olive, 31
Nickel, Louis, 46
Night Operator (book), 189n2
Niles, Michigan, 31
North Bloomfield, Connecticut, 65
North Branch, Minnesota, 85
North Carolina Railroad, 40
North Dakota Launderers Association, 176n32
North Missouri Railroad, 16

North Pennsylvania Railroad, 21
North Redwood Falls, Minnesota, 85, 87
Northboro, Iowa, 99
Northern Pacific Railroad, 49–50, 57, 78, 145, 148
Norwich & Worcester Railroad, 8

Oak Hill, Kansas, 154
Odessa, Minnesota, 183n62
Oelwein, Iowa, 101
Official Railway Guide, 42–43, 165, 176n29
Ohio River & Western Railway, 184n65
Old Colony Railroad, 97
Old Time Depot (print), *viii*
Old Time Telegraphers' and Historical Association, 168
Olympian Hiawatha (passenger train), 145
Omaha Road. *See* Chicago St. Paul, Minneapolis & Omaha Railway
Order of Railroad Telegraphers, xii, 105, 107–109, *110*, 111–112, 114–116, 141, 149–153, 174n3
Order of Railway Conductors, 105
Ormonde, Illinois, 133

Pacific Electric Railway, xii
Packard, Frank Lucius, 160, 189n2
Palmer, Howard, 187n3
Parcel Post Act (1913), 50
Parker, Arlene, 103
Pasco, Washington, 168
Paterson, New Jersey, 7
Paterson & Hudson River Rail Road, 7, 14; Pennsylvania Railroad, 21, 31–32, 39, 63–64, 82, 113, 178n51. *See also* Long Island Railroad; Pittsburgh, Cincinnati, Columbus & St. Louis Railway; Pittsburgh, Fort Wayne & Chicago Railroad; Ohio River & Western Railway; Vandalia Railroad
Perry, Oklahoma, *146*
Petersburg Rail Road, 8
Philadelphia, Pennsylvania, 7
Philadelphia & Reading Railroad, 31, 63, 179n63
Phillipsburg, Kansas, 103
photographs, 166
Piermont, New York, 19

Pierre, Rapid City & North Western Railway, 46, 72, 184n73
Pierre, South Dakota, 46
Pierson, Michigan, 179n63
Pinkney, Michigan, 163
Pippin, Orlando, 102
Pittsburgh, Cincinnati, Chicago & St. Louis Railway, 43
Pittsburgh, Fort Wayne & Chicago Railroad, 91
Plowden, David, 188n20
Port Jervis, New York, 19–20
Port Royal Railroad, 95
Postal Telegraph Company, 37, 108
Powderly, Terence V., 106–107
Pullman, George, 110
Pullman, Illinois, 109
Pullman Company, 42
Pullman Place Car Company, 109

Quanah, Acme & Pacific Railway, 92
Quincy Coal Company, 98

Railhill Locomotive Trials, 1
Railroad Magazine, 160
Railroad Man's Magazine, 160
Railroad regulation, 136–138
Railroad Retirement Act (1937), 100, 141
Railroad School of literature, 159
Railroad Station Historical Society, 159
Railroad Stories (magazine), 160
Railroaders (book), 102
Railroadiana, 164–166
Railroadina Collectors Association, 165
Railway Commercial Training School, 38
Railway Express Agency, 51, 88
Rainbolt, Phyllis, *147*
REA Express, 51, 156
Reid Newfoundland Railway, 93
Reisch, Floyd, *147*
Revere, Massachusetts, 22
Richardson, Henry Hobson, 166
Richford, Vermont, 56
Rigolets, Louisiana, 70
Rio Grande Railroad. *See* Denver & Rio Grande Railroad
Riverside, Illinois, 189n34
Roaring Springs, Texas, 92

Robertsville, Ohio, 33
Robinette, Lamar, 125
Rocket (locomotive), 1
Rockford, Iowa, 101
Rock Island Railroad. *See* Chicago, Rock Island & Pacific Railroad
Roebuck, Alvah, 87
Roseville, California, 31
Rural Electrification Administration, 122
Russell, Minnesota, 102
Russellville, Texas, 92–93

Saint-Gaudens, Augustus, 166
St. Louis, Iron Mountain & Southern Railroad, 31, 106
St. Louis–San Francisco Railway, 85, 109, *110*, 125
St. Paul & Duluth Railroad, 85
Salem, Iowa 34
Sanders, D. C., 36–37
Santa Fe Railway. *See* Atchison, Topeka & Santa Fe Railway
Saturday Evening Post, 145, 160
Schenectady & Troy Railroad, 5
Schribner's (magazine), 160
Seaboard Airline Railroad, 179n63
Sears, Richard Warren, 85, *86*, 87
Sears, Roebuck & Company, 44, 85, *86*
Sheldon, North Dakota, 145
Shelley, Kate, *32*, 33
Sheridan, Missouri, *83*
Shippensburg, Pennsylvania, 10
Silver Meteor (passenger train), 145
Sioux City, Iowa, 48, 102
Snograss, Bert, 55
Snyder, Nebraska, 127
Snyder, Roy, 139
Soo Line Railroad. *See* Minneapolis, St. Paul & Sault Ste. Marie Railroad
South Carolina Canal & Rail Road Company, 2–3
South Dakota Public Utilities Commission, 149–151
Southern Express Company, 51
Southern Pacific Railroad, 31, 34, 39, 65–66, 69, 105, 127, 153, 160, 178n57, 179n63; Southern Railway, 51, *163*. *See also* Alabama Great Southern Railway;

East Tennessee, Virginia & Georgia Railroad
Southwestern Limited (passenger train), 140
Spanish influenza pandemic, 67, 69
Spearman, Frank Hamilton, 159
Spirit Lake, Iowa, 101
Spokane, Coeur d'Alene & Palouse Railway, *xi*
Spokane, Portland & Seattle Railway, 52
Sprague, Lucian, *86*
Spring Valley, Ohio, *43*
Stager, Anson, 24
Staggers Act (1980), 154, 157
standard time zones, 44
Station Agent (film)
Station Agent's Blue Book, 89
station agents-operators: background, 28–30; "boomers," 99–102, 182n35; commercial telegraphing, 89; community involvement, 103–105; compensation, 6, 39–41; criminality, 98–99; custodial agents, 32–34; definition of, ix; duties, x–xi. 6–7, 16, 35, 42–52, 176n24; emergence, 3–6; emergency messages, 60–61; employment advantages, xi; employment post–World War II, 145–149, 157, 186n1; express work, 88; featherbedding, 149–154, 188n16; hiring practices, 27–30; housing, 116–120, *121*, 122–127, 184n72; job stress, strain, and complaints, 89–99; kindnesses, 139; legacies, 159–169; mobility, 99–102; nonrailroad activities, 82–85, 87–88; nontraditional and unusual duties, 65–70; optimism post–World War II, 141; penmanship, 60, 178n58; people of color, 30; regulations, 138, 149; resourcefulness, 61, 64–65; retirements, 188n20; romances, 102–103; Rule G, 100; telegraph communications, 29, 35–37, 48–49; telegraph schools, 37, 38; telephone communication, 113–115; train control, 11–16, 52, 54, 55, 56, 57, 58, 59–60, 61, 63–65, 157, 178n51, 178n,61–179n61; union activities, 105–109; wives, 127–128, *129*, 130–134; women, 30–35, 41
Stephenson, George, 1
Stephenson, Robert, 1

Stimson, H. A. (Al), 95
Stockton, Illinois, 88, 105
Stockton & Darlington Railway, 1
Stourbridge Lion (locomotive), 2
Stronghurst, Illinois, 131–132
Sumpter Valley Railway, 76–77
Sunbury, Iowa, 101
Super-Chief (passenger train), 145
Super-Railroads for a Dynamic American Economy (book), 145
Surface Transportation Board, 157

Tacoma, Washington, 148
Talmage, James, 98
Tangeman, Nebraska, 128
Tarkio, Missouri, 99
Telegraph: American landline Morse code, 175n15; Civil War, 24; invention of, 17–19; 19 and 31 train orders, 177n50, 178n57; OS messages, 175n13; quadruplex telegraph, 26; railroad–private company relationship 25–26; train dispatching 19–23; train order volume, 178n58
Telegraphers' Protective Union, 105–106
Telephone dispatching, 112–115, 184n65
Terminal Railroad Association of St. Louis, 101
Texas & Pacific Railroad, 69, 106
Thornburg, Iowa, 101
Tickets, 6
Tidd, C. P., 98
Tikonka, Iowa, *126*
ime internal system, 11–14, 22, 24
imetable and train-order system, 54, 58, 62, 112
Tipton, Indiana, 178n58
Tipton, Iowa, 101
Toledo, Peoria & Western Railroad, *68*
Toledo, St. Louis & Western Railroad, 118
rack warrants, 62, 157
rain dispatchers, 27–28, 31, 45 54, 61–62, 101, 111–114, 116, 157, 177n49
Transportation Act (1958), 154
Transportation Communications International Union, 116
Travelers Insurance Company, 84

Travelers' Official Railway Guide, 42

Tripoli, Iowa, 47

Turner's, New York, 19–20

Twentieth Century Limited (passenger train), 140

Union, Nebraska, 128, 130–131

Union Pacific Railroad, 11–12, 43, 101, 109, 118, 120, 123, 156, 162–163, 166

Uniontown, Alabama, 137

US Military Rail Roads, 24, 273n27

US Military Telegraph Corps, 24

US Naval Observatory, 90

US Railroad Administration, 116

Vail, Alfred, 18

Valdosta, Georgia, 70, 72

Valdosta, Moutrie & Western Railroad, 72

Valentines' School of Telegraphy, 38

Van Cleve, Iowa, *66*

Van Nest, C. B., 138

Vandalia Railroad, 44

Varnville, South Carolina, 95

Veblen, Thorstein, ix

Vickers, S. L., 105

Victoria, Minnesota, 85, 187n12

Villisca, Iowa, 70

Volker, Louisa, 31

Volland, Kansas, 179n63

Wabash, Indiana, *xi*

Wabash Railroad, 98, 106, 139. *See also* North Missouri Railroad

Wagner, H. O., 130

Walker, Iowa, 101

Wanstead, Ontario, 179n63

Wapello, Iowa, 101

Waukee, Iowa, 157

Waukegan, Illinois, 84

Wayland, Iowa, 138

Webb, Dayton, 146

Webster City, Iowa, 101

Wells, Martin, 70

Wells Fargo Express Company, 51

Wendte, South Dakota, 46

West Brimfield, Massachusetts, 96

West Haven, Illinois, *40*

West Manayunk, Pennsylvania, 179n63

West Point Foundry Association, 2

Westboro, Missouri, 99

Western Electric Company, 115

Western Union Telegraph Company, 25, 37, 46, 48, 89, 98, 106, 108, 133, 149, 156

Wheeling, West Virginia, 2

Wheeling & Lake Erie Railway, 33

Whispering Smith (book), 159–160

Whitehall, Montana, 168

Wilder, Laura Ingalls, 122

Williams, Harry, 88

Williams, "Red," 85

Wilson's Mills, North Carolina, 40

Winchester & Potomac Railroad, 7

Wisconsin Public Service Commission, 188n15

Wisham, George, 98

Wolbach, Nebraska, 118

Wood, Robert, *86*

Woods, North Dakota, 145

Woodworth, Jimmie, 122

Wooster, Clarence M., 66

yellow fever, 69

Zanesville & Western Railroad, 36

Zurich, Montana, 69

H. ROGER GRANT is author of numerous books, including *Visionary Railroader, John W. Barriger III, Railroaders without Borders, Railroads and the American People,* and *A Mighty Fine Road.* He is Kathryn and Calhoun Lemon Professor of History at Clemson University.

.

CPSIA information can be obtained
at www.ICGtesting.com
Printed in the USA
BVHW041436131022
649369BV00001B/1